Mission-Based Management

Mission-Based Management

*Leading Your Not-for-Profit
in the 21st Century*

Third Edition

PETER C. BRINCKERHOFF

John Wiley & Sons, Inc.

Published by John Wiley & Sons, Inc., Hoboken, New Jersey.

Published simultaneously in Canada.

For general information on our other products and services, or technical support, please
contact our Customer Care Department within the United States at 800-762-2974, outside
the United States at 317-572-3993 or fax 317-572-4002.

Wiley also publishes its books in a variety of electronic formats. Some content that
appears in print may not be available in electronic books.

For more information about Wiley products, visit our Web site at http://www.wiley.com.

Library of Congress Cataloging-in-Publication Data

Brinckerhoff, Peter C., 1952–
   Mission-based management : leading your not-for-profit in the 21st century / Peter C.
Brinckerhoff. –
3rd ed.
     p. cm.
   Includes index.
   ISBN 978-0-470-43207-5 (cloth : acid-free paper)
  1. Nonprofit organizations—Management.   2. Associations, institutions,
etc.—Management.   I. Title.
   HD62.6.B74 2010
   658'.048–dc22   2009019194

Printed in the United States of America

10 9 8 7 6 5 4 3 2 1

This book is dedicated to my mother:
Inger Melchior Hansen Brinckerhoff, 1924–1994
by far the best writer in the family.

Contents

Acknowledgments   xi

Preface to the Third Edition   xiii

About the Author   xv

CHAPTER 1   Introduction   1

A look at three core philosophies, who the book
is written for, how the book is designed, and how
to get the most from reading it.

CHAPTER 2   Where We Were, Where We Are, Where We Are Going   13

A brief history of the nonprofit world, an examination
of the relationship between nonprofits and their funders,
and an updated prediction of the nonprofit world for
the next ten years.

CHAPTER 3   What Works: The Characteristics of a Successful
            Nonprofit   31

An updated list of the ten things that a nonprofit
needs to continue to do its mission well in the
twenty-first century.

CHAPTER 4   The Mission Is the Reason   39

How to get the most benefit from the reason that
nonprofits exist. For many, the mission is an
underutilized resource. A discussion on updating
and then using a motivational mission statement.

CHAPTER 5   Being Ethical, Accountable, and Transparent   55

Effective nonprofits are highly ethical, accountable to their communities, and transparent both inside and outside the organization. The best ways to do this on the highest moral plane possible is covered.

CHAPTER 6   A Businesslike Board of Directors   73

What an effective board is, and what the board's and the staff's respective roles are. Reducing board liability and recruiting and retaining a board will be covered as well.

CHAPTER 7   Leading Your People   97

A new approach to nonprofit leadership that succeeds in today's high-speed, information-driven environment, also including better communications, evaluations, and rewards.

CHAPTER 8   Embracing Technology for Mission   123

How to use technology to better serve, manage, inform, market, empower, and compete in today's all-tech, all-the-time environment.

CHAPTER 9   Creating a Social Entrepreneur   143

How to develop a culture that takes reasonable risks on behalf of the people it serves. The criteria of a social entrepreneur. How to focus on your core competencies and remain flexible.

CHAPTER 10   Developing a Bias for Marketing   171

The best way to bring your entire team into the marketing process, to discover who your markets really are, and how to meet their needs and wants. The characteristics of a market-driven and mission-based organization. Why asking is so important.

CHAPTER 11 Financial Empowerment 195

The eight key characteristics of a financially empowered nonprofit, better internal reporting, and how a nonprofit can keep what it earns.

CHAPTER 12 A Vision for the Future 233

How to plan where you are going, and how to get the most from the planning process as well as from the plan itself. Sample plan outlines.

CHAPTER 13 The Controls That Set You Free 255

The way to get the most from nine different kinds of policies, including a tested method for their development and enforcement.

CHAPTER 14 A National Agenda: Empowering Our Nonprofits 275

A new way of looking at nonprofits for everyone to consider: funders, donors, volunteers, staff, board, the · public, and the press. What we all need to do together to improve, free, embolden, and empower the nonprofits that are so essential to our community.

CHAPTER 15 Final Words 289

Index 293

Acknowledgments

No book like this is the author's sole product. In my case, much of the theory, case studies, and applications presented here have been developed over my thirty-five years as a nonprofit manager, volunteer, board member, consultant, and trainer. My consulting firm, Corporate Alternatives, has worked with thousands of nonprofits since 1982, and the exceptional efforts of the staff and volunteers of the organizations with which I have worked show up here repeatedly. My students at the Kellogg School of Management at Northwestern University have also provided me with fascinating insights into their perceptions on what nonprofits are and should be.

This book is therefore a compendium of consultation, research, applications, and experience, and like any observer in any field, I have incorporated ideas and experiences of others to apply to the field of nonprofits. Where appropriate, and when not violating confidentiality, these people have been noted in the text. Where they are not acknowledged, they are still greatly appreciated.

For this third edition, I would also like to particularly thank my technology experts, Ben Brinckerhoff and Dan Mayer, founders of Devver.net. Their understanding of both technology and the potential for technology to help nonprofits was crucial to major improvements to this text.

Preface to the Third Edition

It has been a long, strange road for all of us since the second edition of *Mission-Based Management* was published in 2000. As I read through the second edition, in preparation for writing this edition, I was repeatedly amazed at how much of the world we, and in particular the nonprofit sector, have changed; how many steps we have taken forward and how many back. While much of what I wrote in the last edition still holds true, particularly the core principles, so many of the trends that were just becoming evident then are completely absorbing now. For example, in 2000, most nonprofits had just gotten their first Web site, were feeling their way on how to use e-mail to its fullest extent, and nobody, not even a 16-year-old, had heard of texting. Many of us still carried beepers . . . so last century.

In 2000, the economy was booming, federal deficits were "a thing of the past," and very few if any of us would have been able to answer the question: Who is Osama bin Laden? When the second edition came out, Bill Clinton was president, Al Gore was ahead in the race to succeed him, and Barack Obama was a state senator in Illinois, just beginning to think about running for the U.S. Senate in 2004.

So much has changed on so many levels, and it is time for a refreshed set of priorities for the mission-based manager. I have looked at, and revised, the characteristics of a successful mission-based organization. I have given you an updated set of predictions for the next ten years, added an entire chapter on ethics, accountability, and transparency, and brought the chapters on financial empowerment, marketing, and social entrepreneurship into agreement with the books I have written on those subjects since *Mission-Based Management* was published. I have also edited and updated the discussion questions at the end of each chapter to allow you to generate better conversations with your staff and board about which parts of the book most apply to your organization's unique needs.

It is a fascinating and exciting time to be in the nonprofit world. We have more challenges, more opportunity, and more ways to respond to the increasing community needs that are at our doors. As a nation, as a planet, we need our nonprofits more than ever, certainly more than we did in 2000. We have to take our mission to a new level and a new *Mission-Based Management* will help you, your board, and staff get there.

About the Author

Peter C. Brinckerhoff has spent his entire adult life working in, around, and for nonprofits. He is dedicated to the concept that a nonprofit organization is a mission-based business, in the business of doing its mission.

When Brinckerhoff formed his firm, Corporate Alternatives, Inc., in 1982, it was the first consulting and training company in the United States dedicated exclusively to the management concerns of 501(c)(3) organizations.

A former VISTA Volunteer, Brinckerhoff knows how nonprofits work from his experience as a volunteer, his work as a staff member, and later as executive director of two regional nonprofits, and from his service on numerous state, local, and national nonprofit boards. He brings this understanding of the many perspectives in a nonprofit organization to his work.

Brinckerhoff is an award-winning author, with eight books and two workbooks in print, and more than sixty articles published in the nonprofit press. Three of his books, *Mission-Based Management* (John Wiley & Sons, 2000), *Financial Empowerment* (John Wiley & Sons, 1998), and *Generations, The Challenge of a Lifetime for Your Nonprofit* (Fieldstone Alliance, 2007), each won the prestigious Terry McAdam Award from the Alliance for Nonprofit Management. The award is given for "The Best New Nonprofit Book" each year. He is the only author to win the award multiple times. Brinckerhoff's books are used as texts in courses at the undergraduate and graduate nonprofit management programs in more than 100 colleges and universities worldwide.

Brinckerhoff is also a highly acclaimed speaker and lecturer, presenting his ideas on how to make nonprofits more effective to dozens of audiences throughout North America, Europe, and Asia each year.

From 2003 to 2007, Brinckerhoff was an Adjunct Professor of Nonprofit Management at the Kellogg School of Management at Northwestern University. He taught the core graduate course in the Nonprofit Management program at Kellogg. In addition, Brinckerhoff has guest lectured at the graduate level at Boston University, University of Colorado, University of Illinois, and Vanderbilt University.

Brinckerhoff received his bachelor's degree from the University of Pennsylvania, and his master's degree in Public Health Administration from Tulane University. Raised in Connecticut, Brinckerhoff and his family lived in Springfield, IL, from 1977 to 2007. He and his wife now call Union Hall, VA, home.

The author can be contacted by e-mail at peter@missionbased.com.

CHAPTER 1

Introduction

Welcome. This book is intended for you, the leadership of our nation's nonprofit charitable organizations. It is designed to give you a different insight into how top-quality nonprofits *really* run, what works, what does not, and how to ensure that your organization is one of the ones that works, both this year and throughout the twenty-first century. It is intended to help you become a mission-based manager.

In this introductory chapter we'll review the core philosophies on which I have based the book, examine the reasons that I feel the book is needed, and then take the first look at what the book holds and the best ways for you as a reader and a management practitioner to use it. By the end of the chapter, you should have a better understanding of my philosophical perspective and also be ready to get the most from the book as a whole.

Three Core Philosophies

Before you continue, you need to know that the material in this book is based on three philosophies. These philosophies have been the core of my consulting, training, and writing since 1982, and they express better than anything I have seen my beliefs about what your organization is and what it can become.

First: Nonprofits Are Businesses

Your organization is a *mission-based* business, in the business of doing mission. For-profits chase profits—nonprofits pursue their mission. But just because you are not primarily motivated by profit does not give you a license to be sloppy or to ignore a good idea simply because it was initially developed for the for-profit sector. Let's take another minute to examine this because it is really important to what you are going to read in the rest of the book.

1

In the past decade many nonprofits made the decision to stop being a charity and start being a mission-based business. What's the difference? In both cases, the stewards of the organization (paid staff or governing and nongoverning volunteers) are responsible for getting the most high-quality mission they can out the door using all the resources available. The difference lies in how a charity and how a mission-based business view their resources.

A *charity* views its resources as a combination of four things: people, money, buildings, and equipment. If you think about it, your organization has some combination of these four things, too. The charity uses these four resources to provide mission, and when the resources are used up, mission stops.

A *mission-based business* also has the same combination of four resources: people, money, buildings, and equipment. But it looks beyond just those four and also considers business tools in performing mission. Thus, it utilizes the techniques that business has spent literally billions of dollars and thousands of person-years honing and it turns them to mission. What is the result? Good marketing becomes good mission; good human resources (HR) becomes good mission; good inventory management, good cash flow management, good business planning, all of these become good and better mission. More high-quality mission out the door. And, if this is done right—and here is the key—the other four resources *last longer*.

This philosophy is certainly not as shocking to most readers (or perhaps even a new idea) as it was when I wrote the first edition of *Mission-Based Management* in 1992. Only eight years earlier, in 1984, I had told a national audience that nonprofits needed to become more businesslike in their pursuit of mission, and I was not only booed, people actually threw things at the stage. We've come a long way since then.

But there are still people who are uncomfortable with the idea of using business skills in nonprofits. They worry that if we act too much like a business, we'll become a business and lose our mission focus. I agree—mission is always first. *Always*. But if we don't use these business tools, we won't do as much mission as we could. It's a balancing act: Stay on the mission track but use the best tools of business when they are appropriate.

A story may illustrate this issue best. In 2006, I was presenting for a full day on *Mission-Based Management* to a group of board members and CEO/executive directors from about two hundred nonprofits in California. I had given the content of this chapter and Chapter 3 in my first segment of the morning and, at the break, a man approached me to tell me he was really uncomfortable with the idea of using business tools in nonprofits. I learned that he was the board president of a homeless shelter and, in his other life, the president of a local bank. In fact, I found out later that he had an MBA from Stanford as well as an undergraduate degree from Harvard—a smart, highly educated businessman. But he was really hung up on the concept of, in his words, "using business tools in nonprofits. We're better than that."

I told him that he should never do things in his nonprofit that made him uncomfortable, but that I'd like him to answer three questions. He agreed.

First question: "Do you have and use telephones in your homeless shelter?" He said they did, but looked confused. Second question: "Do you have and use a copier at the shelter?" Again, his answer was a yes, combined with a furrowed brow. Third question: "Do you have and use computers?" A look of understanding came over his face. "Got it," he said. "Okay. Okay, got it."

You see, telephones and copiers and computers were invented first for business, not for nonprofits. They were business tools first. And telephones, copiers, and computers can be used for bad things, but we choose to use them in ways that pursue our mission. Likewise, marketing and cash flow management and HR are business tools that can all be used for bad things, but if we do not use them and use them as *tools for good*, we won't be getting as much mission out the door as we could be. We'll be failing as stewards.

Using good business skills as a mission-based manager does not, I repeat, *not* mean dropping services simply because they lose money, nor does it mean turning people away because they cannot pay. But it does mean paying attention to the bottom line, having a strategic vision, and negotiating in good faith and from a position of strength—in short, being businesslike in pursuit of your mission.

Your organization is a business, and the more businesslike you are, the better it will be for the people you serve.

Second: No One Gives You a Dime

This may come as a surprise, but your organization does not get gifts... Really. No one gives you anything, not government, foundations, United Way, corporations, or individual donors. If you are confused, that is okay. This idea goes against all your training to this point. Try looking at it this way and see if you feel different about yourself and your organization. Let's assume that you come to me for a donation and you convince me that you really need the money for a service or a building. I write you a check for $100. Am I making the donation to you personally? Of course not. Am I giving a gift to your organization? You're getting closer. But what I'm really doing, and what really happens in all of these transactions, is that I am *purchasing services for someone or some family I will never meet*. I am willing to give you money because you gave me what the business community calls an *expectation of outcome*. When I send money to an airline to pay for a plane ticket, I have an *expectation of transportation* in a few days or weeks. When I send money to a concert venue to purchase tickets, I have an *expectation of entertainment* the night of the concert. When I send money to a nonprofit, I have an *expectation of service*.

In other words, and here is the key: You *earn* all the money you get. Don't let anyone tell you that you are a subsidized organization. Subsidies are things that people get without doing anything. I lived in the farm belt in Illinois for thirty years. We had many farmers who were paid by the federal government for *not* growing crops. That's a subsidy. What you get is earned income, *all of it*.

The problem with thinking of your income as gifts is that the organization then acts like a charity. You become stuck in the mentality that you are so poor that the only way you can survive is by the beneficence of people or organizations richer than you. You continue to believe you are not earning your way when, in actuality, you are. It is essential that you and your staff and board understand this and believe it if you are to adopt the characteristics of success that are presented in this book. Why? Because if you keep thinking of yourselves as a poor charity, you will continue to be treated that way and not like the mission-based business that you are.

Third: Nonprofit Does Not Mean No Profit

Let's cut to the chase. Whether you call yourself a not-for-profit or a nonprofit, you should not ever feel bad if you end the year with more money in than out. In short, making money is good for mission. Only by making a profit (yes, a profit) can you grow, serve more people, and try new services. Only by making money can you pay down any debts you have. Profit is not a bad thing in your organization; it's a good thing. It's also not always a possible thing, but we'll get to that in later chapters.

Let's look at this idea in three ways: the legal point of view, the ethical perspective, and from the vantage point of good management.

First, making money in a nonprofit is legal. Nowhere in any state or federal law, and nowhere in any state or federal regulation dealing with taxation or corporate structures, does it say that a nonprofit cannot make money, cannot make a profit. In fact, the Internal Revenue Service (IRS) code dealing with 501(c)(3) organizations says "... the *profits* of the corporation shall not inure to the benefit of ..." This clause precludes staff or board from inappropriately benefiting from the organization's profits, but the key to the phrase is that the IRS anticipates and accepts profits. Profits in a nonprofit are *legal*.

If you or anyone in your organization thinks that I am wrong about profits being legal, consider this: Your organization is considered tax-exempt (by reason of your 501(c)(3) status), but from what kind of *federal* taxes? I know you may not pay sales or property taxes, but those are state or local exemptions. At the federal level, you are exempt from what the IRS terms *income tax*. Now, for you and me, income tax means that every April we add up all of our income from the prior year and pay the IRS a portion of that. But the tax your nonprofit organization is subject to is a business tax, and guess what? Businesses do not pay tax on what you and I would term *income*; they pay taxes on *profits*. They add up all their revenue, subtract all their expenses, and pay, in taxes, a portion of their profits. *Income* to the IRS means *profits* to you and me. Thus, your organization has an exemption against paying taxes on its profits. Here is the question: *If you cannot make a profit, why do you need a tax exemption?*

In fact, the entire issue of nonprofits not being able to make money is just so much smoke, and it runs right in the face of the intention of Congress in giving you the charitable status you have. In the early 1950s, when the last substantive work was done on federal nonprofit statutes, Congress decided we needed more nonprofits, so it allowed your organization to keep what it earns and reinvest it in the community. They wanted to encourage our sector and did not think that we should be taxed for doing good things related to our mission. What's happened since? All of us have screwed it all up by not allowing nonprofits to keep what they earn. When I say all of us, I mean funders, the press, the public, and those of us in nonprofits. We all bought into the idea that nonprofits should be poor, and it has deeply damaged the sector and our ability to do good mission. By keeping non-profits poor, always scraping by from year to year or from payroll to payroll, we've sapped much of the ability to innovate, experiment, and come out with better services for people in need.

Profits in your nonprofit are also *essential*, a key element in financial empowerment, a subject that we will cover at length. As I said earlier, with-out profits, you cannot grow, you cannot innovate and try new ways to serve your communities, you cannot recruit and retain excellent staff, and you cannot take prudent risks on behalf of your clientele. You will see in later chapters that I contend that you need to make money as an organiza-tion at least seven out of ten years. To do less is not good mission-based management.

But what about the ethical perspective? This is *hard*. By not spending every dime you have every year on service, you necessarily will wind up saying no to someone who needs or wants your services, perhaps someone who is hungry, undereducated, or in need of spiritual help. And I doubt that anyone reading this book came to the nonprofit sector to say, "No, we won't help you." But if you say yes to everyone now, you won't have any funds for next year. I am just as sure that your organization is not in business to solve a *short-term* problem as I am that you do not want to turn people away. Nearly all nonprofits are struggling to solve *long-term* issues: hunger, homelessness, drug addiction, the need for more education, arts, environmental quality, and on and on. Long-term problems require your organization to be around for the long term. Keep your organization poor and it won't be. Again, this is a balancing act, one of many you have to do. Focus too much on mission and not enough on money and you are out of business. Focus too much on money and not enough on mission and you become just a business.

One more point here: I am not contending that you need to have every single service you provide be profitable every year. You do not, and you probably should not. There will be services that are so mission-rich that they can be money-poor. Services that only you provide in your community that do not pay for themselves or that are mission-critical. But if all you provide are mission-rich/money-poor services, you will soon be out of business and no good to anyone. Again you need a balance, and you need to use the business skill of return-on-investment (ROI) to maintain the right balance.

For-profit businesses are concerned about their financial ROI, and rightly so. If they invest funds in a building or a piece of equipment or staff expansion, they want to know how quickly they get their investment back and at what rate.

Nonprofit businesses need to also be concerned about ROI as well, but unlike for-profits, we have two returns: the *financial* return and the *mission* return. Thus, if you invest money in Service X, you should be asking, "Does this service make money or lose money AND does it do a lot of mission or only a little?"

 HANDS ON: Always consider the expenses in your income and expense form as investments in mission. If you do that, you will need to think about the return on that investment, both in financial and mission forms. The financial return is pretty easy to calculate, but the mission return is much more difficult. We will talk about ways to do this calculation later. ■

I'm sure you have services that are mission-rich and money-poor, and if you are like 90 percent of nonprofits, you invest resources in a service that does NO mission. For example, if you run a soup kitchen, you provide a very, very mission-rich service. But it doesn't pay for itself because you are giving food away. But this is fine because on the two-ROI scale it balances out: mission-rich, money-poor.

So what's the service that does no mission? It's variously called development, or fund-raising, which by itself does *no* mission. Only if the service *makes money* can it spin off funds to help other mission-rich/money-poor services, like the soup kitchen. Thus, you need to make sure your fund-raising is not haphazard, or done poorly. It needs to make money! This underscores another theme that we'll return to a lot in the book: You have to do whatever you do *well*. Really well.

These three philosophies, that you are a mission-based business, that you earn all your money, and that making money is a good mission thing, form the foundation for everything that follows in this book. They are the core of mission-based management. If you agree with them, if you find yourself nodding and saying, "That's great!" you are going to enjoy the book and get a great deal out of it. If you are uncomfortable with the philosophies, I hope that the remainder of this chapter and the issues raised in Chapters 2 and 3 will convince you of the validity of these philosophies. If that does not work, then I think that the remainder of the book will convince you that there are many, many business applications that can improve your ability to do better mission more efficiently and effectively.

We will return to these philosophies at the end of the book (Chapter 14), to look at how your funders can adopt them to give you more leeway to do your job. But for the majority of the book, we will concentrate on how you can make them a reality in your own management style, in your own mission-based organization.

Why Is This Third Edition Needed Now?

The 1980s were an extremely turbulent time for U.S. nonprofits. During the Reagan administration years of 1981 to 1989, the vast majority of nonprofits—those that depend on government funding for the majority of their incomes—had their perspective on life radically changed. No longer could these organizations depend on government (read: taxpayer) largesse to cover their expenses, nor would regular cost of living adjustments (COLAs) solve their problems. No, nonprofits would have to learn to make do as more independent, more businesslike entities. Wouldn't they?

Those of us in the field thought so. In many organizations, things did change. New businesses sprang up, inside or outside the traditional organization's array of services. Educational opportunities for nonprofit staff slowly became available across the country throughout the decade, not only at the continuing education and seminar level, but as graduate degrees in many top-notch educational institutions. More and more staffs sought and received the one type of course work that they had previously never had access to: basic, as well as advanced, management training.

Unfortunately, many organizations continued to do business as usual. After a brief foray into a new idea or service, they returned to their traditional sources of funding, squeezed more work out of their staffs, and tried to serve the avalanche of new people needing help. (In the human service nonprofit, this higher need for service—from homelessness to public health to literacy—was another result of the Reagan years.) They continued to act like charities rather than nonprofit businesses. Government, foundations, and United Ways for the most part only exacerbated the problems by emphasizing cost controls over strategic planning and marketing, and fundraising over entrepreneurship—two essential components of an excellent organization-for-profit or nonprofit.

The 1990s brought some needed change and some new challenges. Hundreds more colleges and universities developed both undergraduate- and graduate-level nonprofit management programs. Management support organizations sprang up in many states and metropolitan areas, ready to help nonprofits run their organizations more efficiently and effectively. Some funders began to move toward fee-for-service contracting rather than grants. But there were also new challenges. Reimbursement structures based on the managed care model took hold in a wide variety of shapes at the federal and state level, requiring measurement of outcomes rather than process for the first time. After decades of punishing "duplication of service," some funders started to worry about costs to such an extent that social service and educational organizations nationwide began a movement to merge. Competition for dollars, for good staff, for good volunteers, and for people to serve became much more intense. On the good side, the federal deficit was closed and surpluses began. The economy was good, and technology began to provide real returns to all of us. The other great change was the emphasis on what was termed capacity building by foundations. This movement, of funding training, better use of technology, benefits, and other indirect costs, was a terrific improvement over the days when funders only funded "direct costs" and ignored the essential back-office functions that enable service for any nonprofit.

Then came the roller coaster ride of the Bush years in the early twenty-first century with the tech bubble, the war on terror, the housing bubble, and the crash that followed. The economy grew and contracted, grew and collapsed. Donors couldn't figure out day-to-day how much money they had, millions worldwide lost jobs, and corporations cut back charitable giving and some simply vanished. We went from good times to bad times so incredibly quickly that our heads spun. And all of us realized that the old rules (prudent management, prudent investing, and prudent levels of debt) were not outdated at all.

At the same time, society began to be aware that the Boomer generation was aging and that a hand-off to GenX was imminent. The differences between the generations became near war in many organizations.

Excellent use of technology became more and more important in all parts of society, and nonprofits struggled to keep abreast of changes that could make the difference between connecting with a new generation and being ignored by the young.

As a result of all these changes, there is a pressing need for a rethinking of the best ways to govern and manage our nonprofits. This book is intended to help you find those techniques that will help you do more mission and to make the transition from an administrator of a charity to a mission-based manager. I know, from consulting and training thousands of nonprofit staff and boards since 1982, that the organizations that *are* succeeding in meeting the needs of the people they serve, the organizations that *are* financially stable, the organizations that *will* meet the challenges of the future have the characteristics discussed in later chapters. I also firmly believe that if your organization has those characteristics, or acquires them *and consistently works to improve them*, you will succeed in serving the people who are depending on you. Unfortunately, too many nonprofit managers, nonprofit board members, and nonprofit funders are still stuck in the 1990s. And they are getting further behind every day.

Mission-based management is good management. It is more than stewardship, a term that has become widely used in the nonprofit field in recent years. It is a philosophy that says, "I will use all the best tools at my disposal to help my organization excel in the pursuit of its mission. The mission is the reason that we are here, but that is no excuse for sloppy or slipshod management. We would never tolerate poor quality in services. We won't tolerate poor quality in management either."

Mission-Based Management, Third Edition

You already know that much has changed since the first edition of *Mission-Based Management* in 1994 and the second edition in 2000. The format for all of the *Mission-Based Management* series books has evolved as well. There are now more features in the chapters than before that should give you, the reader, more value for your time. The book is designed to be used as a guide and as a reference for you to return to over and over. I know that your time is limited and that you will be tempted to jump right to the parts that you are most interested in, perhaps "Developing a Bias for Marketing" (Chapter 10) or "Financial Empowerment" (Chapter 11). To the extent possible, I urge you to read the book from front to back. The chapters are in the order presented for a reason: They build upon one another. Issues raised in the early chapters are discussed further in later ones; problems that surface in one chapter sometimes reappear in another. To get the most from the book, read it in the order that it is presented.

Because much of what I talk about in the remainder of the book is based on teamwork and bringing in lots of staff, board, and outside experts to help, I suggest that you work through this book as a team effort. Have a small group of senior managers, middle managers, and direct service staff read a few chapters and then get together to discuss their application in your organization. Ask the group: "Is what is presented appropriate for our organization? If so, what do we need to do to facilitate any needed changes? If it is not appropriate, why not? Are we doing the best we can in this area? How can we be better?" Use the lists of questions that I have included at the end of each chapter to start these discussions. By reading the book as a team, and by reading it at the same time, you will get a more complete, more organization-wide use of the book, and the benefits of the book will be applied to your organization sooner.

Now, let's turn to the format of the book. By giving you an overview of both the format and the sequence, as well as a brief peek at the benefits that you will get from each chapter, I hope that you will get more from our time together.

The Format

Each chapter starts with an **OVERVIEW**, intended to give you a brief summary of what the chapter will hold. The body of the text comes next, and I try, as much as possible, to give you illustrations and ideas for immediate use. These illustrations and ideas are highlighted by the terms "🖥 **FOR EXAMPLE**" and "✑ **HANDS-ON**," respectively. Look for them in nearly every chapter. Near the end of the chapter is a **RECAP**, which is a brief review of the points that have been covered in the chapter, to allow you to draw all of the material together in your mind. There is also a list of **QUESTIONS FOR DISCUSSION**, which are intended to stimulate group conversations with your staff and volunteers about ways to best use the ideas included in the book.

The Content

The book is broken down into what I call context-setting chapters, working chapters, and the final chapter, which is a call to action for the funders of nonprofits. Let's look at each chapter briefly.

1. Introduction
   ■ This is the chapter you are reading now. It includes a look at three core philosophies: who the book is written for, how the book is designed, and how to get the most from reading it.

Context-Setting Chapters

2. Where We Were, Where We Are, Where We Are Going
   ■ A brief history of the nonprofit world, an examination of the relationship between nonprofits and their funders, and an updated prediction of the nonprofit world for the next ten years.

3. What Works: The Characteristics of a Successful Nonprofit
   - An updated list of the ten things that a nonprofit needs to continue to do its mission well throughout the twenty-first century.

Working Chapters

4. The Mission Is the Reason
   - How to get the most benefit from the reason that nonprofits exist. For many, the mission is an underutilized resource. A discussion on updating and then using a motivational mission statement.
5. Being Ethical, Accountable, and Transparent
   - The best nonprofits are accountable and transparent both inside and outside the organization. The best ways to do this on the highest moral plane possible is covered.
6. A Businesslike Board of Directors
   - What an effective board is, and what the board's and the staff's respective roles are. Reducing board liability and recruiting and retaining a board will be covered as well.
7. Leading Your People
   - A new approach to nonprofit leadership that succeeds in today's high-speed, information-driven environment, also including better communications, evaluations, and rewards. We will also look at ways to engage multiple generations in your mission.
8. Embracing Technology for Mission
   - How to use technology to better manage, inform, market, empower, and compete in today's all-tech, all-the-time environment.
9. Creating a Social Entrepreneur
   - How to develop a culture that takes prudent risks on behalf of the people you serve. The criteria of a social entrepreneur. How to focus on your core competencies and remain flexible.
10. Developing a Bias for Marketing
    - The best way to bring your entire team into the marketing process, to discover who your markets really are, and how to meet their needs and wants. The characteristics of a market-driven and mission-based organization. How to improve 1 percent every day.
11. Financial Empowerment
    - The eight key characteristics of a financially empowered nonprofit, better internal reporting, and how a nonprofit can keep what it earns.
12. A Vision for the Future
    - How to plan where you are going, and how to get the most from the planning process as well as from the plan itself. Sample plan outlines.
13. The Controls That Set You Free
    - The way to get the most from nine different kinds of policies, including a tested method for their development and enforcement.

14. A National Agenda: Empowering Our Nonprofits
    - The other side of the coin: what the funders need to do to improve, free, embolden, and empower the nonprofits with whom they contract.
15. Final Words

Recap

In this chapter we've covered the key philosophies that are the basis for the book and why I think the book is needed. We've also taken the first look at the contents of the book and how it is set up so that you can make the most use of it to benefit your organization and the people that you serve.

I know that you have a tough and challenging job. As a leader of a twenty-first-century nonprofit, you have to concern yourself with many differing and conflicting needs and demands: those of your funders, the people you serve, and your board, staff, community, banker, and peers. You need to ensure that your organization is pursuing its mission with zeal, that it meets the changing needs of the community that you serve, and that you have enough money to make ends meet.

The tools to help you do those things are in the following pages. Good reading and good luck!

CHAPTER 2

Where We Were, Where We Are, Where We Are Going

Overview

Before we start our journey together, it is important to understand how we got here and for you to read my predictions for the next ten years. Without those two pieces of context, it will be harder for you to grasp my ideas for what your organization can become and can accomplish.

In this chapter, we will examine how nonprofits in the United States came to be where they are today, and we will examine the three rules that funders use when they think of you and your organization. We'll then turn to the future and review my six predictions for trends that will profoundly affect you, your organization, and its ability to perform its mission during the next decade.

How We Got Here

The United States, more than any other nation in the world, is blessed with a volunteer spirit of helping others. In other developed countries, volunteering or charitable giving (other than to the church) is much less the cultural norm. This is not to say that people in Europe, South America, Africa, or Asia do not give of their time, talent, or treasure; they do. But not at the level that seems to be indigenous in North America, for reasons we'll examine in a moment. My personal experience with the difference in cultures began early on. My mother was Danish by birth and emigrated to the United States as an infant. There were (and remain) many relatives in Denmark and, during my childhood, many of those relatives came to visit us, often staying at our home.

In those years, my parents would often need to leave to attend one of the board meetings of the many organizations on which they served. (My parents were the original incorporators and first officers of what is arguably the first Association for Retarded Citizens [ARC] in the country in 1951, and served on numerous other nonprofit boards over the succeeding thirty-five years.) When the reason for my parents' absence was explained, it was almost always greeted with puzzled expressions and questions from our Danish guests, such as, "Why would you *give* your time away?" or "Doesn't the government take care of that for you?," to which my parents would reply, "Here, we have a tradition of trying to help each other."

Whether it sprang from a frontier necessity to help and be helped, from our history as a democracy, or just from our national economic abundance, Americans have developed a vast network of charitable nonprofit organizations that assist the poor, rehabilitate the injured, educate the young and old, enrich our senses and sensibilities by providing access to the arts, and fulfill our spiritual needs.

From the beginning of the twentieth century until the onset of Lyndon Johnson's "War on Poverty," most of the funding for these organizations came from locally donated funds raised in the community in which the organization provided services. A few large foundations of national scope, such as Ford and Rockefeller, provided special projects assistance, but mostly the nonprofit community made do with what its local community gave it.

Then, in the 1960s, all that changed. Government, particularly at the federal level, began to provide funding first in the form of grants, and later in the form of "purchase of service" contracts to thousands of locally based private nonprofits. The feds, and later the state, county, and local governments, bought such diverse services as preventive health care; mental health screenings; residential community care for the developmentally disabled; breakfasts and lunches for school children; housing for the poor; art for all; economic development for disadvantaged communities; books for libraries; research on a broad array of social, medical, and scientific issues; and specialized transportation throughout the nation.

With this cascade of funding—the good news—came an avalanche of red tape, bureaucracy, fast growth, reduced local control, and a seemingly endless series of priority changes and reversals—the bad news. This period (primarily 1964–1981) also saw the enormous growth in the sheer number of 501(c)(3)s (many created *specifically* to tap funds authorized in a particular piece of federal legislation) and the concomitant development of a huge cadre of vested interests embodied in the emergence of large professional staffs (within the nonprofits), rapidly growing trade associations, and, perhaps most importantly, a steep rise in the number of government employees whose sole job it was to fund, regulate, and audit these organizations.

In the mid-to-late 1980s and early 1990s, much of the federal funding for nonprofits was passed on to states through what were called "block grants." The concept was that states knew better than the feds what should be done locally. To an extent, this was (and is) true. What happened, though, was another round of hiring, this time of state employees whose job it was to liaise with the federal funding source, write state regulations, hand out funds, and oversee their use. And since the employees were in the same state, they could oversee the funds more rigorously.

This "rise of the staffs," at both the service provider level and within the governments that increasingly were the service provider's single biggest—and sometimes *only*—customer, led to the development of a set of philosophies of funding and oversight that were incredibly damaging to the nonprofits at the time and are still hampering all of us today. The basic tenets of these philosophies are as follows:

- *First: What we say goes.* While being a logical assumption from the point of view of a major (often the only) customer, this tenet often degenerated into the feeling of "Whatever the staff at the Department of XYZ decides is needed in YourTown is what we'll fund, and if you do not need it or if you need something else, well, tough." This attitude, of course, flew directly in the face of time-tested marketing theories of *asking* customers (in this case, the people who were ultimately receiving services) what they wanted. Additionally, this philosophy was in direct conflict with reality: No single broad national or state policy could possibly take into account all of the local variety and uniqueness that shows up in fifty states and 100,000 municipalities. By regularly not recognizing that different communities have different needs, policies and regulations that flowed from this philosophy were and remain doomed from the start.

  But the sheer momentum of dollars flowing from the state and federal capitals spoke louder than the voices of the service recipients. So organizations acquiesced, services were often funded that people neither wanted nor needed, and, when the first budget of the Reagan years came along, these programs were tough to defend against cuts. More on that in a moment.

- *Second: You can't do "well" doing "good."* This tenet is based on the terribly outdated but still overwhelmingly accepted philosophy that nonprofits must virtually take a vow of poverty in order to not appear to be stealing from those to whom they are providing service. This idea also, of course, nicely justifies minimal funding on the part of the main funders, an abundance of auditing and (in my view) unnecessary oversight, and a policy of "use it or lose it," probably the most shortsighted social policy of our generation.

For those of you not familiar with "use it or lose it," it goes like this: If you negotiate a contract or grant amount for service with a funder—say a state or your county—you get to use what is in the grant during the term of the grant period, usually a fiscal year. You may or may not be able to move funds from one budget line to the next depending on how nice your funder is, but by the end of the year, if you have saved funds (or spent less than expected, through excellent management, hunting for discounts on purchases, etc.), you lose the savings because you can't keep what you didn't spend. Further, if you bring in additional income (from donations, earnings, etc.), it may reduce your income dollar for dollar.

With this policy in place, normal and positive incentives get turned on their head. Is there an incentive to save money? Certainly not. Saving funds is work, and if your organization can't keep what you save, why go through the effort? What about earning more outside income? No, that's more work, too, and if the money is just going to be taken away, why take the risk? Does this encourage unnecessary spending at the service level? Certainly, and *everyone* knows it.

Why does it continue? Because the feds and the states are not willing to let nonprofits keep too much money, keep what they earn, or have many, if any, net assets. I call this inane policy "poverty chic," and it has been beaten into all of our heads for so long that most of us believe it. Funders do, many United Ways do, some staffs and boards still do, and the public in general certainly does. How many times have you been questioned about the purchase of "nice" furniture, tried to rationalize raising salaries, or not bought a piece of computer equipment because it *wouldn't look right?* I have, and I work with hundreds of nonprofits who do so regularly.

Has poverty chic saved money? In the short term, certainly. But it has also led in the long term to poorly trained staffs, high staff turnover, a pitiful condition of the national nonprofit physical plant (usually rented instead of owned), a grievous hole in our technological readiness, and essentially no nonfixed assets with which to innovatively address community problems without the funders' further assistance.

The bottom line is that poverty chic has led to many nonprofits' becoming—and remaining—virtual indentured servants of their funders at the same time that the funders are urging the nonprofits to become more independent and self-sufficient. "Use it or lose it" is one way. Underfunding or matching requirements—not paying for the full cost of service—is another. Encouraging monopolies is a third. By being encouraged and forced to be poor, agencies think poor and stay poor. They are underfunded so they must fight fires today to stay alive rather than plan ahead for the future, an action that can save money and provide better service. They make do with old, beat-up, inefficient equipment and buildings, losing money on repairs and the inefficiencies. They are never allowed to "have unseemly" fund balances (either by public pressure or regulation) so they can never grow—without further assistance from the funders.

FOR EXAMPLE: Interestingly, poverty chic only applies in practice to smaller nonprofits. Hospitals, colleges, and universities seem to be exempt. I've talked to hundreds of funders, and as many reporters over the years, who are appalled when a local non-profit has a small endowment or some unrestricted funds but who feel that a hospital or university having the same kind of reserves is fine. They understand that these larger institutions need these funds to grow, to invest in new equipment and services, and to allow the cost of patients and students to be underwritten. But suggest that the same issues confront a local Red Cross or Goodwill and you get a bunch of outraged huffing and puffing. ■

- *Third: What is yours is ours.* This is perhaps my favorite because it underscores so much of what primary government funders and foundations really must feel: that nonprofits that receive their funds are *their* property. In my work, I see this regularly with auditors of state funds (which may account for, say, 50 percent of an organization's budget) feeling that they must examine *every* transaction of the organization, evaluate *all* of the assets, look into *all* of the contracts, and probe *all* the vendor relationships, even if some or most of those assets and contracts and vendors have nothing to do with the specific programs that the state auditor's department funds. The attitude seems to be *"Because we give you money, we have the right to strip you naked and judge you at our whim."*

This attitude, while not only being insulting, forgets the fact that the nonprofit is actually *selling* the government agency or foundation a service and that the payment for this service should not come attached to an unrestricted license to snoop and poke around at will. Remember this: As a for-profit consultant and trainer, I regularly contract with state governments and foundations, and they don't audit *me*. They do not ask me to submit every expense, ask about my mortgage, or look into the resume of my wife or kids; once I do my work, they pay my fee. Why should they then take your organization apart for inspection during and after you do your work for them? Does being a nonprofit make you automatically exempt from the constitutional protection from unreasonable search and seizure? I think not.

The most incredible aspect of this attitude is that *we all put up with it so willingly.* It is a constant amazement to me that there has not been a general revolt against the level of scrutiny, oversight, and general arrogance of the funding sources. How can this have been allowed to evolve? How can the good, intelligent, and well-intentioned people at the local nonprofit level have become so subservient, while the good, intelligent, well-intentioned people at the foundations and state and federal governments developed policies that, in effect, contradict nearly all of their stated intentions, doing much more harm than good? There are two answers—one psychological and one political.

First: The Psychological Answer

The more I think about the relationship between nonprofits and their funders, the more curious it gets. Look at it this way: How many for-profit companies regularly publicly disparage their best customers? Very few. But how often do you and your peers gripe about the state/county/feds/foundations at your national or state association meetings? Every time you are together, right? I thought so.

Moreover, when was the last time that you went to your state/federal/foundation project officer and asked, "How can we make your job easier and do what you want done better and faster?" Never? Again, I thought so. But understand that in the for-profit world, market-driven companies ask those questions of *all* of their customers, especially the big ones, *all* of the time. They are constantly looking for ways to do things better, faster, easier, and cheaper for their customers. They would never fold their arms across their chests and say that the customer that constitutes 70 percent of their income is being unfair. They'd figure out what the customer wanted and give it to them. (If you don't think that your funders are your customers, think again. We'll cover this in great detail in Chapter 10.)

Over the years, I have developed an analogy of the relationship between nonprofits and their primary funders that I think (unfortunately) is very apt. It goes like this:

> *In their relationships with each other, nonprofits and their primary funders (government or foundations) take on the roles and attitudes of eternal adolescents and parents.*

Now, this is not to disparage either group, as both have contributed to the situation, but imagine how you would feel as either a teenager or the parent of a teenager if you were going to be stuck in that often frustrating and antagonistic relationship forever?

In this relationship, the nonprofits (filling the role of the teens) audibly seek more independence, question the wisdom of the funders (who act the parents' part), ask to be left alone (to do their own thing), and generally resent the house rules. But when the car breaks down or when something else goes wrong, they always come to the parent for help/money.

For their part, the funders/"parents" audibly encourage the independence, tolerate the dissension and independence with irritation but benevolence (knowing that they know better), and urge the non-profit/"teens" to try new things ("but nothing too new") and experiment ("but not too far out")—but ultimately to always be home by midnight, submit all friends for inspection, and be prepared for a search of your room at any time ("house rules").

I'm sure you have seen this relationship and probably been a part of it. Once you recognize the relationship for what it is, it is fairly simple to see how it evolved: People who are giving away the money (particularly those who work for the public) want to control how it is spent. Most nonprofits and their staff and board really only want to be left alone to do what they do best: provide mission. Neither group really can envision true independence from the other. And no tradition, law, or social norm makes a nonprofit independent on its twenty-first birthday. Thus, it is easier to grudgingly accept the status quo than to really break apart.

This is *crazy*, and I've been part of it at both a board and staff level. No wonder both sides are so frustrated! And yet, I see it continue over and over and over, even when both sides are aware and acknowledge the problems inherent in not allowing the nonprofits to grow up and leave home. After all, most nonprofits *are* over 21.

Second: The Political Answer

With the media excited about any and all "scandals" they can find, government is reduced to spending millions of dollars to provide oversight to prevent hundreds or thousands of dollars from being misspent. And this is *everyone's* fault. We don't demand that the media print the whole story. We don't demand a cost-benefit analysis of the fraud prevention section of an agency. We just listen to the story that says WELFARE MOM CHEATS AGENCY OF $40,000 and get all worked up about how poorly the agency is run and what a bunch of cheats those welfare moms are. What is the rest of the story? The mom was one of 110,000 funded, of whom 109,999 *didn't cheat*. The $40,000 stolen was out of $298 million of funding, or less than *1/100th of one percent!* And then, no one ever asks how much the agency spent to find and recover that $40,000. Given the norm, probably two or three times what was stolen. Why do we allow this to happen? Because no government agency official wants to be seen as advocating a lax policy that could allow anyone at all to cheat, and in reality the $40,000 is a *lot* of money to most voters—no matter that it is an infinitesimal percentage of the total. So we let it go and we waste a whole lot of money chasing very little.

Thus, nonprofits spend a great deal of their time and (our) money being accountable for the real or imagined sins of others in order to cover the derrières of the funders. Because there is a political liability for the funders if the public perceives that even $1 is misspent, the funders want to control *everything*.

These three rules have done incalculable harm to nonprofits: They have prevented stability, empowerment, and dignity in our nation's charitable sector and steadily eroded our confidence in our ability to manage our own affairs.

 FOR EXAMPLE: To demonstrate this evolution (and its downfall), I'll use as an example a group of nonprofits that was created solely to respond to a succession of federal laws in the 1960s and 1970s, who influenced health care policy for a while and faded away with the end of federal largesse in the 1980s: health planning agencies. (The reader should note that I was integrally involved in health planning from 1974 through 1982 as a volunteer, staffer, and executive director, and thus have a somewhat biased view of what happened.)

Most of you will never have heard of HSAs (health systems agencies) or their predecessors, CHPs (comprehensive health planning agencies), but both were funded primarily with federal funds and grew out of federal concern about rising health care costs, duplication of health care services, and a need to control both. CHPs that were funded from 1968 through 1974 were to enable consumer participation in health policy. In more than two hundred geographic health planning areas of the country, CHPs were to develop health care plans and have limited regulatory authority over hospital and nursing home expansion. HSAs (1974–1984) were the second generation of such agencies, with more money, expanded staffs, a mandate for "consumer" majorities on all boards and committees, and enhanced regulatory powers. The result of this program was more than two hundred new nonprofits with anywhere from four to two hundred staff each, over 100,000 volunteers on boards and committees, and an entire federal and state bureaucracy (I have heard numbers in excess of 350 federal staff when all the regional people were accounted for) just to keep tabs on the locals.

Why? To fulfill the federally designed mandates of cost containment, increased access to care, and consumer empowerment. Did it work? No, and in large part because of the three rules: "What we say goes" turned out to be the most deadly. The federal government decided in just one of many broad, national regulations that there should be no more than 6.1 medical surgical hospital beds per 1,000 population. As a result, HSAs were to turn down applications from hospitals for construction that exceeded that amount, and the funding of the HSAs was in part contingent on achieving that goal. This policy allowed for some local variance, but it had to be rigorously justified and it never adequately took into account important issues such as patient preference, rural accessibility, and relative quality of hospitals. Since these issues are common sense ones, even to nonprofessionals, the regulation was derided, resented, and disliked by almost all of the citizen volunteers upon whose service the entire system depended.

"What is yours is ours" and "You can't do well doing good" also had their own impact: HSAs could not fund-raise without penalty—whatever money they raised was reduced from the next year's budget allotment. They could not keep assets—they were really the federal government's, although HSAs were "independent." Is this the end of the HSAs? Because the federal government funded the program but never really made it a local one when, in 1981, the newly inaugurated President Reagan and his budget director David Stockman attacked the program and tried to zero out its budget; even local volunteers were hesitant to come to its defense. The HSAs were dead in the water. ■

The HSA program cost hundreds of millions of dollars and had thousands of good people at the volunteer, board, and staff level committed to its success, but it went aground on the shoals of too much distrust of local autonomy, an overzealous accounting mechanism, and a high resistance to change.

As long as we do not demand some common sense in government, we will have to live with the ludicrous level of oversight that reduces all regulations to catching the 2 percent of us who are crooks and/or idiots and punishing the 98 percent who are honest and have a brain cell or two. In this environment, you cannot blame the state or federal employees who are caught in the oversight squeeze; they have to assume guilt until innocence is proven, and thus they are never going to fully trust us.

Now, how can we go about breaking both you and your funders out of this relational purgatory? We must, you know, if we are to actually bring the nonprofit world into the second decade of the twenty-first century in some sort of reasonably effective shape. That is really what the rest of the book is about. Hopefully, by giving you some idea of the world you will be working in, and by increasing your skill base, giving you tools, and showing you how other agencies have broken free of the cycle of co-dependence (and that is exactly what it is), you will be better able to do it yourself. Let's start with an examination of the environment you will be working in.

What the Next Ten Years Will Bring

When I look back on my predictions from the 2000 edition of *Mission-Based Management*, my head spins with the changes we've seen. As I wrote that edition, our economy was sound, federal deficits were thought to be a thing of the past, and we in the United States happily considered ourselves on top of the world. So much for hubris.

No matter where we live, or how large or small our organization is, we've become part of a global economy, and what happens on the far side of the world this morning can affect us in very real ways later *today*, not in weeks, months, or years, as in the past. We need and depend upon each other across national borders more than ever, and this is true economically, politically, and socially. Technology has woven us together tightly, opened previously closed doors, and raised previously shut blinds. A donor can find out what our nonprofit spent two years ago (and what the CEO's salary was) in less than a minute. You can give a donation to a specific nonprofit in India as quickly as you can give to one in Indiana. And attention spans? What attention spans? We want it all now, and we want it all customized to each of us.

And, of course, there is the global recession, which is still growing as these words are written. We've been reminded that "old" rules are still valid: Borrow very little, diversify your investments, there is no free lunch. A much different, much more challenging environment presents itself to us over the next decade and beyond.

Nonprofits are, of course, impacted by all of this. What follows is a set of trends that will affect you, and that you as a mission-based manager should consider and prepare for.

Governments with Fewer Resources

We all know that the U.S. federal government is broke (as are most others) but still pushing billions of dollars out the door to stimulate the economy. Most states are in the same predicament, but they can't manufacture funds to purchase services. They have to balance their budgets every year. As this is written in 2009, the most reasonable predictions I see are for a long, deep recession perhaps bottoming out in late 2010 with a slow recovery starting no earlier than 2011. Thus, we won't get back to solid state finances for at least three to five years out—the midpoint of my ten-year prediction horizon. I hope I'm pessimistic, but as good managers we have to go by the mantra "Hope for the best, prepare for the worst." So, here's the deal: You are going to have to muster every iota of time, strength, and savvy to fight for every dollar for the next decade. Remember, even if your nonprofit doesn't take government funds, most nonprofits do. And since their prime source of funds is under real long-term duress, those organizations will continue to compete with your for other funds, from foundations or corporate and individual donors. If you believe your mission is essential, you had better be out convincing others that it is, too.

You should also be aware of four important points regarding this prediction. The first is that even though the *overall* rate of funding from government is dropping, the level of support for the specific programs that your organization provides will vary greatly depending on the political winds. Think about how the feds spent lavishly for ten years in areas that prevent or treat substance abuse—in response to the national movement toward semi-temperance. Then funds flowed to funding for AIDS research, prevention, diagnosis, and treatment, which have gone to entities as widely varied as health departments, hospitals, child welfare departments, drug centers, medical schools, and arts organizations. Now that AIDS is seen by the public and Congress (certainly debatably) as under control, those funds are dwindling. Up through the beginning of the recession in 2008, the U.S. fundee of choice was schools and crime prevention, which didn't last, either. The bottom line: If your area of service is in vogue, you will be hurt a bit less; if not, you may be hurt even more deeply.

The second point is that, in addition to the fact that the rate of funding for your organization is falling, if you are like the majority of your peers, that rate of payment *per unit of service* is probably already woefully short of meeting the needs in your community and may not even be paying your full cost of service. Thus, even if your area of services is "in vogue" and stays steady, that should not be a great deal of comfort. You and your organization will have to look to new sources of income to meet the increasing needs of your community for services. Moreover, if your organization, particularly those in human service or education, gets paid on a fee-for-service basis, wherein you bill the city, county, state, or federal government for services *after* those services are provided, be prepared to be able to come up with more "working capital," the money that you need to pay the bills between the time you provide a service and when you get paid. Why? Because you will be providing more such services, and thus floating more receivables, and the government agencies will be paying you later. (One high official of a state welfare agency told me recently, "We postpone payment one day, just *one* day, and we 'save' $29 million." That's real money, and they need real money now more than ever.)

The third point is related to the second, and it has to do with the need to go outside and look for new sources of funds. As noted above, the traditional place that nonprofits do that is in starting to do fund-raising and increasing applications to foundations. Of course, these have become much more competitive in the past few years as governmental resources stayed static in the face of growing demand. Hundreds of nonprofits that have never gone out to do traditional fund-raising have started doing so in the past few years, and more are entering the arena. This change is occurring at the same time that corporate donations and sponsorships and foundation funding are all waning due to the economy's collapse. Be prepared to improve your fund-raising and grant-writing skills dramatically, or fall by the wayside. If you are in the development world, you need to be good at it. You had better be out there selling that mission as a core competence.

The fourth and final point here is that the confluence of all the first three is that your nonprofit will need to use volunteers more strategically and for more professional tasks over the next ten years. I call these people "unpaid professionals" since the term *volunteer* too often (and inaccurately) brings to mind someone making copies or answering the phone. These new volunteers are not the same as the traditional ones we value so much. They come to the nonprofit giving of their very high talent and skill, but often for a limited time. Think of Doctors Without Borders as a good example. I know that many readers will say, "But what we do is life and death. It requires licensure, certification, and continuing education. We can't just let volunteers do what we do." I understand the barriers to entry but would point out that over 70 percent of the firefighters in the United States are volunteers and the same holds for emergency medical technicians (EMTs), and no one would argue they are not doing not life and death work. And again, think about Doctors Without Borders.

There are nonprofits springing up to deal with this change, including the Experience Corps and some new twists within AmeriCorps. Teach for America is drawing many more applicants than it has positions available. You will see more people being available to come to you for a three-, six-, or twelve-month internship during their careers, not just before or after. And with the Obama administration's call for national service, there will simply be more volunteers out there to choose from.

The key for you is to think strategically about volunteers and to make sure you ramp up your volunteer management skills to make the best use of this remarkable resource.

Generation Change in Full Swing

This is both good news and bad news, and it is not a prediction but a simple fact. Four generations now overlap in our nonprofits, and these four generations are all significantly different (and sometimes clashing) cultures. The older generations (the Silent and Baby Boomer) have much different outlooks on work–life balance, technology, and management styles than do the younger generations (GenX and what I call Gen@). In my 2007 book *Generations: The Challenge of a Lifetime for Your Nonprofit* (St. Paul, MN: Fieldstone Alliance, 2007) I argue that understanding and harnessing the different skills and perspectives of these generations is crucial to the success of your nonprofit and its mission. Not only will we be handing off the management of our national nonprofit sector to the younger generations in the next ten years at the staff level, but we also need to backfill with younger members on our boards, the vast majority of whom were Boomers as of 2008.

Here is some unsettling news if you are a Boomer or Silent Generation manager. We (and I am your age) need to relearn and adapt our management style to fit the younger generations who increasingly make up our staff and board. If we do not, we will alienate the best young people and leave our nonprofit weaker as a result. More on that in Chapter 7, "Leading Your People."

More Demand for Services, Particularly in a Weak Economy

The volume of demand will grow irrevocably, irreversibly, and probably faster than you anticipate, in almost every area of nonprofit service (but particularly in the social services) in a weak economy. If you are in education, the national concern with the decay in our educational structure has already led to more school choice, and "No School Left Behind" has institutionalized testing, often to the detriment of actual learning. If you run a faith-based organization, the continuing national return to the church, synagogue, and mosque will lead to increased need for services and facilities, as well as increases in competition for dollars, as many reputable ministries vie for the same funding sources. In the arts, a better-educated public will want more theater, music, and displays of fine arts nearer and more accessible to them, but only if they can afford them. If you provide a social service, whether to youth, seniors, the homeless, or the mentally or physically disabled, the need for your services will grow faster than the population as a whole.

The reasons for the increase in demand outstripping simple demographic growth are multiple. First, we as a society have turned to nonprofits increasingly for the past thirty years, and we are used to seeking help there. Second, one of the legacies of the last thirty years is a chronic governmental underfunding of social services, particularly low-income housing and job creation assistance that has led to the large number of chronic homeless and "underclass" citizens who are at significantly higher risk of needing services that you provide than the population as a whole. Thus, you cannot just use census projections to predict the need for your services. Since 2000, the disparity between the haves and the have-nots has grown alarmingly. This rift is exacerbated by the current economic downturn. If you are in any field within the nonprofit sector, this fact should unsettle you and factor into your predictions of demand.

Finally, there is one other key issue to ponder here. Not only is raw demand (the number of people presenting themselves for services) going to continue to climb but the cost of serving each of those people will also rise at the same time that income will stay basically static. People are showing up with many more needs than ever before, and to adjust to and serve these needs costs money. As a human services administrator told me in June 2008, "The people we see are broken in so many more ways, and all at once. They come with layer upon layer of problems, and drilling down through all those layers is an imposing, and expensive task." Words to remember.

A More Competitive Environment—And More Failing Nonprofits

This is the biggest single change that you will see during the rest of your career, whether you are 20 or 60. This competition between nonprofits, which began in the early 1990s, has now shown up in everything you do. You are now competing for clients, students, patrons, or parishioners; for funding from traditional sources and for funding from new sources; for donations; for United Way dollars; for visibility; for donated services such as air time and advertising; for clicks and eyeballs on your Web site; and for good volunteers and great staff.

The most disruptive, nerve-wracking, and positive change for many nonprofits is in the area of competing for people to serve. In the past fifteen years, counties, states, and even the federal government have brought more and more programs into the competitive fold. They did this because of the first two trends listed above: limited funds and nearly unlimited demand for services, many of which are entitlements. Caught on the horns of a fiscal dilemma, the solution many purchasers of service have sought is anathema to our entire sector: capitalism. By this I mean putting agencies, many for the very first time, into the risk/reward cycle that is the engine that runs our economy. This, of course, has challenged the monopoly that you once enjoyed. "Monopoly!?" you ask. Absolutely. How many times when asking for funding have you heard the question, "Does this program duplicate anything already serving the same constituency?" Lots, I am sure. The reason: Funders did not want to encourage "duplicate" funding (i.e., competition). Imagine the same scene with your city council approving only one fast-food restaurant or one grocery store in town—to avoid duplication. They would be run out of office for obstructing commerce, interfering with competition, and in general for being too regulatory. But in the nonprofit arena this has been (shortsightedly) considered appropriate.

No more. Funders are looking for the best productivity, the most mission for the money. Volunteers are looking to spend their time wisely. Quality staff want to work with organizations that are financially viable as well as state-of-the-art in terms of service. Businesses that donate services want to associate with top-caliber organizations, not ones that will have their work, finances, or reputation show up in the scandal sheets. And all that information can be had online in a heartbeat.

Here is the good news from the perspective of a funder, donor, citizen/taxpayer, and service recipient: This works, and works well. Not perfectly, not immediately, but the result is better services and lower costs. The bad news: From the perspective of the nonprofit manager, this is hell on wheels. We, as a sector, have not been ready for this. We have been underfunded, thanks to cheap funders and our own inability to discipline ourselves to put aside funds. Few of us have benefited from "capacity-building funds" necessary to get our back-room operations ready to compete. But like it or not, competition is here and increasingly ingrained in the mind-set of our funders and community. In an era of even more limited resources, this competitive trend is only going to grow.

Here are two other spinoffs of competition to consider. First, when foundation, governmental, or corporate funding becomes more competitive, some nonprofits will be unable to compete and will seek more funds from traditional fund-raising, putting even more organizations in that already overpopulated (and highly competitive in its own right) arena. Second, some nonprofit organizations will flat out fail. They will not be able to convince enough of us in our various roles as citizens, governments, or foundations that their mission is worthy enough, and they will close. In late 2008, Paul Light predicted that perhaps as many as 100,000 U.S. nonprofits might fail in the coming eighteen months. I think Paul is optimistic.

Tech . . . Online All the Time

Here is the bottom line. The future of the charitable sector, the future of effective, competitive nonprofits, will come from the successful confluence of mission and technology. This does not mean we will not continue to need face-to-face services or human interaction of all kinds. When I am in the ICU, I do not want the nurse calling it in from home. What I am saying is that until nonprofits embrace (not accept, but *embrace*) technology as a way of doing mission more effectively and efficiently, as a way of reaching and educating more people, as a way of appealing to a new generation of staff and volunteers, until then, we will not be mission successful as we could be. As Jim Collins wisely pointed out in *Good to Great* (New York: Harper-Collins, 2001), technology is an *accelerator* of good ideas, not a *substitute* for one. You've got the good idea: It is your mission. But will you push technology to help you make that good idea, that mission a reality? I think you must. And, here's a hint—your youngest staff have the most intuitive understanding of technology and can help you move this way—if you let them.

More Transparency and Accountability

This is a good thing if it is handled in an atmosphere of making sure that your organization is accountable for what you do, how you do it, and how much you spend—but it can easily turn into a witch hunt (see my earlier discussion of the basic tenets of funders). It can result in a funder who buys a small amount of services from you and demands to know all about everything you do, own, think, and plan.

But we have to live with the contracts we sign. Accountability and the seemingly never-ending amount of paperwork that accompany it will continue to increase as long as the press and the public wonder about us. Accountability is a fact of life and should be seen as a cost of doing business. The oversight may be frustrating and expensive, but we need to spend less time whining about it and more time figuring out how to use technology to make being accountable easier and less costly.

Also remember that accountability and competition go hand in hand. The funders (who have choices of where to send their money) want more accountability and often can get it with a few keystrokes. If you can't measure your real outcomes, in the current environment you may not get much repeat funding. Better use of technology can help you be accountable more efficiently and effectively, but you have to be comfortable with the idea of being accountable in the first place, not just resigned to it.

So there are six areas of change you will need to pay attention to and, most likely, accommodate in the next decade. The remainder of this book will try to give you the tools, techniques, and perspectives to help your organization become more mission-capable and more mission-productive.

Recap

In this chapter, we have reviewed how nonprofits came to where they are today, how your funders really think of you, and the six trends that I believe you are going to have to accommodate to stay viable over the next ten years. These trends are the following:

1. Governments with fewer resources
2. Generation change in full swing
3. More demand for services, particularly in a weak economy
4. A more competitive environment and more failing nonprofits
5. Tech: Online all the time
6. More transparency and accountability

With these predictions in mind, the next question is: How do we adapt and accommodate to these conditions? Even more difficult is the answer to the next question: How do we adapt and accommodate to conditions that may exist in five years that no one can even foresee today? How do we stay close to our mission, stay solvent, stay flexible, and stay sane—all at the same time? How do we harness technology to help us do more of this?

I'm not sure that all of those things are possible (particularly the part about retaining your sanity), but Chapter 3 will detail my observations about the key characteristics of the best, most flexible, most focused nonprofits in the country. By trying to emulate their successes and to integrate their strengths with yours, your organization can move through the next ten years and come out stronger and more mission-capable.

CHAPTER 3

What Works

The Characteristics of a Successful Nonprofit

Overview

This chapter will, in effect, preview the remainder of the book. First, we will turn from the environment to the organization, and I will lay out for you the ten updated characteristics of organizational success that will help you overcome the problems and environmental changes that we reviewed in Chapter 2. Each of the chapters that follow will detail the ways to attain these characteristics. Then I'll define what I contend are the key characteristics of a mission-based manager. There are four different ways that these stewards show their true colors, and we will go over each. By the end of this brief chapter, you will have a good idea of what is in store for you as you read the remainder of the book, and of the standards to which I will be holding you and your organization.

The Ten Characteristics of a Mission-Based Organization

All successful organizations share common characteristics. Since 1982, I have had the opportunity to train thousands of nonprofit staff and board and to consult for hundreds of nonprofits. These consultations often included management reviews, strategic planning, and new business development. In the course of this work, I had the opportunity to talk to staff, board, community members, and the people who the organizations served in depth. As a result, I have had the good fortune to see many, many consistently excellent nonprofits and to talk to their stewards about their strengths and weaknesses, plans and opportunities, their culture and their dreams. It is an examination of those strengths, and how they can work for you and your organization, that make up the rest of this book.

What is striking in these consistently successful organizations is the similarity of these key organizational characteristics. Over and over, I see the same core set of beliefs, values, traditions, policies, and culture on which the organization functions. It does not matter whether the nonprofit is a place of worship, a school, a museum, a hospital, a trade association, or a rehabilitation facility—these key characteristics consistently shine through.

I have attempted to distill these key characteristics into the ten that follow. Any such distillation is fraught with a certain amount of peril. I may group things in ways that don't fit your organization the best, or I may not emphasize a particular item enough. I have tried to put the key components in a logical and workable form, breaking them not only into different segments but separating them in such a way that I hope you can study each, apply the information to your organization, and then put all the pieces back together to make a cohesive whole.

These characteristics have been updated since the second edition of *Mission-Based Management*, and in the intervening years I have had hundreds of requests to put the list of characteristics in priority order. As you will see, mission—which should always come first—is first. After that, I have done my best to order them, but at some peril to the reader. Remember this: They are *all* important. They work together as a group, like the parts of a fine symphony. You cannot be a good social entrepreneur without doing great marketing, or be organizationally tech savvy without investing in your staff. Ignore one or more parts and the whole is greatly diminished. Bring them all together and their synergy outstrips the sum of their individual contributions. So don't perseverate on the order. Just address each one in turn and try to achieve and maintain your mission-based status.

Here are my ten characteristics of successful nonprofits:

1. *A viable mission.* The first rule of nonprofits is *mission, mission, and more mission.* A mission-based organization needs to follow its mission, and to do so it needs a mission that motivates and is understandable, supportable, up-to-date, and needed. Without the mission, what's the point? Unfortunately, at too many nonprofits, there is no point because the mission has become secondary to survival. In Chapter 4 you will learn how to write and use an effective mission statement *effectively.*

2. *Ethical, accountable, and transparent.* We are, after all, just stewards of the community's resources. The best nonprofits understand this and are increasingly transparent in their work. But good accountability and transparency begins at home, *inside* the organization. So does the all-important emphasis on values and ethical decision making. Chapter 5 will cover these topics in detail.

3. *A businesslike board of directors.* Your organization needs a group of governing volunteers that know, understand, and pursue the

organization's mission consistently; are connected to the community; stick to policy; and are the check and balance on the staff—as well as on the people who fund the organization. A board needs the information, experience, character, and support to know how to decide key issues quickly and effectively and, in today's tough environment, they need to know when to say no to a good idea. In Chapter 6, I'll show you how to assess, recruit, and retain just such a board, one that will give you more outcome and policy guidance and less day-to-day manipulation than you thought possible.

4. *A strong, well-educated staff.* Any effective nonprofit needs staff who are advocates for the mission, who manage from the bottom up, and who are constantly trained and training. There is no investment more necessary or more neglected than staff education and training. Chapter 7 will show you the best way to treat, employ, manage, motivate, and retain your staff. You will also learn how to most effectively get staff much more integrally involved in the outcomes of your organization.

5. *Embracing technology for mission.* Far too many charitable organizations still feel that technology is a necessary evil, not the path to better mission. The best mission-based organizations embrace technology as an accelerator of good mission. Technology touches every corner of our lives every hour of every day, and it has permanently changed the ways nonprofits provide services, buy services, hire, manage, communicate, raise funds, and keep abreast of changes in the state of the art. In Chapter 8, I'll show you how to bring your mission and your technology together. Again, the whole is a lot greater than the sum of the parts.

6. *Social entrepreneurs.* Organizations need to be willing to take risks to perform their mission, to try (and often fail) and try again, to look at markets and provide services to support their mission rather than create bureaucracies to continue past (and often outdated) practices. Chapter 9 will give you the best ideas on how to motivate your staff, board, and community to continually take reasonable risks on behalf of the people you serve. It will also show you how to assess your core competencies and match them with the wants of your target markets.

7. *A bias for marketing.* Organizations that understand that *everything* they do is marketing and see every act from service provision to how the phone is answered as a marketing opportunity to pursue their mission. Our marketing discussion will be in Chapter 10, where you will learn who your markets really are, how to give those markets what they want, and how to provide a marketing edge for everyone in your organization.

8. *Financially empowered.* Organizations need to have diversified income, income from nontraditional sources, an endowment, and, therefore, the ability to have an impact on their mission without waiting for help. "Sure," you say, "all of that would be nice if it dropped in my lap."

Well, it doesn't happen on its own. These organizations make it happen. Chapter 11 will show you how to do it in your organization. We'll look at the characteristics of financial empowerment and how to apply them in your organization.

9. *A vision for where they are going.* This is so simple, yet so often ignored. A strategic plan, both the process and the document, is a key to success. Without a plan, the only way you get anywhere is by accident: Isn't what you do too important to be left up to chance? Of course it is, and Chapter 12 will show you why you need to have a plan, what kinds of plans there are, and will lay out a process for you to have a usable, meaningful plan.

10. *A tight set of controls.* These include personnel, finance, operations, media, quality control, and maintenance policies. Good controls free the organization to work on its mission rather than watching its back all the time. In Chapter 13, we'll look at twelve different types of policies and show you where most groups make mistakes, so you don't have to.

In each of the following chapters, we'll discuss the important parts of each of the ten characteristics noted above and leave you with questions for further discussion with board and staff.

What Is a Mission-Based Manager?

If the outcome that I want your organization to have is to be a mission-based business, you and your peers obviously should aspire to become mission-based managers. Such managers have four major skills that we will examine here. Balance, innovation, motivation, and communication are the crux of such individuals' tool chests. Let's look at each in a little more detail.

1. *Mission-based managers* balance *the needs of the community with the available resources of the organization.* Balance is such an important skill. We need to balance our checkbook, our personal and business lives, and our priorities with our resources. This has never been more true in nonprofits than it is today. There are so many people in need, so many community priorities that cry out for attendance. They call to our hearts, and we, as people, want to respond. But in any organization, even yours, there are only so many resources. Even if your organization won the lottery today, there would still be needs to meet when you got done spending all the money.

   Mission-based managers understand that they need to balance pressing needs with available resources and not provide services that they cannot pay for. Does this mean that we accept what we have and do not seek more resources? Of course not. But *mission, mission, and more mission* is only the first rule of nonprofits. It is not the only rule—the second rule is *no money, no mission*. Balance of money and mission, board and staff, close supervision and staff freedom, and work and life is a theme and a challenge that you will see over and over in this book.

2. *Mission-based managers are* innovative *social entrepreneurs, taking reasonable risks on behalf of the people who the organization serves*. True leaders know that consistent innovation is the linchpin of consistent success, and even of continued survival. But innovation is always risky, and it requires an open mind to new ideas and an ability to not fall in love with the way you have always done things—even if you personally invented that tradition. Put simply, a socially entrepreneurial organization must be led by social entrepreneurs, and that leadership must role-model the behaviors that they want from the rest of the organization. Organizational risk also always translates to some degree of personal risk: If you make too many bad risk decisions, you'll probably be out of a job. The problem is that if you do not make any risk-taking calls, everyone will lose his or her job and the mission won't get done. We'll talk a lot more about social entrepreneurism in Chapter 9.

3. *Mission-based managers lead the organization* by example, *and in so doing motivate their staff, their board, and their community*. Successful organizations have people who lead them through the good times and the bad, who keep them on track when there are lots of distractions, and who are able to motivate the rest of the organization with their energy, their vision, and their example. Successful leaders know that they must lead from the front and walk the talk first. In nonprofits, leaders are held to an even higher example than in for-profits. We are all on a pedestal, in the hot klieg lights regarding our behavior. Nonprofit leaders must evidence the values of their organization in their behavior every day, or their staff, their donors, their volunteers, and their community will write them and their organization off. Look at it this way: If a for-profit chief executive officer (CEO) is accused of embezzlement or sexual harassment, it is a small story on page 5 of your newspaper. Does the for-profit suffer in terms of business? Usually not much or not for long—people often do not feel that management impropriety should affect their use of the organization, particularly if it is not a local business. But if a non-profit CEO were accused of that same behavior, what would happen? Right. Page 1 story, fall-off in donations, community trust, volunteer time, and so on. Your actions as a mission-based manager have major repercussions. You need to lead by your values every day. People are watching, both inside and outside of the organization.

4. *Mission-based managers can* communicate *their mission effectively to their staff, their board, the public, their funders, and the community at*

large. There is no way to lead without being a good communicator, and a mission-based manager has to communicate in many ways every day. You have to tell your staff what you want them to do, inquire of your markets what they want, and interact with your board, your funders, and your community all in ways that move your organization forward, not back. The key word here is *effectively,* and that means that the intended message gets to the intended audience. If the wrong message gets out, it means that the organization has taken a small (or huge) step backward. Communications is crucial, and we'll discuss it at length in Chapter 7.

Now you have been exposed to the ten characteristics of successful nonprofits and the four key skills you need to be a competent mission-based manager. As you look at information in the following chapters—information that expands on each of these ten core characteristics of nonprofit success and weaves in the personal skills—ask yourself the following: How does my organization measure up? Do we *really* do all these things or only pay them lip service? How about me? Am I good at balancing things or at motivation? As you continue through the remaining chapters, be brutally frank with yourself. This is not a time for self-delusion. That will only lead to ignoring real problems and deferring any needed changes.

Recap

In this chapter, you have seen the ten characteristics you and your organization need to embrace, adopt, and maintain. To recap, these ten are:

1. A viable mission
2. A businesslike board of directors
3. A strong, well-educated staff
4. Embracing technology
5. Social entrepreneurs
6. A bias for marketing
7. Financially empowered
8. Ethical, accountable, and transparent
9. A vision for where you are going
10. A tight set of controls

These ten characteristics, when achieved as a group, can improve your ability to do your mission, improve your organization's long-term viability, and assure the people you serve that you will be there to serve them for the long haul. They don't show up on their own, and they can't be developed overnight. Moreover, once you attain them all, only hard work and discipline will keep them in place.

Then we turned to the four essential skills of the mission-based manager. I assume that in reading this book, you are trying to not only improve your organization but also your own management style. I included four key skills, and we should look at them again:

1. Mission-based managers *balance* the needs of the community with the available resources of the organization.
2. Mission-based managers are *innovative* social entrepreneurs, taking reasonable risks on behalf of the people who the organization serves.
3. Mission-based managers lead the organization *by example*, and in so doing *motivate* their staff, their board, and their community.
4. Mission based managers can *communicate* effectively to their staff, their board, the public, their funders, and the community at large.

The skills are challenging and are ones that we will work on throughout the book. The characteristics of success and the skills of the mission-based manager play off each other beautifully, reinforcing one another. So you need them all. In the remainder of this book I'll show you how to achieve and maintain both sets.

Questions for Discussion (Chapters 1–3)

1. How do our funders really view us? How do we know?
2. Do we act like a mission-based business? Specifically, how can we get better? Does our staff view us as a charity or as a mission-based business? What about our board? Our funders?
3. In Chapter 2, a number of predictions were made about the next ten years. Which apply to us and how?
4. How many of the ten characteristics that were listed for success do we already have in place in our organization? Of those that are not fully in place, which is the most important for us to develop?
5. What about our personal management skills? Do we measure up to the list?

CHAPTER 4

The Mission Is the Reason

Overview

Let's be realistic: If you are an employee of a nonprofit, you are not in this for the money, nor for a low-stress, short-hour job. If you are a volunteer, you are not spending time with your charity of choice so that you can miss time at home or at work or avoid getting eight hours of sleep at night. If you are a donor, you are drawn by what? The same thing that attracts the staff and volunteers: The *mission*—what the organization *does*.

If that is true, why is the mission even an issue in this book? Why take up time and space on a topic that we all agree is vital? There are more reasons than you might imagine, and in this chapter we'll cover each of them and provide some examples and ideas for you to better utilize your mission as you move your organization ahead. If mission is your most important resource (and it is), you need to get the most from this resource in every way, every day.

In the following pages, we'll first examine the need that you have for a mission statement and how to review and rewrite your mission statement to help you become the organization that you want to be, not merely continue to be the organization you were in the past. We'll then look at the ways that mission statements are misused, underutilized, or completely forgotten. Finally, we will discuss how to use your mission statement as a tool for policy, management, and marketing—in short, how to turn your organization into a mission-based one on a day-to-day basis.

The Mission Statement Is Your Legal Reason for Existence

As noted above, the mission statement is not only the reason you work or volunteer for your organization but it also has important legal implications for staff and board. If you do not perform your mission, in the United States, the IRS can take away your tax-exempt status under section 501(c) of the Internal Revenue Code. The same holds true in other countries around the world. If you bring in too much of your funds from unrelated business income (defined as "income that is derived from activities that do not importantly contribute to the charitable purpose (the mission) of the organization"), you also stand a chance of losing your tax-exempt status, as well as bearing tax liability for any profits from such unrelated businesses.

You may not know that many nonprofits are technically in violation of their mission statement and have unrelated business income that they do not even realize. Usually, this is due to having been established long enough ago that your mission has morphed. For example, if in 1960 you were set up to provide a service in County A but now, as your community has grown, you provide services in Counties A, B, and C, and if your mission statement specifies only County A, you are technically getting unrelated business income from all of the activities that you perform and are reimbursed for in Counties B and C. The same issue arises for nonprofits that were originally set up to provide only mental health services but now do substance abuse; were formed to help the African American community but now assist people from all ethnic backgrounds; or were formed to help senior citizens but now find it useful to provide day care to the elderly *and* the very young. (Note: If this is your situation, see the "Have a Board/Staff Review" section that follows.)

All of this is said to underscore the importance of having a mission that you know, you can live with, and that accurately portrays not only what your organization does now but what you want it to do in the next three to five years.

Writing or Rewriting Your Mission Statement

You all have a mission statement. It is in your articles of incorporation and the forms you submitted to the IRS (or the corresponding government agency if you are outside of the United States) to receive your tax-exempt status. It may also be restated in your bylaws. Every three years (at the same time that you will be writing your strategic plan, discussed in Chapter 12) you need to revisit your mission statement. You need to take the opportunity to get your staff's and board's input into what your mission should be. In most cases, it will be exactly the same as it is now, only you will have a renewed sense of its urgency as a result of the discussion. In any event, there are a number of steps that I suggest you take in reviewing your mission statement.

Find Your Current Mission Statement

If you are like most of your peers, you may have more than one "mission statement." There may be different language in your bylaws, articles of incorporation, or applications for funding. Gather them all up and review them. See where there are differences and similarities. Take the best of all of them and move to the next step.

Note Any Substantive Changes

Have you started to provide services in a new geographic area outside of any listed in your mission statement? Have you added services or a new kind of clientèle? Make sure to consider amending your statement to include this new geography or demography, and make sure that the language you use is up to date.

Have a Board/Staff Review

At a special meeting or at your strategic planning retreat, go over your current mission and any substantive changes, and then talk through whether your current mission statement is inclusive enough for the kind of organization you are shaping. Does it accurately reflect your core values? Does it restrict your flexibility? *Don't* try to rewrite the mission as a group. You will still be there agonizing over syntax and comma placement in 2105. Do talk through the key points or values you want to include, things like "accessible to all parts of the community," "highest quality of service," and "sensitive to different cultural values." In Chapter 5, I will suggest that accountability and transparency should be on your list. Then redraft your mission statement and take it back to the board for review and adoption.

 HANDS ON: Once the mission is rewritten, have it formally adopted by the board of directors or voted on by your membership (meeting whatever stipulations are in the bylaws) *and then send it, with the minutes of the board action, to your state attorney general and to the Internal Revenue Service.* This is critical, as the IRS will judge you under the Unrelated Business Income Tax provisions of the IRS Code based on the mission statement that they have *on file.* If you do not send the amended mission statement to the IRS, they will never know and will judge you on your old, outdated mission statement. ■

Now let's turn our attention to the ways that people misuse or underutilize their mission statement. I have already noted that the mission statement is a resource that you need to use, and unfortunately it is a resource that is often underutilized in many nonprofits.

The Forgotten Mission Statement

What good is your mission statement if no one knows about it? You and your board and staff may review the mission statement every year or two, but if you are like most nonprofits, that is the extent of your use of your mission. I think you need to be reminded of it regularly. We need the mission as a beacon to guide us when we get distracted by the day-to-day ups and downs of life.

FOR EXAMPLE: All three of my children at one time or another played noncompetitive youth soccer. Since Ben, the oldest, played, his younger brother Adam and younger sister Caitlin started at the earliest age allowed: four. Now, at age four, watching soccer is more amusing than exciting, and when Adam started playing, I decided to keep busy by analyzing a little of the group dynamics of the games, practice, and coaching.

Questions sprang to mind. How do you motivate four-year-olds to keep their minds on the game or get them to compete? You have to urge them to "take the ball away" from another child when all they've heard from parents up to that age is "Share now, Susie." At Adam's first game, I wondered, what does the coach say before the game? Will she say, "Win one for the Gipper"? or get technical and say, "Remember play 17! Trevor go left, Andrea go right, pass to Sarah, and she shoots!"?

Not a chance. What she did, and what all soccer coaches of very young players, say is "Look at me. LOOK. AT. ME. Now WHICH WAY ARE WE GOING?" And some, perhaps most, of the children think and point to the goal and say, "THAT WAY!!!" And then the parents line up along the side of the field and remind the kids which way to kick the ball. Why? Because kids get easily distracted, by picking a flower, seeing a friend from school on the other team, or waving to Mom or Dad, and they often kick the ball toward the wrong end of the field. ■

The point of the example is that we, in our organizations, often also get distracted from the goal, from our mission, and it is not as easy for us to refocus on the point of what we do as it is for the kids on the soccer field: You can pick them up and show them where the goal is. Your "goal" is the mission statement, and it needs to be as visible and readily available as the goal on the soccer field.

Remember, distractions are a natural part of the busy world we live and work in. We have annual meeting time, budget time, audit time, Monday, Tuesday, Wednesday . . . Well, you get the idea. It's easy to get off track. Thus, we need to model ourselves after the parents at the soccer game and constantly be reminding each other that the mission *is* the point. By using the mission statement in management and board decisions, by posting it clearly, by incorporating it into personnel evaluations, you can reinforce and remind people all of the time that your mission is paramount. Otherwise, your mission is forgotten among the ashes of the fires that you are putting out each day.

The Mystery Mission Statement

Can you recite your mission statement right now? Probably not, and that's okay for now. But do you at least know the key elements? Does your mission statement specify a particular group of people, geographic area, or type of service? Or does it include some combination of all three? You do need to know that. When was it written? When was it last reviewed by the board and the staff?

One thing is important to remember: Most mission statements are written to be broad statements of charitable activity—usually drafted by attorneys to be as broad as possible, or by advocates of a particular crusade who do not want to offend anyone. They often say, in effect, *"XYZ of YourTown is a nonprofit dedicated to be all things to all people everywhere forever, charitably."* That is fine, but realize that along with that broad, all-inclusive mission can come considerable disagreement in *how* to achieve or at least pursue that mission, as well as an inherent difficulty in getting anyone's attention. I want to work or volunteer for (or donate to) an organization that does something special, something unique. So, bland is not good. On the other hand, if we get too specific, we sometimes confuse people about what we really do.

 HANDS ON: Try this: At your next board meeting and next senior management meeting, ask everyone to get out a piece of paper and write down in one sentence *the single most important thing your organization does.* Then have everyone read his or her answers and write them on the board or on a flipchart. Compare the answers. How many duplications do you have? ■

If you are like the overwhelming number of nonprofits, you'll have few if any duplications. Why? Because *everyone* in the organization comes to it from a different background, perspective, or priority. For example, if you are a human service provider, you have staff who are *doing* while your managers are *managing.* It sounds obvious, but look at how their perspectives will be different. The staff will look at the micro (how the mission affects their job and their part of the organization) and the managers *should* look at the macro (the organization as a whole, or at least their larger part of it). You may well have board members or volunteers who have been recipients of one (but perhaps *only* one) of the services you provide, and their perspective on what you do is colored by their individual and often very personal experiences.

This difference of perspective is a key, and too often overlooked, fact in nonprofits. We are likely to assume that every one of us comes to the organization because we agree on the mission and good works the organization does. Not so. We come together to support what we perceive the mission to be, and it is that mission (our perceived one) that we will advocate and work toward. Obviously, this phenomenon results in a likelihood that we do not agree on the mission, and that can lead to either major conflicts or major strengthening.

Let's look at some real-world examples of this phenomenon.

 FOR EXAMPLE: An Association for Retarded Citizens (ARC) in a Great Plains state was a model of a mission-oriented nonprofit. Formed in the 1950s by parents of retarded children as a voluntary organization dedicated to fighting for funding for their cause, it had, over the years, evolved with the field to provide direct services to persons with developmental disabilities and their families, and employers who employed people with disabilities. The ARC ran twelve residential sites, a vocational workshop, an early-childhood assessment program, and recreational outings as well as support groups and outreach into the community.

Economically, 72 percent of its funding came from state and federal funds, mostly in the form of purchase-of-service, and mostly for less than the actual cost of service provided. The ARC made up for these underpayments by running a traditional (and profitable) "sheltered workshop" where developmentally disabled people do assembly, packaging, and manufacturing for for-profit businesses with assistance from supervisors. The ARC depended on the workshop profits to subsidize many of its other programs.

Then, in 1985, came a change in the philosophy of working with the developmentally disabled, an idea called *supported employment*. In supported employment, agencies like the ARC work with employers to find real jobs in real employment settings, and if the person with the disability needs some assistance, he or she gets the job along with a job coach, who is on site with him or her some or all of the time to ensure that folks stay on task and do the job as it needs to be done.

For the sheltered workshop, this policy was a potential financial disaster. Gone were the least disabled (and thus easiest to work with and most productive) employees. What would be done to keep the workshop profitable? Both the workshop director and the ARC CEO knew that without the profits from the workshop, other services would have to be cut. This would, of course, have an impact on service array, service quality, staff morale, and, eventually, community support and donations.

What should they do? Mandated by the state rules to move people "out into the working community," the ARC was faced with an agency-threatening dilemma unless the staff and board could adjust and adapt. But they did not want to just react; they wanted to respond in a way that they could all support.

The ARC board president called a board/staff retreat to discuss the issue and started with a review of the mission statement: ***"The Mission of the ARC is to work for persons with developmental disabilities and their families to help them achieve their highest potential in school, work, community life, and recreation."*** Even with this broad mission statement, there was stinging disagreement about how to proceed. Some participants wanted to close the workshop, noting that supported employment "works for everyone," no matter how disabled. Some were hesitant about setting a policy (promoting and providing supported employment) that would potentially put clients into a more "risky" job in the real community. Others raised the overall economic impact of potentially reduced profits on the rest of the agency's service array.

The solution? Support the mission. The key phrase? **"Work *for* persons with developmental disabilities."** To the board and staff, this meant allowing clients to choose their options and thus keep both options open. What this resulted in was keeping the workshop open as a work training, transition, and work location, with the eventual goal of having each person with a disability work in the setting *he or she* most liked. To keep profits up, they brought nondisabled staff to supplement the workforce. Thus, the program and the financial viability were preserved, and the solution worked well in light of the mission statement.

Those readers who are professionals or volunteers in the field of developmental disabilities may disagree with the ARC's choices, but the point here is that they let the mission guide them and didn't just react without thinking. ■

FOR EXAMPLE: A nonprofit performance auditorium in the South was in crisis. Like all major performance centers, the Hall, as we shall call it, had gone through tough financial times along with the arts community in general. The Hall not only housed the local symphony, ballet, and opera companies (renting to them at *(continued)*

(*continued*)

a steep discount), but it also reached out beyond its traditionally white, upper-middle-class clientele to the minority and lower-income communities by holding a wide variety of bookings, special performances for children, and so forth.

The financial mainstay of the Hall, however, was its series of Broadway touring productions. The profits from these productions kept the Hall open and allowed it to subsidize the "fine" arts and community outreach.

But ticket sales for the core Broadway series were down. The Hall needed renovations and upkeep that had been postponed for years. The outreach program had brought new nonprofit community groups asking to book the Hall—at a discount, of course. The performing arts nonprofits (symphony, ballet, and opera) were in a financially precarious state as well and could not afford to pay the full cost of the rental of the site but considered the Hall the only dignified place to perform, since it had the best acoustics and ambiance.

What should be done? The board looked at its mission to gain guidance into what the priorities should be: *"The mission of The Hall Inc. shall be to improve the community and cultural experiences of the people of [this state], to foster improvements and expansion of the arts, and to maintain the Hall as a community resource for future generations."*

Now, this broad mission provided some guidance but there were other barriers to a quick fix. First, several members of the board were also members of the symphony, ballet, and opera boards. Thus, their perspective was that the Hall's board should focus on the phrase "foster improvements and expansion of the arts," which to them meant continuing to subsidize their performing arts groups. Several board members were highly successful CEOs who focused on the "maintain the Hall as a community resource for future generations" part of the mission as a mandate to first and foremost break even financially and keep the Hall in excellent physical condition. The third group on the board were community representatives who wanted more access for their own constituencies.

The solution? There was no perfect one, but all of the people around the table understood finance well enough to know that without financial stability there can be no social good. Mission first, but no money, no mission. They agreed to prioritize their social and cultural obligations and budgeted an amount that was affordable for them to subsidize each performing group each year. Then it was up to staff to sell the Broadway series to meet the budget needs. They also set up a five-year capital endowment campaign to facilitate income from a non-arts source each year. Did they satisfy everyone? Not really. But they did acknowledge all of the perspectives around the table and tried to accommodate as many as possible, based on the mission statement. ■

The important points in these stories are many. First, even with a well-written and up-to-date mission statement, your organization will continue to have healthy (I hope) debates on how to implement the mission and on what your values are. That is fine and, as I say, if it is kept on a healthy, positive basis, debates can help the organization mature and keep up with the times. Second, without some common framework around which to discuss, there would have been no starting point for the ARC's or the performance hall's discussions. Their mission statements provided that framework. Third, everyone at your board table and staff meetings comes to the organization with his or her own history, perspective, and agenda. That can be an enriching fact or a divisive one, depending on how the executive director and board chairperson handle it. Use people's diversity of opinion, experience, and perspective to strengthen your organization; do not require everyone to think and act alike.

Getting More from an Underutilized Resource

Staff and board members of a nonprofit have a responsibility to get the most good out of the limited resources that they have. Isn't it ironic that in the day-to-day race to secure more of those resources to allow more of the mission to be realized, people usually forget to use *the mission itself* as a resource?

The mission statement can be a management tool, a rallying cry, a staff motivator, a volunteer recruiter, and a fundraiser. You already have invested in getting the mission statement in line with your values and long-term community needs. Now use that resource in these other areas:

■ *Management tool.* The mission statement should be a regular part of staff and board discussions in questions such as: "Which of the three options that we have before us is most responsive to our mission?" or "Will this type of funding gain us dollars but distract us from our mission?" Use the mission statement as a backstop to make better management and policy decisions. Have copies of your mission statement literally on the table at all meetings.

- *Rallying cry and staff motivator.* The mission statement can be used as a rallying cry and motivator for staff, volunteers, and board in tough times.

> **HANDS ON:** Try this: When the going gets particularly tough, when morale is low, or it seems people have given up hope, ask your staff or your board to list the good things that have happened in the last three weeks or months as a result of your organization's being in business. Get personal, talking about the impact of your organization's services on individuals. Then turn it around and ask them what would have happened if you hadn't been around as an organization. Refocus on the mission statement as a higher calling, a cause worth working and sacrificing for. *Note:* You can't use this exercise every day because it will lose its impact. Save it for when you *really* need it. ■

- *Volunteer recruiter.* Remember the response when President Kennedy called for the formation of the Peace Corps? Or the volunteers who flocked to the Gulf Coast to help after the devastation wrought by Hurricane Katrina? Or perhaps the questions you ask when people ask you to serve on a board or special committee? *Mission,* what the organization *did,* was the key in all of these. Kennedy called for assisting in less developed countries as a way of nonmilitary goodwill in an era of military confrontation. After Katrina, hundreds of nonprofits made it clear what people could and should do to help hurricane victims. When you are recruited for a board job, you ask what services the organization provides—what it *does.*
- *Fund-raiser.* Here, as in the volunteer recruitment area, what you do, what good works are done, and why you do it are all key questions in a donor's mind. The *what* of what you do is up to you, but the *why,* the mission, is the linchpin, and it should be the first rationale for funding. Donors, particularly big ones, like to see organizations that are focused on their mission, not just taking money for any and all purposes.

The Mission That Is Everywhere

Excellent organizations know their mission. It is on the tip of everyone's tongue, and you can ask nearly everyone in the place what the mission is and he or she will repeat it verbatim and give you reasons why *he or she* is the essential link in the chain to get the mission realized. How does this happen? Like the children on the soccer team, it is tough to focus people and it is easy to get distracted. A unified reason for being does not happen by accident. It happens through meaningful repetition. The mission needs to be visible *everywhere*.

Assuming that you have agreed to your revised mission statement, do the following:

- Have your mission statement drawn up in an attractive format and then frame it and place a copy of the framed mission in your reception area(s), staff lounges, and where services are provided. Do not just copy the mission and have people tape it to the wall. Do this right. Also, do not have the first time that the staff people see the mission be the framed copy on the wall. Make sure that they have seen and discussed it in advance.
- Put the mission statement in every document you print. It should be inside the front cover or front and center in at least the following:
  - Your annual report
  - All marketing and public relations material
  - Your board manual
  - Your staff personnel policies
  - Your staff orientation manual (with heavy emphasis on why the mission is so important)
  - Your strategic plan
  - Your Web site (in lots of places), and as a signature on your e-mail
- Use the mission daily as a tool (see above).
- One use I've seen repeatedly is to have the mission statement installed as the screen saver on all of the organization's computers. But it has to be short!

The mission that is everywhere is more likely to become part of the culture and part of the mind-set of the people who work and volunteer for your organization.

Putting Actions behind Your Words

Using the mission statement is a great thing but a perilous risk if not handled correctly. Once you hold the mission statement up as the Holy Grail and take time and resources to print it, post it, and use it at meetings, you hold yourself to a higher standard, one that invites criticism and interpretation from a variety of places. ("Well, *that* decision certainly does not support our mission" from whoever loses in a choice made by management or board.)

The cure for this is threefold: leadership, time, and training. To be more accurate, the real-world components are leadership, time, training, leadership, training, training, training, and leadership.

 FOR EXAMPLE: Everyone has heard of Ross Perot, the computer services billionaire and former presidential candidate. Perot made his money starting and growing Electronic Data Systems (EDS), a computer data services firm that was the first and, for a time, the largest processor of data in the world. Perot built his organization by doing a number of things, including emphasizing customer service, teamwork, and loyalty to each other and the organization, and by having a simple mission and set of values for everyone to work by.

EDS's mission statement was short and simple. Perot had it reduced to a wallet-sized card, which all employees carried so that they could produce it quickly to use in management discussions. For EDS employees, this worked.

At the same time, General Motors was a giant going nowhere. The new GM CEO, Roger Smith, saw the need for more and more information management to tie together the far-flung outposts of his automotive empire, and he contracted with EDS to set up and run the system. Smith got to know Perot, and he admired the lean, can-do attitude that EDS employees exuded and demonstrated in their work for GM. So, Smith proposed that GM buy EDS, in the hopes that the EDS culture would prove to be a "virus" that would spread throughout GM. He and the senior GM management team analyzed what to do to hasten this spread of entrepreneurial spirit, and they focused on the mission statements that everyone on the EDS team whipped out at the drop of a hat. They paid a consultant to come up with a new mission statement for GM, distributed the cards to everyone, and waited for the new "entrepreneurial GM" to emerge fully clothed. It didn't. Not only did the two cultures clash, but the inevitable battle and eventual falling out between Perot and Smith has attained the status of corporate legend. ■

Why didn't the EDS–GM marriage work? There are probably fifty major reasons, and entire books have been written on this subject. Suffice it to say that you cannot change a culture by handing out wallet-sized cards with nice words on them that no one has invested in. (Remember, a consultant had written GM's mission statement.)

Leadership

You need to be seen *living* the mission statement. Once you publicize and invest in your mission statement, you hold yourself up to a higher standard. *You* have to use the mission daily, visibly, and consistently. *You* have to embody its ideals. If the mission says to be culturally sensitive, *you* have to be the most educated and sensitive person in the organization. If the mission says for the organization to be an advocate for children, or a service provider to the most disadvantaged, or an educator of the best and brightest, *you* have to articulate and be a living symbol of the mission. People will be skeptical of the need or value of a revamped mission, and you have to live the mission: Do it, do not just say it.

But saying it, and saying it a lot, also matters. In his wonderful business fable, *The Four Obsessions of the Extraordinary Executive* (San Francisco: Jossey-Bass, 2000), Pat Lencioni shows that one of the key duties of management, and in particular the senior management, is to, in his words, "Over-communicate the core mission." I love this phrase because it means you can't tell people about the mission too much. Say it, say it again and again and again, and then, of course, *live* it.

Time

After leadership, the next key is the hardest—giving it time. You will need to work for many months and even years before the mission becomes ingrained. If you decide to do this (and you need to), you must lead the charge for a long, long time. As new staff and board people come on, they will know no other organization than one driven by the mission, and it will begin to be culturally ingrained. Make sure that a clear discussion of mission is ingrained in your staff recruitment and orientation practices. That way you start with mission first, which is, of course, the way it should be.

Training

Next, there is the need for training, training, training. There is no substitute for training. As we will see in later chapters, investing in your workforce is key, and 40 hours per year per person is the minimum acceptable amount. Whether in orientation, as noted above, or in other training, make at least some of every session about the mission: why it is there and hands-on training about how to use it. Remember, if someone has never managed or provided direct service by a clearly articulated mission before, this is new. Do not expect anyone to know how to do this automatically. Give people a chance to learn, practice, review, and learn more.

FOR EXAMPLE: In the period from 1986 to 1993, and again from 1996 to 1998, Michael Jordan of the Chicago Bulls in the National Basketball Association was, by a wide margin, the best basketball player in the world. And yet, to stay there, *he practiced every day three hours longer than his teammates.* But in the work world, we say, "Oh, I went to a supervision course once, I know how to do that," or "I took accounting in college. I remember that." Wrong. People say, "I've got thirty years of management experience. I've seen it all." Remember, OJT (on-the-job training) is not *practice*; it is the *game.* When you screw up, it is for real. If it is just experience you have, it is almost certainly based on outmoded philosophies, techniques, and technologies. Make learning for yourself and for your staff a lifelong pursuit. Train, train, train. More on this in later chapters. ■

Recap

In this chapter, we have covered the key points of the central crux of your organization, the mission:

- We've reviewed the way to write or rewrite a mission statement to bring it up to date.
- We've reviewed why a forgotten or mystery mission statement is of little or no use.
- We've looked at methods of utilizing your mission as a management, motivation, and policy tool.
- We've suggested methods for you and your staff and board to *live* the mission, not just parrot it.

As you finish this chapter, look around your organization. In how many places can you see and read the mission? Is it on the walls? On people's bulletin boards? Why not? Ask the first five staff you see what the mission is. Listen to their answers. Are they the same? Why not? Look at your marketing material. Is your mission on each and every piece? Why not?

So we agree, I hope, that the mission is a key element in your success. You need to review it, revise it with help from board and as many staff as you can, publicize it, use it daily (starting with your own activities), and train staff and volunteers in how to use the mission as a management and service provision tool. That is the starting point, and if you do not start here, the rest of what is in this book will be of a lot less use to you and your organization.

Questions for Discussion

1. What general improvements would we like to see in our mission statement? Do we have one or many mission statements?
2. Does our mission statement excite us? Is it short enough for us to remember, or does it suffer from comma fault? Is it an effective elevator message?
3. How can we better use the mission statement to recruit, retain, and motivate staff and volunteers?
4. How can we better use our mission statement in management discussions?
5. What specifically can those of us in leadership positions do to evidence our mission daily?

CHAPTER 5

Being Ethical, Accountable, and Transparent

Overview

Your organization's mission is the *why* of your nonprofit. It is your foundation, and that's why it's first on our list of characteristics of a successful nonprofit and the first rule of nonprofits. *Mission, mission, and more mission.* If the mission is *why* your organization is in business, then ethics, accountability, and transparency are the *how* you conduct your mission-based business, or at least they should be.

If you are openly and intentionally ethical, you'll have the best staff, the best board, and a great and trusting reputation in the community. If your organization is accountable for its actions and its outcomes (inside and out, which we'll get to in a minute), your reputation will be burnished and people will see that you not only mean what you say but take responsibility for what you do. If your organization is transparent (again, both inside and out), people will see that you have nothing to hide, while at the same time gaining a greater understanding of not only your mission but your challenges and opportunities. You'll gain more ownership and get more ideas from a wide array of people. Ethics, accountability, and transparency, done right, lead to more inclusion, increased involvement, and a feeling of community.

Over the last five years, the need for higher profiles in all three of these areas has increased dramatically. Technology makes transparency easier and less expensive, but it has also become an expectation of the community, particularly of funders and donors. Ethical lapses by nonprofits make the news far too easily. An emphasis on measurable, meaningful outcomes has spread through the nonprofit world, often for the better, sometimes for worse.

But all those things have to do with how the nonprofit deals with and is seen by the *outside* world. In truth, ethics, accountability, and transparency start *inside* the organization, inside the management team, inside the board.

So that's where we'll start in this chapter. We'll begin by looking at why you need to have more emphasis on ethics, accountability, and transparency, and how that starts inside and works outward. I'll give you a short starting checklist for each area inside your nonprofit and some hands-on ways and cautions for how to proceed.

Then, we'll go through each of our three touchstones in order, starting with ethics then moving to accountability and ending with transparency. The order is intentional: After defining your mission, everything hinges on people trusting that you are the best organization to provide that mission. I'll give you examples of what other organizations are doing right, as well as stories of ones that have gone wrong. We'll look at specific ways you can improve your operations by paying attention to each of these areas, and end with some discussion questions.

By the end of the chapter, we'll have set the framework for all that comes later. And what comes later, whether it be staff, board, technology, marketing, finance, planning, even your internal controls, depends on how you approach the materials covered in this chapter. Think about it. The way your organization embraces or ignores these three items speaks volumes about your organizational values. And values, openly discussed and used as benchmarks, will define your culture, the kind of people you hire, your relationships with the people you serve, the people who pay you, your community, and each other. Your values—how you live them, act on them, promote them, and embrace the high bar they often require—set the stage for everything else.

Please do not pass on this chapter, skipping it because you know you're already ethical and you believe in transparency and accountability. If all that is true (and for most readers, I'm sure it is) I still guarantee you'll pick up some hands-on ideas. And for nearly everyone, I predict you'll be surprised by how you can ramp up your emphasis on these three values for the benefit of your mission. There is nothing more important to your mission success than what you'll read in this chapter. *Nothing*.

Start In and Work Out

The ethics that we show the world start inside us, or they are false. If we talk a great line, advertise our goodness, and seem like the perfect person to the outside world but then are abrupt or dismissive or untruthful in our own home, we are not seen by those closest to us as just abrupt or dismissive, we are seen as a fraud.

So it is in our organizations. If we promote our values outside to our community, but don't live that way inside the organization, not only will we be dismissed by staff, our best employees will leave, morale will plummet, and we won't get the most out of our employees and volunteers since they'll be spending time yammering about how we say one thing and do another. Thus, our attention to ethics, our belief in accountability, and our willingness to make our organizations transparent has to start by doing those things inside the organization, with each other. If we take a values stand, those values have to go for everyone.

 FOR EXAMPLE: I encourage my client organizations to foster a culture of innovation in their organizations. As you'll see when we talk about marketing in Chapter 10, small innovations and small improvements can really add value to the services you provide. A few years ago, I was visiting a new client organization whose CEO had attended one of my marketing seminars a year prior to retaining me to help with the development of a marketing plan. The CEO, who we'll call Michael, was proud of how ingrained innovation was in his nonprofit. "We are all about continuous innovation," he boasted. "We have a culture of innovation. It is on our values statement" (waving his hand at the values on the wall as we walked by), "it's a part of our annual personnel performance evaluations, we talk about it at every staff meeting. We have innovation idea contests, with great rewards and we urge everyone not to fear the new, but give it a try. We're a team of innovators."

I was impressed, to a degree, but worried that the focus on innovation might be overpowering the organization's commitment to mission; perhaps just doing *new* things was good enough, instead of doing the *best* thing. Michael and I spent the morning touring the organization, talking about other things, and we had lunch with his board. That afternoon, while Michael met with his board president, I met with the senior management staff, and while we were discussing the key markets of the organization, I brought up the issue of their innovation culture just to get the staff's take on it. Conversation died, people looked away a bit, and so I pressed them. "Okay, so there is a problem with innovation? Is it the way you're going about it, the emphasis on it, the rewards, what?" I asked.

There was a moment of silence as the senior staff exchanged looks, and then the COO said this: "We *do* innovate lots more than before, and it is generally good. We *do* talk to our staff about their willingness to try new things and, frankly, we are the least change-averse organization I've ever seen. But... well, Michael

(continued)

(*continued*)
talks about personal innovation and growth all the time, which is
fine, but . . . well . . . he does not set a very good example himself.
Understand, I love the guy, and he is a great boss, but he's got a
blind spot here. And," he said, looking at me, "maybe you're the
guy to fix the problem."

"How so? What's the problem?" I asked. The COO responded,
"Michael refuses to learn how to read his own e-mail. He makes
Maggie [his assistant] print it out and then reads it on paper, dic-
tates the responses, and Maggie sends the actual message. And
everyone knows it, jokes about it, and when Michael talks the
innovation talk, people just do not believe him. I've brought it up
with him, we all have," indicating the management team, who all
nodded. "He just doesn't see the damage he's doing to the overall
goal by not adapting to this not exactly new technology." ■

I was, to say the least, astonished. This was 2006, after all, not 1986.
Michael's refusal to walk the walk was hurting his innovation push. We
have to be willing to do what we say, not just have others do it.

As you can see, our push on ethics, accountability, and transparency
has to start inside. If we're going to be accountable to the community, we
have to be accountable to each other on the staff and board. If we're going
to share information and be transparent on our Web site, we need to share
plans, budget, and meeting minutes inside the organization as well. If we're
going to bring ethical decision making into our discussions about mission,
we have to do the same in our decisions about staff discipline, benefits,
and use of vacation time. By starting inside, we role-model to everyone
what we believe, and then when we go outside, we have a firm foundation
to stand on.

So, let's begin. Below is my checklist for getting started with your values inside the organization. When we're done with that, we'll discuss the
specifics of ethics, accountability, and transparency individually and in much
greater detail.

Develop (or Revise) Your Values Statement

Mission first, then values. Ethics, accountability, and transparency are really
values more than anything else. And, like all good values, they are subjective;
people have written for millennia about what is truly ethical behavior, and
you and I could honorably disagree about how much transparency is good
for your nonprofit. But these three values need to be at the core of your
values statement, which, again, is the *how* of your organization. So you need
a list, carefully drawn, of your organizational "hows."

First, remember that values statements need to be written by a board and staff team. They eventually have to be adopted by the board, since they are policy, but start with a group of board and staff together. Here are some hints on developing or revising your values:

■ *Do not just sit down and list a bunch of nice, easy, politically correct terminology and print them up and slap them on the wall.* It's so easy to ask your board/staff team what values you should live by, and let everyone chip in one or two great ideas and then just list them. Think it through. Some values are assumed and don't need to be on the list. For example, I've never seen a nonprofit value statement that included "Thou shalt not kill" or "No stealing." Think through what you want your *core* values to be, what you want to emphasize, what part of your culture you need to change. If you only have a few core values on your list, that's what people will focus on, and they can push the culture in a beneficial direction. In many cases, for example, being more transparent is, while very important, not part of the current culture. If you add transparency (and then do the rest of the things we'll discuss in this chapter), you'll push your organization toward being more transparent. Focus your attention on key values and do not just make a laundry list. And while I urge you to include, in some form, the three core values of ethics, accountability, and transparency, it's up to you. If you feel your organization needs to focus on others core values, great.
■ *Craft values that require regular discussion to implement.* I know this may sound counterintuitive but hear me out. Values are not digital; they are analog. Think of two clocks, one digital, one analog. You look at one that says "It is 10:14 A.M.," while the other tells you "It is about quarter after ten." The latter clock is like your values—they get you close but you have to interpret the rest.

 FOR EXAMPLE: What's the most talked about corporate value of the last decade? Google's only value statement, the wonderful, all-encompassing, and ultimately vague
"Don't be evil."
You may remember hearing that the first time and thinking, "Cool!" or "Weird!" or "We'll see." And every time Google announces some new project or application, critics hold up the "Don't be evil" flag and wave it vigorously. Inside the organization there are, according to many staff, *raging* debates on whether those same new Web features or aggregations of information violate the core value.

(continued)

(*continued*)

And this debate, both inside and out, is *exactly* what the Google management wanted. By setting a high bar, and one certainly open to interpretation, they kept the discussion going and going and going . . . and the focus *stayed on the value.* ■

■ *Don't have values (or policies, or rules, for that matter) that you all can't live with.* You'll see more about how to figure out the implications of your values in a minute, but remember that once you set a rule, it has to be for everyone. Once you state a value, you have to be willing to not only live with it yourself but also, as a manager, *enforce* it. To not do so is disingenuous: unethical.

■ *Once you have a draft set of values, share them with everyone in the organization, in writing, online, and then in discussion groups.* Remember transparency? Here's your first taste of what it's like inside the organization. Post the values and ask your staff to consider each value statement and what, if anything, will have to change in their area of the organization if they are adopted. Tell them to make a list and come prepared to fully discuss the implications. Then have an outside facilitator (because these meetings can be very interesting) come and walk your staff through one or more discussion groups about the values and their meaning to mission. Take any and all suggestions under consideration.

■ *Amend the values, based on the discussions, and have the board consider and, ultimately, adopt them.* Once adopted, go back to the staff, show how their input helped, and then start the discussion about implementation. Increase the discussion of the values (along with the mission) at staff meetings. Ask everyone (and encourage your direct reports to do it with their staff) whether the decision under discussion agrees with the values. Use the values as you do the mission: as a discussion tool to keep them front and center—where they should be.

 HANDS ON: Remember Michael, the CEO who refused to live by his own innovation credo, and the damage he did? Always be willing to listen to your staff calling you out if something that you have done violates one or more of your organizational values. This is *hard,* and when you've messed up (and all of us do), it requires you to role-model one of our key values: accountability. You need to say, "Yep, you're right. That was a mistake on my part, and I am sorry. Thanks for pointing it out, and I'll work on that." And then *do* work on "that," whatever it may be. ■

Include Values in Recruitment, Orientation, Personnel Evaluation, and Your Staff and Board Decision Processes

The values that just sit on the wall aren't on the table during decision making. The values that are window dressing aren't on people's minds as they interact with each other. The values that are discussed as an afterthought show that you consider them, well, an afterthought. Start at the beginning: in recruitment for board, staff, and volunteers. You should already be talking about mission—include the values as well and how important they are to you. This should come from the top, from you as a manager. Remember in Chapter 4 I told you what author Pat Lencioni tells us—that one of the key necessary obsessions of a good manager is to "over-communicate the core mission." I agree, and I think this extends to values. You need to be talking about mission *and values* to potential staff, volunteers, and board members right away. Once they come on board, the values (and their meaning) should be part of orientation. Evidencing values should be part of performance evaluations, and I suggest an annual staff/board meeting to discuss how well the organization did in syncing its values to its mission.

Be Transparent with Your Values, Which Will Hold You More Accountable

Put the values on your Web site, on more than one page—for example, on your recruitment pages for volunteers and employees, on the entry pages describing your services, and on your pages for donors. Inside the organization, post the mission statement (we talked about that in Chapter 4) and the values prominently in many places around the organization.

 HANDS ON: Hold a small ceremony when you post the first copy of your values to indicate their importance, to commend staff for their input, and to remind everyone to discuss the values regularly and hold each other accountable to them. ■

Hold the mission and values up high and people will both see them and they'll hold you accountable to act by them—which is a good thing.

Once you have your values and have ingrained them in your policies and reviews, you need to live them day by day, week by week, month by month, decision by decision, and policy by policy. This is not an on–off switch that you throw and things just happen. You've got to work at it. The good news is that most nonprofits are already doing something in each of these areas, so you are probably not starting from a standing start, and that's great.

There are a lot of specifics to attend to in each of my three core values, and we'll address each in order. But before we do, I have to emphasize one more thing. These three values, when crafted from within, build on each other and form a virtuous circle. You use your ethics to make better decisions. Being more accountable for those decisions makes all of us, no matter how pure our hearts are, think more about those decisions and what the most ethical decision is. Finally, being transparent and letting everyone see our decisions holds us even more accountable, and the circle starts over and reinforces itself. Will this be hard? Sure, sometimes. But two things are sure: First, the more you do all three as a set the easier it gets; and second, the people who benefit most are the people you serve.

Now to specifics.

Ethics in a Nonprofit

What are *good* ethics? Thousands of pages and millions of person-hours of discussion have been spent arguing out the answer to that simple question. I once knew a Ph.D. in philosophy, whose dissertation had been on that very question, who admitted a decade after getting her degree that she was still unsure of the answer. So let's agree that we won't nail down the definition of the best or even of good ethics for every situation. One thing I do know (and learned in a wonderful course my senior year in high school) is that all ethics are *situational*: I can tell you with *absolute* assurance that I won't steal a carton of eggs today, but ask me when my children are starving and I may well give you a different answer.

We'd like to think that our ethics are timeless and absolute but, for everyone but saints, they really aren't and the same holds true in nonprofits. Sometimes, and more often than we *ever* imagined before we moved into management, we have to choose the *least worst* option. That is hard and always opens us up to criticism. But just because ethics aren't absolute doesn't mean we can't use them to help us create a better mission-oriented culture or to make better, *more* ethical decisions.

There are two management credos that I've always used both inside and outside my organizations. Certainly, when I was a young executive director (my first executive director job came when I was 27), I messed this up a lot. I tried to live by these words, and I often failed, then got up, and tried again. I still miss the mark some days; however, I hope my percentage of success is better now! Here they are, and I'll bet they are not new to you:

Treat others the way you'd like to be treated.
The right thing to do is also the smart thing to do, and vice versa.

These sound simple, even trite, but when you think about it, they are *profound* in their implications. Just look at the "treat others" credo. How do people want to be treated? With respect—for their person, their feelings, their opinion, their honesty. People want to be informed, they want to be asked to help, they want to be recognized as individuals, and they want to be able to measure in some way their contributions. Do any of those sound like things *you don't* want? So if you want to be treated that way, you have to treat others that way, and that may require changes in your management style. You may have to ask for others' input more, or take the time to learn more about your employees' lives beyond work, or to be more inclusive in decision making, even delegate more. Once you *say* you are going to act on the "treat others" mantra, you have to both do it and accept others holding you accountable for it.

On the other hand, "The right thing is the smart thing" is a bit tougher to nail down. What this really says is that taking short cuts (ethically or otherwise) does not pay off in the long run. It also gives backup to staff and board who hold out against such shortcuts, giving them the philosophical support they need to speak up or object in a difficult situation.

 HANDS ON: My suggestion on these two credos is to introduce them to the management team and board as operating guidance. They aren't really values but they can help guide decision making and give people benchmarks for accountability. Once you list them, actualize the "treat others" credo by starting with a discussion about how the people you serve want to be treated and inquire if your organization has deficits in any area. Then meet with your direct reports and ask them how their staff want to be treated . . . and repeat the examination of things that may need to be changed. Understand that once you go through this activity, your people should (and hopefully will) call you out when you do not meet the mark. ■

 HANDS ON: To actualize the "right thing is the smart thing" credo, after introducing it, bring it into the discussion the next time the management team is engaged in a debate on a proposed course of action. Ask everyone: "Is everyone comfortable that either option A or B is the 'right' thing to do? If not, why not?" And then use your values to see if you can focus and come to a consensus on which option to pursue. In some cases, of course, the discussion will end with you alone having to make the decision, but you want the input and perspectives from your team before you have to make any decision, particularly the tough ones. ■

As always, your ethics as the leader will show the way and set the tone for the rest of the staff. If they see you are doing the right thing, they will too. If they hear you are bringing your organizational ethics and values into discussions with them, they'll do the same with their staff. On the other hand, if you see your long-time staff taking shortcuts or not acting ethically, look to your own actions first.

John Maxwell, the noted leadership author, says repeatedly in his books that if a leader looks at his or her employees and does not like what he or she sees, then it's probably due to the leader being a bad example. Maxwell notes that people who are unethical or who take short cuts will not be comfortable in a culture that does not tolerate that behavior. This is true for all kinds of behavior, such as off-color (particularly sexually suggestive or harassing) jokes or language, upbraiding an employee in front of peers, missing deadlines, or chronic lateness. Organizations that don't tolerate those behaviors don't have them because people who cannot change their behaviors leave. Conversely, if the behaviors are present—they must be being tolerated and perhaps they even start from the top. Consider that if you look out and don't like what you see.

With ethics, or more accurately with ethical lapses, you really do need a zero-tolerance culture. That does not mean that you fire someone if he or she slips and makes one behavioral or ethical mistake. We all do that, and if we were all fired the first time we messed up, well, we would all have been fired pretty quickly. But understanding fallibility does not mean that you can ignore a key behavioral or ethical lapse. You have to put people on notice right away that you saw the mistake and remind them that such behavior is just not acceptable, that you're sure they won't do it again. And leave it at that—unless it repeats.

 FOR EXAMPLE: As I said previously, I was appointed to my first executive director job at age 27. I was, with one exception, the youngest person on a staff of twenty, and pretty quickly I got my first management test. A midmanager, perhaps ten years older than me, started coming back late from lunch about three months into my tenure, but worse, he came back smelling like a brewery. The first time I smelled his breath, I made some lame comment like "Long lunch, John?" to see if he would say anything. He didn't, and I hoped it would pass. Of course, it didn't, and a few days later the same thing occurred—late and loaded. Now I had a real knot in my stomach. I went home, talked to my wife, we kicked the problem around, and then I went for a long run and tried to figure out what the best plan of action would be. Ignore it? That was a nonstarter. Fire the guy? I had no "proof." Dress him down at the next staff meeting? Not a good idea. What I did know was that I had to deal with the issue and soon. Like the next day. No sleep that night!

The next morning I went and found John and asked him to come see me in my office. When he came in, I closed the door and said to him, "John, I'm worried about you. Is anything going on in your life that you want to talk about?" John looked confused and said no, everything was fine. "Really?" I asked. "Because I figured that if there was not something going on you would not have started taking long lunches and coming back smelling of alcohol. And when I've talked to you after lunch, John, frankly, you act like you are more than a little drunk." John looked startled and began to make excuses. It was the allergy medication he was on. It was stress. It was blah blah blah. I let him run the course and when he finally stopped, I said, "Okay, John. Two things and you can go. First, I don't care if it is your meds or any other thing, you have to be back on time from lunch and be sharp in the afternoon. Starting today. No more, no third chance. Second, if you do have a problem with drinking, I want to help. We can get you into a program and will support you in any way we can. That's up to you, but what's up to me is that I need *all* of you here all the time. Okay?"

The bad behavior stopped that day, which was actually pretty remarkable, given that things could have gotten ugly, or John could have quit. But the most interesting thing was that John became my most hard-working and loyal employee for the rest of the time I was executive director. ∎

You as leader have to set the standards. Set the bar high—and people will meet your expectations. Set the bar low—and people will meet your expectations. Your choice.

 HANDS ON: Building an ethical culture starts with you, but it also starts at the point of recruitment—you as CEO or senior manager should meet with all potential hires and talk to them about your mission, your values, and the behavior that is expected. This will weed out some potential employees who don't feel comfortable being held to that standard. Then, when a new employee is hired, match him or her up with a mentor who is one of your ethical stars. Give the new hire a big dose of expectations right away. Ingrain the culture early and often. ∎

Finally, talk about ethics regularly. If you have a book club (which I strongly recommend), read a book now and then about ethical management and talk through any applications for your organization. You don't want to build a culture that has a holier-than-thou-attitude, nor do you want to empower an ethics gestapo. But you do want to acknowledge ethics and the ethical dilemmas we all face as a real part of management and the way we treat each other. It is the right thing to do—and thus the smart thing to do.

Accountability

I have lost track of the number of friends, family, peers, and neighbors who have bemoaned our culture's general lack of accountability. All too often we see someone, perhaps a celebrity or politician, who when confronted with anything from a traffic ticket to a felony casts the blame elsewhere, on his or her upbringing, lack of understanding family, bad luck, the phase of the moon. And, again too often, society seems to buy or even enable such excuses. When former Illinois Governor George Ryan was indicted for racketeering (he later was convicted and went to prison), one Chicago paper seemed to excuse his behavior by noting that he had started his political career in Joliet, historically a haven of organized crime and political corruption. As if that explained it.

We all learn early (except, apparently, George) that we need to be accountable for our actions and our choices. This is even more true in non-profits. As I said early in the book, when we work for nonprofits, our actions and choices are scrutinized much more than those of people in the for-profit world. One value that will please our community greatly is being openly accountable for what we do because, when we do that, we're accountable for the resources the community has entrusted us with.

And, like ethics, accountability starts with the leader. You have to be willing to say, "I'm sorry. My bad. Won't happen again," and mean it. I know that there is a tendency, particularly for new managers and executives, to think you have to exude an aura of perfection; that if you appear fallible the people you supervise will lose respect for you. Wrong. Everyone knows that everyone is fallible. And all the people you supervise know when you make a mistake. What they're waiting for is what you do next—how you lead *through* your errors.

 HANDS ON: Remember this: If your staff sees you never admitting to errors, they'll assume that's what you want—perfection. In response, they will stop admitting errors, too. Which would you rather have, an employee come to you early, admitting to a small mistake, or having him or her cover up the error until it turns into a major problem? ■

Once you've set the example, the next issue is what the organization should be accountable for. Certainly accomplishing the goals in its short- and long-range plans, absolutely staying within its budget, without question keeping to the appropriate level of quality of services, and always being a prudent steward of the resources you manage. While you may "know" when you're on track, a better management style is to measure. In fact, I agree totally with the classic management credo "You can't manage what you don't measure." In this discussion, let's turn that around and say that you can't be accountable for goals and outcomes if you don't set them and then measure your results.

Thus, a key part of accountability (again, once you set the leadership stage) is to benchmark your organization against itself over time and against other peer organizations. I know that most nonprofits are already looking at outcomes and some of those are terrific, some not so much. A great resource for you in this area either to get started or improve your measurement is *Benchmarking for Nonprofits* by Jason Saul (St. Paul, MN: Fieldstone Alliance, 2004).

Setting and measuring outcomes is very important and fraught with a variety of potholes and dangers. Let's go over some rules.

First, measure outcomes not activities. Think of activities as a spinning wheel held in place. Round and round it goes, using up energy but not getting anywhere. "We held twenty-three staff meetings last year" is an **activity** measure. "We planned and coordinated staff duties, and reduced overtime 14 percent" is an **outcome** measure, even though it was the meetings that facilitated the outcome. Activity alone is not worth measuring.

 FOR EXAMPLE: Early on in my executive director job, I had many, many meetings with state officials and their subordinates. Even if I was just meeting with a program manager, and the only people who really needed to be in the room were the two of us, there were always three or four other state staff attending. The extra staff would sit there, pens and notepads in hand, and not contribute a whit to the meeting. No matter which agency, section, or program I worked with, the behavior was the same. Need one staff person? Bring four. Need two? Bring seven.

After six months or so of this, I asked one of my running buddies, himself a state employee, what the deal was. Why bring so many people? "Oh," he laughed, "that's easy to answer... It's scratch my back, I'll scratch yours." I was confused. He explained, "We have to hand in activity reports every month that document how busy we are. If we're not busy, we may get reassigned, given

(continued)

(*continued*)

more duties, or even laid off. So manager A invites manager B, D, and G to his meetings; manager B reciprocates, and on it goes. That way we all stay busy." I was, to say the least, unimpressed. Or perhaps, as a taxpayer, I was simply depressed. ■

Second, measure against mission. Remember in Chapters 1 and 2 we talked about the fact that every action, every choice, every investment of resources in a nonprofit should result in more mission or improve the capacity of the nonprofit to do mission of higher quality or with more efficiency. If that's true, what you want to measure are things that move you toward those objectives. More staff education? Great, but did it result in fewer errors, higher-quality standards, more efficiency? A new Web site? Awesome, but did it result in higher referrals or more donations? You can only look at (and truly understand) so many measurements. Make sure the ones you use are meaningful to the mission.

 HANDS ON: Don't make the decision on what to measure or on what are priority benchmarks by yourself. Ask, ask, ask, and then listen. Your staff, your peer organizations, your board, even your funders will have ideas about what's important to measure and how to hold your organization accountable in a mission-based way. ■

Third, go very public. Once you've gotten the outcomes and benchmarks set, post the goals, post the benchmarks, and, most important, post the results where everyone can see them. Celebrate the successes and discuss and recommit when you do not make your goal. Put the key benchmarks right on your Web site for the world to see. Hold yourself, your staff, your board, and your funders all accountable for your outcomes and the success of your mission.

 HANDS ON: Remember to focus the benchmarks you post to have the most effect and be most appropriate for each area of the organization. If you have a residential program and a day component, post the residential and organization-wide goals for the residential people to see, not the day-program goals. You want people to focus on the goals that they can impact. And, if the residential staff want to know the day program goals, they can go online to see all of them. ■

Speaking of putting things online, that is part of the last component of our virtuous cycle, transparency.

Transparency

Transparency is such a buzzword. It's used so often that it is easy to ignore. Yeah, yeah, yeah, transparency shmansparency. Blah blah blah. Don't fall into that trap. The concept of transparency is crucial, but the benefits of becoming transparent go deeper than the common usage.

When the vast majority of people use the term *transparency,* they mean organizational transparency from the outside in: letting people in the community see what is going on inside the organization. During his run for the U.S. presidency, candidate Obama talked repeatedly about making government more transparent—for example, putting Congressional "earmarks" online for the public to see. In nonprofits, outside-in transparency is not only important, it is an expectation of most funders, donors, and the media. Moreover, the initiative for this has already been taken away from you: Anyone can find out about your organization on one of many nonprofit online watchdog sites, such as Guidestar.com. Thus, you already live with some outside-in transparency, whether you like it or not. And that outside oversight will do what I said earlier—hold you accountable for your decisions, and that will result in more careful decision making.

But an equal, some would say greater, benefit from transparency results if you become an internally transparent organization. Sharing information inside your organization, in meetings, on your Web site, in your decision making will transform not only your culture but improve employee engagement and ownership, develop richer sets of solutions to thorny problems, and keep your best people on board, both employees and board members. We'll discuss this much more in Chapter 7's discussion on staff, and give you lots of hands-on ideas for how to use technology to ramp up your transparency in Chapter 8, so let's leave it at this for now: The virtuous cycle works inside the organization as well as outside. If your decisions are available for everyone to see, you'll be held accountable. If the organization acts on its ethics and values, that accountability will hold you to a higher standard. Who wins? Ultimately the people you serve.

Before we end this chapter, I want to return for a moment to the outside-in part of transparency and discuss the minimum information (usually in .pdf format) that should be easily accessible on your Web site. Here's my list:

- Your most recent IRS 990 or 990N reports and the 990T if you file it.
- Your two more recent audits along with management letters.
- Your current strategic plan, or a summary of your goals and objectives.

- An annual report of your outcomes for the last two years, put in human terms. Don't just say "Occupancy up 12.4 percent"; instead note that "253 more families got housing last year than the year before."
- A listing of your board members with links to their biographical information and experience to answer the question "Why are these people good policy makers and fiduciaries?"
- A listing of your management team with links to their biographical information and experience to answer the same question.
- And when people ask for something else, put it on your transparency page. You should have nothing to hide. Take the barriers to knowledge down and let the virtuous circle do its job.

Recap

In this chapter, we've moved from mission to values and focused on three values that give us the *how* for your organization. The way we approach ethics, accountability, and transparency is crucial to our mission success, and without intentionally dealing with each, our organizations will flounder if not founder. Remember, the mission is the why of your nonprofit. These values are the how. Don't skip them.

We started by discussing the fact that dealing with these values has to start inside the organization, not outside. I gave you a short checklist for your values, which was the following:

1. Develop (or revise) your values statement
2. Include values in recruitment, orientation, personnel evaluation, and your staff and board decision processes
3. Be transparent with your values, which will hold you more accountable

We also discussed, for the first time, the concept of the virtuous circle of ethics, accountability, and transparency.

Next, we dealt with each value in turn, starting with ethics. I showed you my key ethical guidelines, which were the following:

Treat others the way you want to be treated.
The right thing to do is the smart thing to do, and vice versa.

We talked about the implications of those statements and how to use them in your organization.

Then we turned to accountability, and we noted that being accountable is something far too lacking in our culture but that also starts inside the organization before it can credibly go outside. I urged you to use benchmarks as part of your outcome measures and gave you a list of guidelines:

> **First, measure outcomes not activities.**
> **Second, measure against mission.**
> **Third, go very public.**

Finally, we briefly covered the keys of transparency and how it completes the virtuous circle. I noted that we would deal more with transparency in the chapters on staff and technology, but I urged you to be transparent inside and out. I closed with my list of things you needed to post on the transparency pages of your Web site.

Now, and only now, are you ready to proceed to the working chapters about staff and board, marketing and technology, and all the rest. With your mission and your values set, you have the framework and the guidance to improve the other important parts of your nonprofit and to make sure that it pursues mission in the best, most effective way.

Questions for Discussion

1. Do we need to develop (or revisit) our values statement to include ethics, accountability, and/or transparency?
2. What can we do to turn these values into action?
3. How can we have better, deeper discussions about the ethics of our key decisions? How do we remind people that "the right thing is the smart thing"?
4. Do we share information enough inside and outside the organization? Where can we improve?
5. Do we use internal and external benchmarks to their fullest? Are there places we can experiment with this?

CHAPTER 6

A Businesslike Board of Directors

Overview

Whether you are a staff member or a board member, you know that the board of directors is a key component of your organization. For starters, you *have* to have one; it is a legal requirement in state and federal statutes. Second, the board can provide an excellent resource of judgment and leadership, a connection with the rest of the community, and a partnership with staff that can strengthen the organization and its services. In other words, the board *should* be a key resource for the organization. Unfortunately, it is often anything but that.

Too often, boards either totally dominate an organization, thus blocking the staff's ability to do their jobs, or are so subservient to staff "expertise" that the staff, in effect, manipulate the board at will. Neither are effective uses of resources, and both are counterproductive. In the worst case, both problems—board dominance and staff dominance—occur in the same organization. How can that be? Simple, the staff *think* the board is dominating while at the same time the board members *think* the staff is running roughshod over them! Gridlock in governance!

How do you optimize your board as a resource? How do you analyze what your organization needs from a board and then go out and recruit one that meets those needs? What should the respective roles of the staff and the board be? In this chapter, I will tell you about those things as well as about how to reduce your board's liability. I will show you how to get the most effective board, why board people *really* serve and how you can meet those needs and wants, and how to evaluate your board. With the things you learn in this chapter, you can really turn your board into the effective policy-setting, check-and-balance resource that it needs to be.

Board Effectiveness

The first thing you need to do in order to make your board a better-utilized resource is to benchmark your board against some target characteristics of effectiveness. An effective board has most, if not all, of the following characteristics:

- *It understands the organization's mission and acts to implement that mission for the benefit of the organization's constituency consistently and professionally.* If it is to be effective, a board must first and foremost understand and support the organization's mission (see Chapter 4). It must also be consistent in the development of policy to implement that mission; if it favors one method of implementation one week and another the next, it will be doing more harm than good.
- *It acts as a policy setter and check-and-balance with the staff.* With one exception (a start-up nonprofit in which the board often *is* the staff), the board must act *only* as policy setter and check-and-balance. It must not allow itself, nor any of its members, to get seduced into trying to run the day-to-day activities of the organization or to be a "back-seat driver" in relation to the staff's duties. The board hired the staff, and running the organization's day-to-day activities is what the staff is paid to accomplish. The staff is supposed to be professionals (if the right people were hired). The board should set the broad policy and let the staff implement it. The board has more important things to do; things that only a board can do.
- *It works primarily with the executive director/CEO and evaluates that person at least annually.* Rule 3 of nonprofits: **The executive director/CEO works for the board, and the rest of the staff work for the ED/CEO.** The board cannot be effective if it allows itself to be bogged down in both personal and personnel issues that are most appropriate for staff members to handle on their own. Thus, board members who acquiesce to letting staff people other than the CEO or executive director call them and complain are asking for trouble. I know that this is not always easy, particularly in small towns where everyone knows everyone else, but it is the prime rule of nonprofit board/staff management. As with any relationship, the one between the board and the executive director can only flourish if both parties let the other know how they are doing. Many board people tell me that they are not experts in the executive director's discipline (i.e., they are not a minister, teacher, artist, or social worker) so they cannot evaluate her or him. This concern, while understandable, neglects what the board does know and can evaluate. The board can evaluate how the executive director interacts with and supports the board, how close the staff comes to staying

within the budget, completing tasks in the long-range plan, achieving fund-raising or outreach goals, reducing staff turnover, and so on. The board can and should set measurable goals for the executive director and then evaluate his or her ability to meet those goals. Moreover, the board should evaluate the executive director in formal terms at least annually. To board members who are reluctant to evaluate, I say this: You want to be evaluated in your job. If you want to keep your exec, give him or her the same courtesy: Let your executive director know how he or she is doing.

■ *It changes over time, filling its membership fully by recruiting new members to meet the changing needs of the organization.* Your organization does not look like it did five years ago in terms of funding, programs, or staff. But it may very well be identical or close to it in board makeup. If the board is a resource, shouldn't its constitution change with the changing needs of the organization? Of course it should. Boards should *not* be perpetual. You should build board turnover into your bylaws. My suggestion is a three-year term, with a maximum of two successive terms before a particular board member goes off for at least a year. Thus, one-third of your board is up for renewal each year, and this gives you a chance to evaluate them and recruit both new people and new skills regularly. Also, a three-year term works well with my recommendations on strategic plans (see Chapter 12), which include a planning retreat every three years or at least once in every board member's term of office. The issue of how you assess what kind of board you need and how you recruit them will be covered later in this chapter.

■ *It elects qualified officers and appoints qualified committee chairs.* As in so many of life's endeavors, the difference between success and failure can often be leadership. Think of some of the great leaders of key organizations in our past: Presidents like Washington, Lincoln, and Franklin Roosevelt, and visionaries like Martin Luther King Jr., Susan B. Anthony, Mahatma Gandhi, and countless others led their groups at a time when they were most needed. Just because you may not be involved with a national or trend-setting organization does not mean you don't need leaders on your board or to head your committees. It also does not mean that all your leaders need to be officers or committee chairs, but it certainly helps. Effective boards have people in officer and committee chair roles who know their jobs (and their limitations), get them done effectively, and are willing to commit the time to do so. They show up with their homework done, lead their groups through the decisions that need to be made, and represent the organization without bias with funders, donors, the media, and the public. Your organization needs a leadership development track, where new members are assessed after a

time and potential leaders are put onto an "officer track," assigning them
first to committee chairs, then officer slots, and, finally, if appropriate,
the board presidency.

■ *It supports the organization in public.* Elaine was elected to the board of
the XYZ agency four months ago. She has been to every meeting since
her election and has had, in her own words, "a steep learning curve"
about the agency, its works, its staff, and its funding problems. Elaine
is at a social engagement at a friend's house when she is approached
by Phil, whom she has not seen since her election to the board. Phil
mentions that he has heard that Elaine is now on XYZ's board. Elaine's
response:

> *(Sigh) Yes, I got talked into being on the board. I'm not sure that
> I won't regret it, what with all of its financial problems. I had no
> idea how big XYZ is, how many staff and services it has, nor how
> financially fragile it is. I mean, they are good people and all, but they
> are working under tremendous strain. I don't really see how they are
> going to continue at their present pace or their present funding. But
> I am learning a lot, and I guess I'll be able to help at some point,
> once I figure out what is really going on.*

Or

> *(Smile) Yes, I started about four months ago, and talk about an
> education! I had no idea how big and diversified it is. I'm really
> impressed by the staff. They are good people and are doing miracles
> with, shall we say, minimal resources. I'm learning a lot, and hope
> that I can really contribute once I get my feet on the ground.*

If XYZ's mission was close to your heart, which answer would you like
to have your Elaine giving? If you are or have been a board member, do you
hear yourself echoed in the first or the second answer? And what if Elaine's
friend Phil happens to be on the United Way allocation committee for this
year, or is an officer at XYZ's bank, or is a potential referral source for new
clients? What message do you prefer he get?

Another problem I see a lot is this: It is also critical that board people
realize that they are "on the Board team" and must support that team—even
if they do not agree with every decision made at every board meeting.
Once board members start to criticize board decisions or complain about
the agency outside of the boardroom, the ability of board members to act
as an effective team starts to go down the black hole of internal conflict.
And leadership is key in making sure this does not happen. More on that in
a bit.

Barriers to Board Effectiveness

What are the main barriers that get in the way? It's always beneficial to highlight the most common places that boards trip up. A board *cannot* be an effective resource for the organization if:

- *The members of the board do not know basic and up-to-date information about the organization's mission, programs, and purposes.* This sounds so elementary on the face of it that one would think that of course people on boards have that kind of information. Don't be so sure. Board members come to the table with different ideas and backgrounds, and their perceptions of the mission (as we discussed in Chapter 4) may be as different as night and day. This also extends to the organization's programs and services. They may not even be aware of some programs' existence. Thus, orientation, on a consistent basis, is a key to board effectiveness.

 HANDS ON: At *every* board meeting, reserve 15 minutes for ongoing board orientation. Cover a single program, a new state law affecting your organization, or new developments in your field. Orientation should be a continuous, never-ending process. Too often it is done at one only meeting at the beginning of the board member's term, provided in a language (your jargon) that the board member does not yet understand. Think back to your own orientation when you joined the staff of your employer. How much do you remember? Not much, and you have worked there 40 hours a week ever since. Now add to that "working" only three to four hours a month as a board member does, and you may get the picture about why they do not keep 100 percent up to speed. Help them keep current by dedicating 15 minutes per meeting. ■

- *It doesn't get accurate and timely information from staff.* There is no excuse for inaccurate information going out to the board, and even less excuse for not sending it to members in advance. If board members are to set policy and to be a check-and-balance for the organization, they need to see the meeting materials in advance—and that does not mean 10 minutes in advance of the meeting. As a rule, three days is the minimum for materials to be *in the hands* of board members before a meeting. Also make sure that all the information that the board needs is posted on the board section of your Web site so that members can access it if they misplace their paper information.

Another part of this barrier is staff not telling board members about key or controversial issues until they read it in the paper, get an e-mail from a concerned friend, or see it on the evening news. This is, to understate the issue, not smart. Whether the news is good or bad, if you are a staff manager, let the board members hear it from you, not through the grapevine or from the press. If the news is good, the board members feel like insiders. If it is bad, you get to tell them the whole story first, not after they have read (and been prejudiced by) whatever spin the media or rumor mill puts on the story. Keep your board well informed, in person, online, or by telephone, but keep them informed.

■ *It frequently is lacking a quorum.* How can you take action without a quorum? You cannot. If the board members are not there, three things happen. First, board people who are not present cannot add their contributions to the discussion and decision. Second, if a bare quorum is present, decisions that are made will not have the strength of a wider board ownership and may later be subject to being overturned, or at least not supported fully. Finally, board members are liable for actions taken in their absence (see the section entitled "Board Members' Legal Liability").

I tell executive directors all the time what I was told (and did not like hearing) as an executive myself years ago: *If you consistently do not have a quorum, it is your (the executive director's) fault, no one else's.* Why, you ask? Because board members are people like all the rest of us. They make choices about how to spend the 24 hours they are given each day. All of us have more things to choose from than we have hours to do them in. Thus, going to a board meeting is a *choice*, one that competes with family time, work, sports, television, chores, hobbies, socializing, or sleep, to name a few. As a staff member, you are *competing* for your board members' time and you have to *earn* their attendance by meeting their needs and wants. You need these people at the meetings. It is your job to entice them there and to keep them coming.

 HANDS ON: You also need a tool to help you entice by enforcement. All boards should have attendance requirements that are discussed during recruitment and are enforced rigorously. For example, if you have twelve meetings a year, each board member must come to nine per year, or not be renewed for membership. Missing three in a row is cause for probation, with one more miss leading to termination. If this sounds tough, it is designed to be. You are a mission-oriented business, and you can't get your business done without board attendance. Be upfront with your board people and let them know you can no longer have them be casual about attendance. They need to be on or off the board, not both.

Finally, remember (and remind your board that) board members are liable for actions taken at meetings that they miss. That fact alone should entice them to come to meetings. This fact will be discussed in more depth later in this chapter. ■

- *It is not given anything meaningful to do.* I make the assumption that you want talented and accomplished people on your board, ones who can contribute to your organization with their skills, experience, and expertise. Given that, why would you not give these people anything to do that challenges them? Too many boards are perfunctory: Call the meeting to order, take attendance, review the minutes of the last meeting, approve three committee reports, and go home. As the classic television commercial said all too well, if a bit annoyingly, "Where's the beef?" If you treat your board members as though they are incapable of doing real work, the good board members will leave, and you will not have a quorum, yet again.
- *The board leadership is weak.* Weak leadership often results in internal strife, chaos, and lack of direction. Also, boards sometimes need strong leaders to stand up to strong staffs. Additionally, good leaders make sure that everyone gets to speak, while weak leaders will often let one person dominate. This leads to less input and ownership and can fatally undermine the board's feeling of being a team. Finally, weak leaders do not inspire good people to keep coming to the board meetings or to contribute or take risks on behalf of the organization.
- *Its meetings have no agenda and are not well facilitated.* The lack of an agenda is an open invitation to anarchy and meetings that go on for centuries. You simply must have an agenda and stick to it. The agenda needs to be sent out in advance with meeting materials, and, if possible, the agenda should be somewhat standardized from meeting to meeting. That's the easy part: Facilitation is a whole other issue. It is a skill, one that your committee chairs and board president needs. It requires that they encourage people to speak and allow them to contribute, but at the same time keep the meeting on track and bring each issue to closure in a timely fashion. That is a big order, and too big an order for a lot of board presidents whom I have observed.
- *Its committee structure is not effective, and every policy decision comes before the full board for lengthy debate.* There is simply not enough time in a single board meeting (no matter how long it may drag on) to get effective policy and oversight accomplished solely by the board as a whole. To use the board effectively, you need a committee structure

that allows for persons on (and sometimes not yet on) the board to use their particular expertise and focus on a particular issue, such as finance, personnel, fund-raising, or planning. Then, once the board delegates the details of a particular area to the committees, the board discussion should be limited and, in most cases, perfunctory. If every issue that is discussed at committee meetings is discussed over again at the board level, why have committees? Also remember that having nonboard members on your committees is fine and widens your net of involvement. Just make sure that your committee chair and a majority of each committee are board members.

■ *The staff lacks the skills to support the board—or worse, makes a systematic effort to ignore the board or undermine its effectiveness.* Staff members have a role in making the board work well: They need to be supportive, but guiding (the key functions will be reviewed later). But if the paid staff do not help make the board effective, it won't be; if they undermine the board to try to seize or hold power, the checks and balances get negated and there is a terrible risk of the organization's not staying focused on its mission, not keeping up with changes in the community, and thus being out of touch. Additionally, if staff members are not supportive, good board members will either walk out or attempt to take over the day-to-day activities of the organization, both of which are situations you want to avoid.

Board Members' Responsibilities

In attempting to mold a better board, we need to define the specific responsibilities that they have. As we have already noted, the members of the board of directors are the representatives of the community; they protect the community's interest while advancing the organization's mission in the same fashion that a for-profit corporate board represents the stockholders and promotes the corporate goals.

Even with this philosophical background, it is important to list specifics. The board is responsible for seeing that the items listed below are accomplished, but they may not actually do each of these things personally. If there are paid staff, certain tasks such as filing Internal Revenue Service (IRS) forms are left for staff to do the mechanics, but board members are still responsible for ensuring that they are done.

Other authors have talked extensively about the roles of boards, particularly Brian O'Connell's excellent *Board Member's Book* (New York: Foundation Center, 1999). In this text, O'Connell notes the need for clear definition of roles, particularly between boards and staffs. Barbara Burgess, in *The Nonprofit Management Handbook* (Hoboken, NJ: John Wiley & Sons, 1997), lists three governing functions of boards:

1. To preserve the integrity of the trust
2. To set policy
3. To support and promote the organization

Although I agree with this list, I think we need to expand on the roles a bit.

A board of directors must:

- *Fulfill all of the IRS and state nonprofit reporting requirements.* This includes taxes, FICA, annual reports, the IRS 990 form, Unrelated Business Income Tax (UBIT) estimations, and filing the 900T as appropriate, and operating as called for under section 501(c) of the Internal Revenue Code.
- *Set policy and establish organizational goals.* Boards are responsible for broad policy and must do long-range planning to set those policies in place.
- *Hire the executive director/CEO.* No one else can or should do this important job.
- *Evaluate the executive director's performance in writing at least annually.* No excuses, accept no substitutes.
- *Ensure that fiscal policies are in place and followed.* Boards should be very concerned about financial oversight, and that means good cash, receivables, payables, and budgeting policies.
- *Help develop and adopt budgets.* The board must have final say about how the resources of the organization are allocated, and this is most clearly embodied in the budget. Staff (at all levels) should help draft the budget, but the board has the final say. Once adopted, the budget essentially becomes a contract between the board and the staff.
- *Review and amend bylaws every two years.* This ensures that they are up-to-date with current regulations and that they reflect current board thinking on attendance, board selection, standing committees, and officers and the like.
- *Ensure compliance with the funding stream's policies and regulations.* Nearly every nonprofit has at least one major source of funding: government, United Way, foundations. Every funding source has a different way of monitoring expenses and auditing past work. When you sign a contract to take someone's money, you also agree to comply with their regulations. These may include such diverse items as having a drug-free workplace, not discriminating in employment, or keeping all records related to the contract for five years. Read the fine print before you sign, and then make sure that you can meet all of the provisions. If you are a board member and you do not fulfill your contractual obligation, it is your head on the platter.

- *Establish personnel policies and monitor their compliance.* More organizations get in trouble with people problems than with any other kind. Have good personnel policies, review them every two years with a professional, and build in checks and balances to ensure that they are followed *to the letter every time.*
- *Nominate and elect officers.* Most bylaws have the board do this function at the annual meeting.
- *Represent the organization in public within the constraints of the organization's media policy.* This is important (remember Elaine) but also something any board member should approach with caution. Hint: If you are a board member and asked to speak or present about your nonprofit, always take a staff member as backup.
- *Help recruit new board members.* The board needs to replenish itself. Good recruitment calls for a board/staff partnership, but board involvement is key.
- *Raise funds, but not full time.* In the first edition of *Mission-Based Management*, I said that a board doing fund-raising oversight was sufficient. That ramped up in the second edition to "raise funds," and for good reason. Development is so incredibly competitive that there is no place to hide for board members. Not only must they take an active role in fund-raising, they themselves must give money to the organization. That said, this area has a deep and dangerous pothole: boards that *only* fund-raising, or whose primary reason for being recruited to the board is to raise funds. Look at all the responsibilities listed above. If all the board does is concern itself with raising money, how can it adequately perform the rest of its fiduciary duties? It cannot. So fund-raising is an important board duty, but it is not the only, or even the primary, job of a board.
- *Perform volunteer program work.* If the organization has a volunteer component, I strongly urge board members to at least try some hands-on volunteer work to get to know the organization better. For example, I tell the school boards I work with that they can't do their jobs adequately unless, at least once a year, they ride a school bus, read to first graders, and serve lunch in the high-school cafeteria. Such hands-on exposure should be common for board members and an integral part of the board leadership track.

Staff Responsibilities to the Board

As with any other relationship, "it takes two." Staff members have to support the board if the board is to be effective; it is not only the board that must contribute to the overall relationship. What follows are the minimal expectations that the board should have of its staff:

- *The board should expect accurate, timely, honest, and focused information.* The board needs to be able to rely totally on the staff to provide it with honest and unbiased information and to provide that information well in advance of meetings. Staff members are professionals, and the board should solicit their advice and ideas. Too often, I see boards who want "just the facts, ma'am" (like the *Dragnet* cops of old) and feel that if they ask for any suggestions from staff, they will be overrun, dominated, or manipulated. I disagree. The board hired the staff as the paid experts. Let them contribute to the discussion, but make sure that everyone is aware that the board has the final say on policy.
- *The board should be regularly informed of new developments.* As the paid experts, the staff needs to inform the board of new developments in the organization as well as in the field in which the organization operates.
- *The board should expect staff to gather information, analyze it, and make recommendations to the board*—in essence, to be technical advisors to the board. As noted previously, it is key that the staff be the responsible conduits of information for the board. The staff also needs to focus the board on what is essential. Here, staff members walk a very thin line, one where they are right on the edge of controlling rather than assisting. If the only information that they provide the board is self-serving, or supports only the staff position, the staff members have not done their jobs. In fact, they have violated their trust.
- *The board should expect staff to report fiscal information regularly.* We had a local nonprofit organization that went out of business very suddenly one day perhaps fifteen years ago. Staff (more than 100) came to work one morning to find the doors locked and a sign saying OUT OF BUSINESS. The organization had run out of money and no one—other than the executive director and the financial manager, both staff members—had known it was in trouble. It was a major scandal for our small town, and when I ran into some of the board members, I asked them what had happened. Their (admittedly lame) excuse was that they had not seen financials for a year! I had no sympathy for the board members—none at all. Not providing regular (as in monthly) financials, annual budgets, and cash flow projections to the board is totally unprofessional for staff. Board members: If financials stop being regular, start *demanding* them. This is cause for *extreme* concern and urgency of action. Find out what is going on and accept no excuses. You need to see the financials.

- *The board should encourage staff to make optimum use of the board as a resource.* The staff has a responsibility to be familiar with the skills, connections, and talents of the board and to make use of these skills and talents to the best interest of the organization. Board members, if a staff person calls you up to ask for your expertise, remember: He or she *should* be doing this. You can always say no, thanks. But do not resent the question.
- *The board should expect staff to develop a process for and to educate all new board members and to orient all board members on an ongoing basis.* As noted earlier, board members come to only one or two meetings a month (including committee meetings), so they need regular orientation in addition to their initial overview of the agency.
- *The board should expect staff to provide support for board recruitment and development.* The process I lay out later in this chapter will demonstrate a board/staff partnership in this key area.
- *The board should expect staff to support board committees and provide them with necessary information and expertise they need.* Just as with the board as a whole, someone needs to provide support to the committees, to get them the information, and to provide technical assistance and advice.
- *The board should expect staff to attend all meetings of the board unless excused therefrom.* I am a strong supporter of board meetings being open to staff—it breaks down the mythical barrier between the board and staff and lets staff know what goes on at these important meetings. I also am a strong advocate of staff, other than just the executive director, making presentations to the board. For example, the financial manager can present the financials, the program director can present items about the programs, and so on. This is not only good development for the staff members involved, but it makes the executive director look good as well. He or she has hired great people!

There is a great deal on both the board's and staff's plates in this relationship, but if the staff members do their part, and the board does its part, the relationship will truly benefit the organization.

Board Members' Legal Liabilities

In addition to a long list of responsibilities, boards also have legal liabilities as a result of their board membership. Board members are *fiduciaries*, defined as a person, association, or corporation that has a duty to act for another in a specified area. As such, they have a fiduciary responsibility to the organizations they serve. In financial terms, this means that board members are responsible for the proper utilization, management, or invest-ment of property and other assets placed in their trust. They are legally responsible for the management and control of the organization—and the resulting actions or accidents.

This is a pretty heavy responsibility, but it does not mean that a board member should worry about liability for every corporate loss or mishap that occurs. Most states protect nonprofit board members from liability for errors of judgment as long as they act responsibly, in good faith, and with the best interests of the corporation and its mission foremost. All of this must be balanced with the board's overall role. As I have said repeatedly, the board should be interested in results, not details of operation. The board's involvement in programs and operations should be limited to setting overall policy and monitoring results, unless there are extenuating circumstances.

FOR EXAMPLE: A medium-sized nonprofit school found that it was unable to pay its bills. In order to stay afloat, the director began borrowing heavily from employee withholding (FICA) taxes. The board had no idea this was going on until the IRS contacted the board president and demanded payment of the back taxes. By the time the board of directors was aware of this, the school had closed and the few remaining assets had been liquidated to pay creditors. The IRS, of course, still wanted its money. It took the board to court to pursue the payment of the taxes by the fiducia-ries, arguing that the board members were ultimately responsible for the financial actions or inactions of the organization. The law-suits dragged on for years, and there was always the nagging concern that the board members would be held personally liable for the organization's outstanding debts. The answer? Yes, they would, and to the tune of thousands of dollars for each board member. ■

This is not a scenario you want to repeat. But it is a true story and one that I hear repetitions of annually. To avoid this and other embarrassments, you need to be aware there are two common violations of fiduciary duties (or of being prudent):

1. *Failure to follow fundamental management principles.* This is the pro-cess of making a decision that a prudent person would not make if provided the same information. It occurs when a board:
   - Doesn't develop plans or budgets.
   - Doesn't read staff reports to see if there are problems.
   - Doesn't pay attention to problems raised in reports.

- Doesn't demand a reasonable standard of reporting and control (like the board of the organization that went out of business overnight).
- Ignores repeated warnings from staff, volunteers, or outside experts.
- Does not attend meetings

2. *Operating the organization in a way that benefits one or more board members directly.* This is known as self-dealing or "inurement of benefit" and is flat out illegal. To help avoid this, your organization needs to have strong conflict-of-interest policies and enforce them. More on that below.

Avoiding Liability

Let's focus on some proven ways to avoid liability:

- First, if you are a board member, take your responsibility as a board member seriously. Come to the meetings, read the material in advance, and be willing to ask questions.
- Take the time to read and understand the organization's bylaws and mission statement, and act in accordance with these documents. If actions conflict with either the bylaws or the mission, speak out.
- Stay informed of what is going on within the organization's programs and administration.
- Set policies only after reviewing the facts carefully. Never make decisions in a vacuum; demand documentation.
- Read the financial statements before each meeting. Demand a format that can be understood and some training in how to use the reports in your role as a board member.
- Make sure that your organization has a long-range (three-to-five-year) plan and that board and staff contribute to its generation, revisions, and monitoring.
- Make sure that minimum statutory or technical requirements are met: filing annual reports (such as the IRS 990, 990N, or 990T), timely payment of withholding taxes, contracting with a certified public accountant for an independent audit of the agency's books annually, meeting the legal and regulatory requirements of the agency's funding sources, and so forth.
- Demand minutes from all meetings that list who voted which way on all significant items. List dissenting members by name.
- Adopt and enforce a conflict-of-interest policy that discourages any business transactions between directors and the corporation, unless conducted openly and with stringent safeguards.

- Know the state laws regulating voluntary organizations to ensure compliance. The board's attorney should review these laws closely to determine how the state handles the issue of board members' liability. A report to the board should be made on these issues.
- Have directors' and officers' insurance *if* such insurance buys you more than state and federal statutes that protect governing volunteers. Ask your insurance agent to show you why the policy exceeds the statutes in protection.

Following these suggestions should greatly reduce the risk that board members face and make it an acceptable risk for them to continue serving on the board. Finally, remember that many states have laws that reduce the board members' individual liability for actions taken in good faith. Make a good faith effort and you will be in much better shape.

Building a Better Board

How can you build a better board? First, you need to look at the needs you have in terms of expertise on the board. Then you should assess when those needs will become critical. For example, if your strategic plan has a goal to add a new building in three years, within a year you need to recruit a board member with construction experience and perhaps someone who can help you through the maze of financing options on your board. Finally, you need to develop and implement a recruitment program that fills slots in an orderly and planned manner.

 HANDS ON: Let me say here that I believe that you need a huge and varied skill set on a board, but that a businesslike board should have two broad categories of members. First, you need *advocates* for your mission—people who passionately believe in what you do. These people keep you honest to the first rule of nonprofits: mission, mission, and more mission. The second kind of people you need are *businesspeople*, and these folks keep you honest to the second rule of nonprofits: no money, no mission. These two groups provide a dynamic and very healthy tension on the board and help the organization balance the needs of the two primary rules. ■

In assessing the type of board member expertise you need, you should pay attention to three things:

1. Your organization's current programs (what you are now)
2. Your strategic plan (what you want to be in three to five years)
3. Your funding sources' regulations (what the payers' require)

The criteria of need can be objective, such as "ethnicity," "age," or "county of residence," or subjective, such as "community leader" or "political connections." Exhibit 6.1 allows you to assess those criteria important to you, add your own criteria, and assess your current status.

As you can see from the checklist in Exhibit 6.1, the types of board members that you will need vary greatly and can change over time. I served on a board that, at the time I joined, had no one with finance, architectural, or building skills, and yet the organization had just acquired a sixty-bed residential facility and was planning on buying or renting twenty small homes within the coming five years. We needed people with those skills and recruited them. Eight years later, as I went off the board, the skills needs had changed again from property acquisition and financing to fund-raising, marketing, and property management. Your needs will change, too. Do not make your categories for board service static. Review them regularly, at the same time you review your strategic plan.

EXHIBIT 6.1   Board Assessment Tool

Characteristic/Expertise	On Board?	Need This Skill			
		Now	1 Year	2 Years	3 Years
Gender					
Ethnicity (various)					
Funder's mandate					
Age group (various)					
Location (county, city, etc.)					
Advocate					
Legislative					
Clergy					
Customer					
Ethnicity					
Legal					
Accounting					
Finance/banking					
Marketing					
Personnel					
Construction					
Fund-raising					
Small business					

Board Recruitment

Now that you have established the board that you want and the schedule on which you will recruit those skills, you will need to organize a consistent recruitment program to constantly be prospecting for high-quality board members. As noted above, the quality of the board member is as important as the "slot" she or he fills.

There are five keys to good board recruitment and retention:

1. *Consistent recruitment.* This means that you do not just deal with board recruitment the week before the nominations committee meets or the afternoon before the annual meeting. Finding quality volunteers to sit on your policy-setting board is a constant job, and the process should encourage consistent effort.
2. *The recruitment effort is a joint board/staff task.* Board members need to be involved in the job of recruiting and assessing potential board candidates. So do staff. The effort should be split between the two groups, but if both are not involved, the outcome will not be optimal.
3. *Provide well-defined and clearly stated expectations of the board members.* There is no substitute for clearly stating to potential board members the expectations of them. That way, if they do not feel that they can meet those expectations, they can decline an offer to serve and save you the trouble of recruiting another person later. Examples of such expectations include:
   - You must attend ten of twelve monthly meetings.
   - You must serve on one board committee (most meet monthly) after your first six months on the board.
   - You are expected to read your board mailings before you come to the meeting.
   - You must work at our annual XYZ (fund-raising) event and either sell twenty tickets or donate $100 dollars yourself.
4. *Enforcement of these expectations.* Having rules and then not enforcing them is a waste of time, effort, and political capital. As noted in Chapter 5, it also violates our ethical goals; say what you mean and mean what you say. If you have these expectations, and board members can't or won't meet them, let them know that they will either be voted off the board or not nominated for renewal. When you let people know in advance, and in writing, about your expectations, then there is little area for them to complain. That doesn't mean that they won't complain, or that "firing" a board member is ever easy. It's not, particularly if your culture has not enforced any expectations on them in the past.

5. *Evaluation of recruitment efforts.* How many of the available board slots did you fill? Did you double up on the important ones? How many of your recruits stayed the first full year? How do you know these things? You track your efforts. As with any good process, you learn from your mistakes only if you know about them. You can build on your successes, but only if you are aware of them. Evaluate, evaluate, evaluate.

Board Orientation and Education

Orientation

There are some essential parts of good board orientation. First, and unlike the way that most organizations orient their boards, orientation should be a never-ending discipline. It should occur at *every* board meeting and, in the best-run organizations, extend to brief, focused discussions at committee meetings as well. However, the process does have to start somewhere, and that somewhere is not the hour before the first board meeting of a new year. Rather, good orientation starts at the first interview for potential board candidates. At that time, not only does the future board member get an oral briefing into mission, programs, funding, and philosophy, he or she should also get that key document: the board manual. After someone is elected to the board, he or she should get a number of things provided in addition to the board manual, a copy of your mission statement (and organizational values if you have those developed), the current budget, the most recent two audits, the last three or four monthly financial statements, and all of the organization's promotional material. If you also want to provide information on key funding sources, fine. Do not overwhelm a new board member with a 200-page manual. These basics will get him or her started. Additionally, as we'll talk about in more depth when we discuss technology, your Web site should include a password-protected area for board members only. This area should include information that is deeper and wider than the manual can ever accommodate, and it should be kept up to date.

Second, new board members need a personal oral orientation to the organization. That usually means a tour of the facility(ies), hopefully at the time that actual services are being provided. The board member may also choose (or be required) to serve as a volunteer for a short time as a hands-on practicum. A week or so after the tour, the board member should be called to see what questions have popped up.

 HANDS ON: One very successful and important adjunct to orientation is board mentoring. The board president asks a veteran board member to mentor each new board member for three to six months. The mentor meets the new board member for coffee or lunch before the first board meeting that the new member attends. They discuss board duties, perhaps the handouts, agenda, etc. Before the first meeting, the mentor and new member meet in the parking lot, walk in together, and the mentor introduces the new member to all current members. Then for the next few meetings, the mentor and new member sit together so that the new member can quietly ask the "dumb questions" that, while not being dumb at all, often do not get asked otherwise. Between meetings, the mentor calls to check in and is available by phone and e-mail to chat. It is a method to increase the likelihood of meeting the new member's wants and assuring that problems or questions are resolved early. This works, and it is not an imposition on anyone. ■

Third, make sure that at his or her first meeting, the new member is formally introduced and welcomed at the beginning of the meeting by the board president.

The Board Manual

The board manual (I do not like the term *orientation manual* because board members should regularly return to this document for reference—even after they are veterans) provides board members with an organized, single-reference source for questions about your organization. More and more, this information is online as well as in paper. You should give your board members the choice of which format they prefer. The manual should include at least the following:

- The organization's current bylaws and charter
- The organization's mission statement
- A table of organization with a listing of all key staff people and a *brief* description of what they do for the agency (*DON'T* send job descriptions unless requested)
- A list of current board members with their addresses, place of employment and title, work and home phone numbers, e-mail addresses, and what officer or committee chair positions they hold
- A list of the board committees, with a listing of current members and a brief explanation of what each committees does
- A flowchart of funding: where it comes from, where it goes (pie charts are particularly good for this purpose)

- A list of programs with a two-sentence description of each program
- A listing of frequently used acronyms/jargon and their meaning
- A list of board responsibilities (adapted from earlier in this chapter)
- A list of staff responsibilities (adapted from earlier in this chapter)
- A list of officer responsibilities

Committees of the Board

As noted earlier, you need a structure of committees to make the board work. The board does not have the time to review every single issue at length to the level of detail and scrutiny it may merit at every meeting. Thus, the board needs to delegate the "grunt" work to the committees. Your organization needs to determine what type of committees it needs to serve your board of directors. Some committees may outlive their usefulness over time; others, such as your finance and audit committees, will always be needed. Standing committees are those committees that are established on a permanent basis and may be described in the bylaws. Ad hoc committees are those assigned to carry out specific functions, make recommendations to the entire board, and then disband.

It is important to reiterate what I said earlier: that committee membership does not need to be solely composed of board members. Indeed, I suggest to all my client organizations that some committee members can also come from the pool of potential board members (and are an excellent training ground for board membership) and from persons who have a specific interest in helping the organization but do not want the long-term commitment that board membership requires. Just remember that the committee chair and the majority of committee members should always be board members.

An Effective Committee Structure

Your committees should do the following:

- Provide expertise to the board by gathering a group of experts on a given subject in a committee where they can share ideas and make recommendations based on the issues at hand.
- Reduce or eliminate the board's need to deal with every detail of operation. Working committees take assignments from the board, deal with them effectively, and return with solutions to recommend to the board. Committees will also come before the board with ideas and recommendations that their committee members have developed.
- Permit broader participation by all board members, as well as nonboard members.

The president, in consultation with the executive director, should make all committee assignments based on each board member's expertise and special talents, as well as personal preference. This should be done on an annual basis. Each board member should know several weeks before the first board meeting of the year which committee(s) he or she will serve on for the year. Board members should be notified in writing on which committee they will serve, who the chairman is, when and where the committee usually meets, and who the other committee members will be. The dates, times, and locations of all committee meetings should be posted on the board part of the Web site, and minutes from all prior meetings should be available there as well.

 HANDS ON: Some board members will not be happy with their committee assignments. One way to solve this is to ask each board member on which committee he or she would prefer to serve before the decision is made. At the last board meeting of the year, provide each board member with a written checklist of available committee assignments that must be returned to the president by the deadline noted. (Make it clear that it is not always possible to place them on the committee of their choice, but every effort will be made to do so. If they do not submit the form by the deadline noted, their assignment will be made by the president.) Then, based on this and the organization's needs, make assignments. ■

As noted in the discussion of board responsibilities, every board member should serve on at least one committee. However, don't ask new members to serve right away. Let them ease into their duties for five or six months and then give them an assignment. Try to keep committee membership small and focused. Five to nine people seems to work well for most groups. An odd number of members provides a tiebreaker if you need it.

Finally, I strongly recommend having all committee appointments be one year in length. That way, the president and the committee chair can constantly be improving the committees and adjusting to the changes on the board, on the staff, and in the industry. This does not mean that a particular board member might not serve on one particular committee for six years; it just ensures the maximum flexibility for the president.

What Committees Need to Operate

Committees, like boards, need certain things to operate effectively and efficiently. As I have noted repeatedly, an effective committee structure is crucial to an effective board, so staff need to ensure that the following elements are present:

- A clear understanding of their role and what their limitations are
- Quality, supportive staffing
- A committee chairperson who is:
  - A leader
  - Knowledgeable
  - Experienced in group leadership
  - Able to encourage participation by all committee members
  - Capable of facilitating a meeting and keeping members on track without inhibiting valuable new discussion
  - Able to bring the group to a timely conclusion and/or a decision
- Committee members who:
  - Complete their assignments on time
  - Do their homework between meetings
  - Are reasonable and thoughtful
  - Understand the importance and impact of their decisions

One final reiteration of an earlier admonition about committees: If you find that committee reports to the board are simply the basis for rehashing everything at length, you are not using your committee structure well. I understand that some critical issues will deserve a great deal of board attention and time, but if you see that you are simply holding the committee meeting over again at the board meeting, work to cut short the debate and have the board accept or reject committee recommendations, not reinvent them. One technique that works well for board members who feel the need to know everything about everything is to invite them (in public at the board meeting) to attend the committee meetings and have input there.

Recap

In this chapter, we have set the stage for building a better board of directors for your organization. You have learned about what makes an effective board and the barriers to that effectiveness. We have reviewed the responsibilities of the board to the organization and listed the expectations that the board should have of the staff. We also went over the legal liabilities of the board and suggested ways to reduce and avoid liability.

A quick review here of the crucial criteria and responsibilities from this chapter is in order. First, the characteristics of a businesslike board:

- It understands the organization's mission and acts to implement that mission for the benefit of the organization's constituency consistently and professionally.
- It acts as a policy setter and check-and-balance with the staff.
- It works primarily with the executive director and evaluates the executive director at least annually.
- It changes over time, filling its membership fully by recruiting new members to meet the changing needs of the organization.
- It elects qualified officers and appoints qualified committee chairs.
- It supports the organization in public.

The responsibilities of the board were listed as follows:

- Fulfill all of the IRS and state nonprofit reporting requirements
- Set policy and establish organizational goals
- Hire an executive director
- Evaluate the executive director's performance in writing at least annually
- Assure that fiscal policies are in place and followed
- Help develop and adopt budgets
- Review and amend bylaws every two years
- Ensure compliance with funding stream's policies and regulations
- Establish personnel policies and monitor their compliance
- Nominate and elect officers
- Represent the organization in public
- Help recruit new board members
- Raise funds, but not full time
- Perform volunteer program work

Finally, the staff responsibilities to the board were listed:

- The board should expect accurate, timely, honest, and focused information.
- The board should be regularly informed of new developments.
- The board should expect staff to gather information, analyze it, and make recommendations to the board—in essence, to be technical advisors to the board.
- The board should expect staff to report fiscal information regularly.
- The board should encourage staff to make the optimum use of the board as a resource.
- The board should expect staff to develop a process for and to educate all new board members and to orient all board members on an ongoing basis.

- The board should expect staff to provide support for board recruitment and development.
- The board should expect staff to support board committees and provide them with necessary information and expertise they need.
- The board should expect staff to attend all meetings of the board unless excused therefrom.

Your board is a crucial resource, one that needs to be used to its fullest if you are to provide the best mission in your community. You need a strong board.

You also need a strong staff, which is the other side of the coin in most nonprofits. That is the subject of Chapter 7.

Questions for Discussion

1. Do we have a businesslike board now? How can we get there?
2. Is the list of board responsibilities valid for our agency? How should we improve and amend our list?
3. What about staff responsibilities to the board? Do we do all these things now? Does our board agree? Where can we improve?
4. How can we ramp up our orientation process to be constant and consistent?
5. Is there value in having ongoing board recruitment? Why? How can we move toward that goal?

CHAPTER 7

Leading Your People

Overview

An essential component in successful nonprofits is building and retaining a strong staff, one that embraces the mission, knows the field of endeavor that the organization has embarked on, and manages all of its resources as effectively and efficiently as possible to produce high-quality mission every single day. Remember, the resources of your organization also include the traditional ones; some combination of people, money, buildings, and equipment. But let's also not forget the mission-value of your governing and nongoverning volunteers, and the business techniques we discussed earlier. Of all these, though, the most visible resource for most nonprofits, at least after the mission, and certainly the most expensive resource, are the employees, which is the subject of this chapter. You need to maximize the effectiveness of your staff, and to do that you need to be an effective mission-based manager.

Throughout this chapter, I will walk you through the information you need in order to become a more effective leader of your staff, valuing and empowering them. We'll look at a management style that is literally upside down, as well as some competing management styles and their advantages and disadvantages. We'll look long and hard at ways to communicate better. I'll show you some new thoughts on delegation, how to double your outcomes in evaluations, and how to set up a staff reward program that really rewards rather than punishes. By the end of the chapter, you will have a clearer understanding of how to better manage that crucial organizational asset—your staff.

First, some facts to set the framework from which I will advise you: Your staff is one of the "markets" that you need to attend to. As I noted in Chapter 2, you are increasingly in competition for good staff. Second, you can't, and probably never will, pay like the private sector, whether for a secretary, a driver, a line staff person, or an administrator. Thus, you have to give folks who work with you something more than just a check to keep them coming to work for you.

To a certain extent, this something is your mission statement, and we discussed this at length in Chapter 4. But beyond that, it is your culture and the way you as staff treat each other and hang in there together as a team that will keep people wanting to be employed with you. A wise executive director once told me, "There are two reasons and only two that our staff show up for work every day: the mission and the way we treat each other. So we need to talk more about mission and treat each other better." Let's look at how we can do both.

The Inverted Pyramid of Management

Look at Exhibit 7.1, the traditional management pyramid. This organizational structure, which is familiar to almost everyone, was not, believe it or not, developed at the same time as the pyramids in Egypt or Central America. In fact, it was developed after World War II by the Rand Corporation for the use of global U.S. corporations to help them manage their firms. And it worked for nearly thirty years. Rather, it worked until there was serious competition.

EXHIBIT 7.1   Traditional Management Pyramid

You see, after the war, the United States really had a twenty-year window in which it had the only serious manufacturing, medical, research, and higher-education capabilities in the world. Much of the industrial world lay in ruins and spent that time rebuilding and recovering from the destruction of the war. The United States had free rein, until the Europeans and Japanese and then the Koreans and other Asian countries recovered. Then, from the mid-1970s through the mid-1980s, those countries ate our lunch. Remember when the Japanese bought Rockefeller Center and we thought it was a harbinger of things to come?

It was not, and one of the many reasons why was the abandonment of the traditional management structure. Companies became flatter (with fewer levels between the line staff and the senior executives), and they also flipped themselves around and realized that the people who were really the most important in any organization were the people who do the actual manufacturing or provide the actual service: the line staff. World-class firms like Cisco Systems, Marriott, Federal Express, Lands' End, and Google all have turned their organizations around by valuing their line staff more and their executives less. This kind of structure empowers staff, pushes decisions to the line of service, and makes use of all of the resources of the organization. In a competitive, globalized marketplace, it is the model that succeeds.

The same holds true for nonprofits. Most nonprofits simply copied the for-profit world and still use the old traditional model. Until the nonprofit world was subjected to serious competition, it worked just fine. No longer. Successful nonprofits realize that they too must value their staff, educate and empower them, and bring everyone into the effort to provide total customer satisfaction. If they don't, they will not be around much longer.

In this organizational model (again, look at Exhibit 7.1), the executive director is at the top of the heap, with associate or assistant directors and assorted middle management between the executive and the line staff, who are portrayed at the bottom of the pile.

Now, let's turn that all on its head. Take a look at Exhibit 7.2. Note that the box that the executive director occupies is at the bottom, and the line staff at the top, with the people who you serve at the very top. This symbolism (and that is all it is if you don't live this style of management all the time) is important because many organizations need to rethink what is the most important thing that they do, who is most important, and where their internal priorities are.

Let's look at the major tenets of my version of the inverted pyramid, and then examine some examples.

- *The only reason there are staff is because of the mission: There are people to serve.* The only reason there are managers is because the staff doing the service need support. The executive director is not the most

EXHIBIT 7.2   The Preferred Management Model

important person in the nonprofit. He or she may be the most powerful, but not the most important. If all staff members realize that management exists to find and manage resources to allow line staff to do their jobs, then the priorities become much clearer, the roles begin to change a bit, and the organization starts to head in the correct direction.

- *Managers are enablers, not "restrictors."* Good management should be a supportive, assistive function rather than a harsh power game, telling people what they can and can't do. As an enabler, your role is to support your staff in accomplishing the goals of the organization. This support means doing what it takes to get the job done. It includes fighting for resources for your people, fixing things that aren't right, getting distractions large and small out of the way, and participating in budget and planning activities, no matter what your level in the organization. This fundamental principle allows you to see your job in very human terms. Your job as a supervisor is to take some of the load off of the people you supervise and let them do their jobs.
- *The supervisor/supervised relationship is two-way.* The relationships you develop with your staff, like any other relationships, are two-way. That means that both the supervisor and the supervised have a responsibility to make things work. Additionally, if the closer you go

toward the people you serve, the more important people doing the service are, then the supervisor—instead of spending time restricting and controlling—should be facilitating getting resources to his or her employees. As we all know, relationships will not work if you always talk and never listen, if you only give ideas and are never receptive to those of your staff, or if you make all the decisions and do not delegate. This idea works in great sync with our concepts of ethics, accountability, and transparency. More on this idea later.

- *Treat others the way you would want to be treated.* Again, we started with this as a major part of our ethical framework in Chapter 5, and it is so important it needs to be revisited here. Honesty, fairness, and consistency are the key characteristics of a successful manager. Honesty means not promising to do something you cannot deliver ("I'll get back to you on that tomorrow"), fairness means treating all of your staff equally (what goes for Assad has to go for Amie), and consistency means asking for rules to be followed and then enforcing them when you say you will. Say what you mean and mean what you say.

- *Be a leader, but be willing to follow.* This means that you are a leader who takes risks on behalf of your staff. It also means you let your staff take the lead when they are right or when they have a better solution to a problem. (This happens more than you or I want to admit.) It also means being very human and part of the team, so that you pitch in and do the most menial task when it is necessary to help support your staff. If there is a rush item to get out, like a mailing or preparing handouts for a board meeting, and everyone is hustling around, pitch in: run copies, lug boxes, drive the van. We all know that you are very busy, but these small efforts go a long way with staff people; they remember them and it makes you more accessible to them.

- *If you are going to help your staff, you need to keep in touch.* Knowing what is going on with your line staff has never been more important. The further you are from line work, the more important it is. Make the time to work with line workers. My rule is one day per quarter at the very least, and more if the size and locations that you operate allow it. This task (which too many managers think is a waste of time) is, in truth, an essential component of the job. The most popular term for this was coined by Tom Peters in *In Search of Excellence* (New York: Warner Books, 1982). He called it "Management by wandering around." Peters talked about keeping in touch by being on site, on the factory floor, or at the place that service is being provided. In his wonderful 2007 book, *The Three Signs of a Miserable Job* (San Francisco: Jossey-Bass, 2007), Pat Lencioni notes that people want to be "known." Employees want their supervisors (and their coworkers) to take the time to know them as people, not just as employees. Leadership guru John Maxwell echoes this in his book *Developing the Leader within You* (Nashville, TN: Thomas Nelson, 2005) when he notes that "People don't care how much you know until they know that you care." You need to get out of your office, stop hiding behind your "open door" policy, and get to know your people.

In addition to just being there, I also have seen over and over the positive effects of also having management *do* some line work at regular intervals.

 HANDS ON: Do a monthly stint as a volunteer, a quarterly day as a line worker, or simply have breakfast or lunch with line staff once a week. You've got to keep in touch with your people, and that means starting by understanding what they do. For example, if you run a hospital, work as a security guard or as a volunteer who greets new patients for a day. If you run a human service organization, open a case, be a meals-on-wheels driver, or sit in on an encounter or support group. If you run a school, teach an hour a week or a day a month as a guest teacher. The essential philosophy: This is *not* taking time away from your job. *This is an essential part of your job!* You will learn more about your organization, how it really runs, and what staff really need to get the mission accomplished than you would ever believe.

Many of the senior staff at McDonald's work one week a year behind the counter at a restaurant to keep in touch. It doesn't matter that most of them worked at a McDonald's as teenagers. They need to work on site *now* to know what works and what doesn't *now*. ■

■ *When you and your staff are praised, pass it around. When you are criticized, take the fall.* You are responsible for the results of both you and your staff. But when someone praises you (individually or as a group), pass the praise on directly: "Well, thank you, Mayor, for those kind words, but I am just the CEO. The real work, and thus the real praise, should go to our outreach staff." Pass the praise around.

Also, go out of your way to compliment deserving individual and group efforts. Positive reinforcement (if sincere and deserved) is always appreciated. This can be constant and informal or may include employee recognition, which we'll discuss later in this chapter.

The reverse is true when you are criticized—as an individual or as your part of the organization: If you are the chief staff person, you take the fall. Never, ever, ever blame someone else. There are three reasons for this. First, even if whatever went wrong is really not your fault, you are in charge. The captain on the bridge of a ship is responsible for the actions of his or her people. Second, nothing you do will bring more loyalty or build more morale than stepping in front of the blame bullet for your staff people: "Well [board president], I know we missed the deadline. I'm doing all I can to minimize the damage, and I've already apologized to the affected people. It won't happen again."

Finally, it is always easy to blame your staff for something that doesn't go right. But remember, it may really *be* your fault, as a result of your not clearly communicating instructions or picking the wrong person to complete a task. We'll look at delegation and communications later in the chapter.

The inverted pyramid works, slowly but surely. However, to make it work, it has to be *lived*, every day in every way. Once you set yourself up as believing this philosophy, it is easy to fall off the pedestal. If you just flip your organizational chart on its head and do not follow it up with real and consistent actions to support the concept, you will lose ground with your staff.

With those tenets in mind, let's look at several applications of the principal of the inverted pyramid and how it works.

 FOR EXAMPLE: My wife, Chris, was a special education teacher in our local public school district for thirty-three years until her retirement in 2007, and for many of those years she worked in a building that was first a 5th- and 6th-grade center and later a middle school.

As background, all teachers everywhere are required to come in for planning days and meetings a few days before the children return in the late summer or early fall, and these are not days that most teachers look forward to. The schools are still hot, the meetings are dull, the kids are not yet there, and there is too much to get done in too short a time.

The year this story took place, Chris went in for her planning days with even more trepidation. The 5th- and 6th-grade center she was assigned to was new; she knew only some of the staff and didn't know the principal at all, although she had heard through the grapevine that the principal was "incredible."

After her first day of meetings, Chris came home totally pumped up and excited. She almost could not tell me the story fast enough. "It was incredible. Our principal, Phyllis, was amazing.

(continued)

(continued)

She came into our first all-faculty meeting and said: '*I am the principal here, but I'm not the most important person in the school. The kids are. And since you deal more with the students than I do, you're more important to their education than I am.* So what do I do? I am the person who ensures that you get the resources you need and the necessary environment to allow you to teach to your maximum potential. You, as teachers, are what this school is all about: teaching children. My job is to get you the resources you need, as well as removing the distractions you don't need. If you need supplies, see me and I'll get them. If you need a disruptive child removed from the room, I'll do it. If you can't get parental support, I'll help you. My job is not to sit on you; it is to help you teach.'"

Chris went on: "You could have heard a pin drop. No one had ever been talked to by a principal like that before. I actually heard our union rep say, as we walked out, 'Who needs money if we're treated like that?'"

Chris taught at that school for the next twenty years (the remainder of her teaching career), and you could not have gotten her to leave for any money. Phyllis moved on to another school after the first five years, leaving her successor and her successor's successor to carry on the tradition of management that she started. The school is among the most recognized in the nation and has become a magnet school where twice as many students are on the waiting list as are in the school. Its students are blessed with great teachers, who are well treated and who want to be there every day to teach. The school is a great place to learn. Not only do kids like it there, but their test scores are up, there are innovative teaching techniques being tried, and it's fun to teach there. Teachers work more hours (in and out of school) than any school I know of and there is also a waiting list to get on the faculty. ■

This example shows what can be done in a short time with a commitment of one person. Admittedly, Phyllis had a clean slate (a new faculty) to start with, but she also had to overcome tradition, past morale problems, and inertia. She did it by letting the teachers know in word and deed that she valued them as professionals and as individuals. What more do any of us really want? And Phyllis made the changes stick—they outlasted her tenure as principal.

FOR EXAMPLE: As a result of my work, I travel a great deal. I usually stay in hotels that are the choice of the conference planners at the conventions where I speak or at hotels close to clients with whom I am consulting. In both cases, someone else decides where I stay. When I am lucky enough to check into a Marriott, at *any level* of Marriott, from a resort to the Fairfield Inn, I know my needs will be met. I know that everything will work, that I will be treated like a valued customer, and that whatever I need will be provided. This is particularly important when I am conducting training, as I need to ensure that the LCD projector, microphone, and room temperature all are working well (and in many places this is an iffy proposition at best), and that other last-minute details are attended to. What I don't want are hassles, bad attitudes, or to be told "can't" or "won't."

In the thirty years that I have been traveling for business, I have probably stayed at two hundred Marriotts, and I have never, ever met anyone (bellhop, restaurant server, housekeeping staff, audio visual tech) who works in any of those hotels and not been greeted with a "Good morning, sir. How are you today?" And it was said like they meant it. I can recount dozens of times staff went out of their way to make me feel special or to willingly and immediately fix a small problem that I had. Like the night I arrived at a Marriott in Washington, D.C., at 2:00 A.M. after interminable travel delays, only to find that my reservation was for a different Marriott across town. What did the clerk do? Dismiss me and tell me to go elsewhere? No, first, he called the other hotel to assure that my room was still available, and then, sensing my exhaustion and frustration, offered me a room at "his" hotel—the hotel that I was standing in—even though they had no rooms at my reserved rate. I gratefully accepted the latter offer, and five minutes later was escorted into a three-room suite, complete with fruit basket! On another occasion, I was off to a meeting and walked by a pleasant matronly housekeeping supervisor who greeted me with a cheery "Good morning," then told me to wait while she very tactfully straightened my tie, and added, "Go get 'em!" What a great way to start my day!

Both of these people made my stay memorable by doing a little extra thing that they were both encouraged and empowered to do. The desk clerk had been given the authority to upgrade my reservation (or actually to give me one without a reservation), and the housekeeping staff person was simply motivated and pleasant.

(*continued*)

(*Continued*)

Both of these were the result of good management practices and the upside-down pyramid.

Marriott as a corporation believes in the phrase of their CEO: *Take care of your employees and they will take care of you.* They constantly train and motivate their line staff, drilling into them the concept that they, and not the management, will make the hotel succeed or fail, and to have the line people surface ideas on ways to make the guests more comfortable. They delegate responsibility and authority. The company invests in its people and it pays off. ■

Other examples abound in the proprietary world. When was the last time you met a curt or unfriendly UPS or Federal Express delivery person? Or talked to a brusque salesperson from Lands' End? You don't. Why? Because these organizations value their people, they tell them so all the time, and they show them by their actions. *All* of the staff at the Disney properties are provided costumes—not uniforms—and even the trash collectors at their parks go through a solid week of training in how to interact with customers *before* they get their trash collection training.

Think of each of these and other organizations, such as airlines, restaurants, and the like. Who do you deal with nearly all the time in these organizations? *The lowest paid people in the company.* At the airline, it's the ticket agent or the baggage clerk or the flight attendant. At a hotel, it's the concierge, bellhop, or desk clerk. At a restaurant, it's the greeter or server. It's these people who really shape your experience with the company. And, in successful companies, it is these people who are the most valued.

Who are these people in your organization? Who do your clients, donors, volunteers, and referral sources deal with most? If you are the executive director (unless you are a one-person shop), it's probably not you. Treat the people who actually *do* the mission with respect and you'll get a lot more out of them.

Styles of Supervision

There are four broad categories of management styles listed below. In truth, as managers we all fit into at least one and probably more than one at different times. As you read these, think about how each does or does not fit into our inverted-pyramid model.

1. *Attila the Hun.* We've all worked for Attila, or a direct descendant. This person is *the* boss. No question about it. He or she maintains a "directing

behavior," lays down the law, and expects it to be followed to the letter. He or she looks at the staff as stepping stones *up* the management ladder. Attila is quick to criticize and judge and has never heard of the words "thank you." Attila is obeyed but usually not respected. Attila also gets results, at least in the short term, but when Attila is not present, a great deal of staff time is spent griping . . . about Attila.

2. *One of the gang.* These managers usually come "up from the ranks" but never adjust to the new role. They want to remain one of the gang, so they try to minimize or eliminate the distinctions between them and their staff. They never understand that once they cross the bridge to become a supervisor, they are never again peers. They can still be friends with those who they supervise, but they can never be pals. This person has difficulty in completing performance appraisals and usually cannot discipline at all. Morale can be good if you work for one of the gang, but over time productivity tends to slip, as this person may be liked but is rarely respected. Often he or she favors his or her former peers over other staff, causing resentment and discord.

3. *All business.* These managers are thoroughly professional, but distant. They do not fraternize or socialize with their direct reports, and they place great emphasis on plans, goals, objectives, budgets, and performance. They never take the time to truly get to know their people, and this is key to good communications and effective delegation. I cannot envision this manager stuffing envelopes or filling in at the reception desk in a pinch.

4. *Coach/Conductor.* Both a coach and an orchestra conductor get the job done, but, and this is crucial, *through the actions of others.* The coach and the conductor both know that they themselves *don't play*, that others do, and that their success is contingent upon the success of their team. They cajole, praise, and discipline when it is necessary. These managers exemplify team spirit with enthusiasm, but they maintain a long-term view of the organization. A coach/conductor helps his or her staff to grow and attain their maximum potential.

Obviously, I would prefer if all of us were coaches/conductors. But it would be naive to assume that everyone can adopt that style. Besides, in the real world, we all need to be Attila once in a while—hopefully for only short periods at long intervals! The most important thing is to adapt your style to let people know you value them. If you are demanding, fine, but be demanding of the right things, things that focus attention on mission and line staff and quality of outcome, not things that inflate your ego or make people cower before you. And make sure that if you are demanding of others, you are even more demanding of yourself.

Your style as a manager, as well as your priorities in terms of staff and mission, are inherent parts of bringing about the organizational direction that will allow you to succeed.

Communications

To succeed with your staff, you will need to be able to communicate with them: to find out what they need to get their job done, to delegate tasks, to plan budgets, or to figure out what to buy for lunch—all these things require good communications. It often seems that *communication* is a five-syllable word meaning trouble, as in "What we have here is a failure to communicate." I can hardly think of one of the nonprofits that I have consulted with over the past twenty-five years—even the well-run ones—who didn't complain about inadequate (or poor or awful) internal communications. This seems to be an area where everyone would like to see improvement (or are unsatisfied with the way things are now). Why?

There are a number of reasons. First, many people assume that they need to know everything that goes on in the organization. They do not, but that's irrelevant. They *feel* that they should be better informed, and thus will be discontented until they *feel* that they are being at least adequately informed. (Often, these people will simultaneously complain about too many meetings, too many e-mails, and not enough time to do their "real" jobs.) The second reason is that many nonprofits are changing quickly and growing rapidly. As a result, the staff, particularly those who have been employed for a number of years, often feel that they "used to know everything and everyone around here" and now feel isolated. This problem is most acute if the organization has multiple buildings or sites.

Obviously, the issue of communications is essential, not only to good operational management but also to good morale. Good communications is as much perception as reality, and it is based on the following tenets.

Trust

If the staff don't trust the management to give them full, accurate, and timely information, the rest of these techniques are a waste of time. The staff will still complain about the lack of communication from top management.

 FOR EXAMPLE: A client agency of mine was having problems with employee morale. The executive director had been on the job two years and had instituted a number of staff and organizational

changes that I felt were terrific but that had met with very traditional resistance to change from many of the staff. This agency
provided distinctly different services at two separate sites, and thus
staff did not all get to see each other a great deal.

The agency was planning to construct a new building to
house some of its services. At the time the events described
here occurred, the agency had developed architectural plans, had
acquired a site, and had a date for the initiation of construction
and a target for completion. It also knew the budget and which
major components of the agency would move to the site upon
completion. The agency was to build the building as a shell first,
and then later would divide the shell into components to house
various programs.

As soon as the site had been purchased, all staff who had
not been in on the early planning were informed of the project
and told everything listed above. Approximately two weeks later,
I was scheduled to come in to run some focus groups of staff
to discuss the results of an employee survey that our firm had
administered for the agency. In the survey, communications had
come up over and over again as a real deficit in the management
area.

During my discussions with staff, one staff person (I'll call her
Linda) and I had the following conversation (the notation "PCB"
means yours truly.)

Linda: Senior management never tells us *anything* till after the
fact.

PCB: Give me an example.

Linda: Well, take this new building we just heard about. We just
haven't been told *anything* about the project, and it's
important to us.

PCB: Of course it is. What did the management staff tell you
specifically?

Linda: Well, I know that the building is being built at the corner
of Adams Street and 15th, and that it will house the intake,
client assessment, and rehabilitation divisions.

PCB: Did they tell you anything else?

Linda: No, *nothing*. See what I mean?

PCB: No information on schedule, budgets, or anything else?

Linda: I do know that they are laying the foundation next week
and that we are scheduled to occupy next April. I think
my division will move in first.

(*continued*)

(continued)

> **PCB:** Sounds like you know everything there is to know about this project. I actually just met with your executive director and the architect, and that's pretty much all *they* know.
>
> **Linda:** *(After a pause)* Well, they always tell us so *late*.

You get the picture I'm sure. Linda did not trust the management staff, for whatever reason. And, no matter what the management people told her, no matter if she was included in senior management meetings, she would not be happy. If, however, she had trusted the senior management, she would have had a different outlook on the same information. ■

All Communication Is Two-Way

The most important part of communications is not what you say but what your staff hears. It is not what you send but what your staff receives. It is not what you write but what your staff reads. All of us have the mystery filter in our houses; you know the one that comes between you and your spouse or you and your kids. It is the filter that comes between your mouth and their ears and results in the conversation: "No, I didn't say THAT. What I said WAS ..." etc., etc., etc. There is little protection against miscommunication, but we can do more to check on what people heard so that we correct the initial miscommunication.

 HANDS ON: To vividly demonstrate the concept of miscommunication to your management staff, try this exercise with your staff. At a staff meeting, read off the following list (exactly) *without warning*. Read it slowly and deliberately:

> BED, REST, SLUMBER, SNOOZE, PILLOW, SHEET, NAP, MATTRESS, SNORE, DREAM.

Now ask the staff to write down as many as they can remember. Give them a minute or two. Ask how many people got six words (ask them to raise their hands). Some will have gotten six. Ask if anyone got eight. Compliment them. Ask who wrote down the word "bed," the first word you read. About half will have. Compliment them. Ask who wrote down "dream," the last word you read. About the same number will have. Now, and this is the key, ask whoever wrote down the word "sleep" to raise their hands—and keep their hands up. If your group is like the dozens I've done this with, over half will have written down sleep, and *you never read it!* Have everyone look around to see how many hands were raised.

Make the point with your staff that the reason that they wrote down "sleep" was that they associated it with the rest of the words you read, but that they felt so strongly that they heard it, that they *wrote it down.* Now, if you were to have gone back to them in a week and asked for notes on what you said, they would have written proof (documentation) that you said "sleep" because they wrote it down!

We need to ensure that our instructions and communications are understood. ■

Let's examine the issue of communications from the viewpoint of results. When do your staff fail to complete a task correctly? When

- *They don't know what they are supposed to do.* None of us is very good on this one. Think about it: You tell your staff something and then ask, "Do you understand?" or even worse, "You understand, don't you?" Now, who is going to say to his or her boss, in effect, "No, I don't understand; I'm stupid"? We do not give people much of a chance to say no, or to ask for help.
- *They don't know how to do the task.* Same issues as above.
- *They think they are doing it right, but haven't received any feedback.* If you are not around to talk to or observe staff while they are working on the project, you cannot guide them away from mistakes. Thus, little problems become big ones. If people are not given some supervision or being observed, particularly the first time they do a job, they may very well, with good intentions, do it completely wrong, and in a way that could have been prevented if you had been around enough to catch the little mistake before it got to be a big one.
- *They don't know why they should complete the task.* The *why* is so important. Telling people *why* they need to do something puts it in context; it gives the assignment a rationale, a purpose, and a priority. In terms of accurate communications, think of the difference in the message sent by someone saying, "Please put together a spreadsheet of our cash flow projections" or "Please put together a spreadsheet of our cash flow projections because I need to present them to the finance committee on Thursday night." The first assignment gives the bare bones. The second gives context and would probably lead to a clearer, more

complete (and neat) cash flow being presented. Tell people *why* something needs to be done. Do not assume that they don't care about the why. Let them make that choice.

■ *They hear something different than what you say and you are not in control of what your staff hears.* Remember our list without the word "sleep"? Need I say more?

In order to get over the worst of these, when you give instructions to someone, particularly on something new, follow this order:

1. **Explain** how to do it.
2. **Demonstrate** how to do it (if possible).
3. **Request** an explanation of how to do it.
4. **Invite** the employee to demonstrate it for you (if possible).

Now, you can't just treat staff like a small child and say, "What did I just say?" in a condescending voice. But what you can do is ask, "Please tell me what we just agreed you'd do, so that I can make sure I didn't tell you wrong." In an inverted-pyramid management scheme, and if you agree that you are responsible for getting the communications across, ask for feedback with the assumption that you have not communicated whatever needs to be communicated accurately or thoroughly. At the end of meetings, ask everyone at the table to reiterate what it is that they agreed to do at the meeting, and by when. Don't tell them what they agreed to; you want to hear it in their words.

Delegation

There is enough good material on delegation to fill three shelves at your local library, and we all know that good managers are ones who delegate effectively, so I won't try to convince you that you should be delegating more. Rather, I'll try to pass on some ideas on how to delegate better. Delegation is particularly tough on first-time supervisors who still want to "do" rather than "manage." After all, if you hadn't been good at the "doing," you probably wouldn't have gotten promoted. But since you now are a supervisor, you have a different job, and not enough time to both do and supervise. You need to delegate the jobs that your staff can do now or learn fairly quickly. To be successful, you need to attend to the following rules:

■ *Delegate authority with responsibility.* This is critical: Your employees must feel that they have the authority to decide as well as to do. If you require them to get back to you on every little detail, you might as well do it yourself, and your staff person will be very frustrated to boot. The further toward the line staff that decision authority can be pushed, the better.

- *Challenge your staff supportively.* Do not just give them a job and a deadline and then kick them out the door of your office. Learn how to offer support and advice without having them lean on you for everything. Also, push them a bit, forcing them to try new tasks if you feel they can learn them. Back off in the level of supervision as quickly as you can, but let them know that you are there as a safety net.

- *Know your staff.* We've talked about this already a great deal, and it's really important to being able to do good delegation and communications. You just have to take the time to know your people so that you know their skills, their strengths and weaknesses, their likes and dislikes, their potential, and their pitfalls. You just have to have this information if you are going to use them to their maximum potential. Remember we talked about Peters and his maxim "Management by wandering around"? Be out there, look and listen more than you talk. This will allow you to know your people.

- *Recognize that mistakes will (and should) be made.* It is how we learn. Honest mistakes honestly made are okay. Once. Don't let people make the same mistake twice. But be assuring and helpful, noting that you also have made your share of goof-ups. If people don't make mistakes, and don't learn, they won't ever grow. Adopt the maxim "Do something!" as your credo, and you will have gone a long way toward better delegating.

- *Admit that other people can do some things better than you can.* It really is true. You'll be amazed at how well other people can do what you have always done, often without your help. It will be different, but often—if you are really honest—better than the way you have done it in the past. Remember, be a leader but willing to follow.

 HANDS ON: Try this with your staff. Make a copy of the figure below:

IX

Hand it out at a staff meeting and tell people *exactly* the following:

"Take this, add one line, and turn this into a six."

(*continued*)

(*continued*)

Give the staff people a minute or two to get the right answer, and perhaps one in ten will. The answer, by the way, is:

SIX

I used to use this exercise to teach people to learn how to solve problems in different ways. But, in 1988, my then-six-year-old son Benjamin was talking to me as I was preparing for a presentation. He was asking the age-old question, "What do you do at work, Daddy?" and I was trying my best to explain the job of management consultant and trainer in terms that he could understand. I told him that "I teach grownups." "Like in school?" he asked. "Yes, like that. I teach them things about where they work." "Do you play games?" he wanted to know. "Yes, sometimes," and as I said that I saw (and here's a blast from the past) a *transparency* that had the IX on it. Aha! "Benjamin," I said, showing him the IX just as on the preceding page. "Take the pencil and with one line, turn this into a six." With no hesitation at all, he grabbed the pencil, added an "S" before the IX and said, "Like this?" I was floored. I mean, I knew he was smart (*my* child and all that parental pride), but only about 10 percent of adults get this at all, much less immediately. What was going on?

What was going on, of course, was that Benjamin, as a first grader, had not learned about Roman numerals. When he looked at an "IX," he saw an "icks," not a "nine," which is what adults see. In short, we as adults have *too much information, too much education, too much knowledge* to solve this problem. Later that week, I was visiting Benjamin's classroom, and I asked the teacher if I could repeat the activity with the class. Of thirty kids in the room, all thirty got it immediately. ■

The point here is, don't assume that because you have a college diploma or a master's or a doctorate or twenty years on the job that you can solve every problem better than someone without those degrees or experience. Sometimes you'll be *too smart to solve the problem*.

 POSTSCRIPT TO THE STORY: As I was preparing the first edition of this book in 1992, Benjamin, then 10, asked me how the book was coming, and if there were any stories about him in the book. I told him yes and summarized the story for him. When I finished, he asked to see the problem; for me to let him do it again.

He couldn't come up with the answer. I laughed and asked him what he saw on the page, and he said, "Dad, how can you turn a nine into a six with one line?" I showed him, and informed him that he now knew too much to solve the problem: He had learned about Roman numerals. At this point, Benjamin's then-seven-year-old brother Adam walked in. Benjamin (who like all big brothers thought he knew it *all*) handed Adam the "IX" and asked him to turn it into a six. You guessed it. Adam, with no hesitation, replayed his brother's actions from four years before. He grabbed a pencil and wrote an "S" in front of the "IX." I still treasure the memory of the look on Ben's face as he realized he did not automatically know more than his little brother just because he was three years older. ■

Communicate clearly. Back to communications, again. Remember:

- **Explain** how to do it.
- **Demonstrate** how to do it (if possible).
- **Request** an explanation of how to do it.
- **Invite** the employee to demonstrate it for you (if possible).

Good delegation is the path to supportive management: You help people grow by good delegation. They wither without new challenges.

Evaluation

I make the assumption in writing this section that you already have an evaluation policy and an evaluation tool in place. If you do not have such a policy, you need one, starting today.

At a minimum, you and your management team should provide a written and oral evaluation of every staff member, volunteer, and board member every year. Why? Because without evaluations, without confronting the bad and acknowledging the good, people don't grow. It is also the only documentation that you have of a person's capability (or lack thereof), his or her contributions to the organization, and the like. It is the easiest management task to procrastinate on, but it is an essential component of good management.

That having been said, there are some keys to the way we encourage a staff evaluation process to be established and conducted. These may be different than you have seen before, but they are well tested and they work.

All Evaluations Should Be Two-Way

As discussed in the opening pages of this chapter, the relationship between a supervisor and the supervisee is just that—a relationship. It will not work if both parties do not participate and try to make it work.

For example, if the worker does not get clear instructions from the supervisor, or does not get them in a way that he or she can best understand and follow them, then the worker will fail to do the job up to the supervisor's expectations. In a normal evaluation setting, that problem would be the employee's fault, with no encouragement to the worker to point out the supervisor's communications problem. Therefore, your employee evaluations should have parts where the employee is evaluated, goals are reviewed, and so forth, as well as parts where the supervisor is evaluated in terms of his or her interaction with the employee.

There is no question that for many supervisors this is a *terribly* threatening change. Supervisors are used to doing the evaluation, not being evaluated. For staff, this can be very nerve-wracking as well. Evaluate my boss? No way! But it does work, can work, and should work in an organization that sees management as support and staff as critical. We'll cover *how* you do it in the methodology below.

Evaluations Should Be Oral and Written

You write out evaluations so that you have to think about them, so that people can read and think about them, and so that you have documentation of what was said. You do them orally as well, so that each person has to face the other with both the good and bad parts of the evaluation. It opens yet another channel in the communications array.

There Should Be No Surprises at Evaluations

If you and your staff are communicating well and regularly, if you are dealing with the good and bad immediately rather than waiting for an annual review, then there should be no bombshells between supervisor and worker. If there are big surprises, then the rest of the communications system is breaking down, and you should use the evaluation process as an early-warning sign of that breakdown.

Set and Evaluate Goals for Both People

Three or four goals for the next evaluation period are important. If accomplished, they provide a feeling of satisfaction and accomplishment. If not, they provide a challenge for improvement. Again, the goals should be for the supervisor *and* the worker.

Evaluations Should Never Be Just Numerical

I feel that the biggest mistake that we all have made in the past ten years in the area of evaluations is the trend to totally numerical rankings or ratings for evaluations. I understand the need for quantification in many evaluation/compensation systems; you need a number to calculate a bonus or a raise. But numbers without context are meaningless. They provide no guidance for the employee, and a record of no value in the future.

 FOR EXAMPLE: Agency A has a form that asks for a supervisor to rate an employee in ten categories such as "Enthusiasm," "Attendance," "Work Quality," "Interaction with Clients," "Interaction with Staff," and the like on a 1 to 10 scale, with 10 being "Exceptional" and 1 being "Totally Unacceptable." Thus, a supervisor can go down the list and rank John or Mary a 7 for "Interaction with Staff" and a 5 for "Interaction with Clients" and be done with the whole rating in a minute. Now, the supervisor gives the evaluation to John or Mary and tries to compare the rating with last year's. John went from a 7 to an 8 in "Work Quality." But why? The supervisor cannot *really* remember. Worse, if next year there is a new supervisor, he or she will have absolutely no background as to *why* John was rated an 8 as opposed to a 7, or a 2 for that matter. ■

I strongly prefer written evaluations with questions that require thought and answers in complete sentences. If you must use a quantified scale, fine, but require written justification for each numerical rating.

Include the Mission and Values as Evaluation Criteria

Everyone should have as part of his or her evaluation criteria an item with wording to the effect of "In what ways did [the person being evaluated] pursue the mission or embody our mission and values this year?" This, once again, reinforces the mission statement as a focus for the work ethic at your organization.

Develop Criteria That Are Important to the Organization and to the Individual Job Being Evaluated

Don't rely on standard evaluation forms. Work with your people to establish criteria that reflect your culture, mission, and values, as well as those that are focused on the job being evaluated. For example, I feel that people who supervise should have a component of their evaluation that deals with how the people who they supervise have evaluated them. This supports the theory of management as a support function. Another example would be to limit an evaluation criterion for "Interaction with Customers" to only those who *have* such interaction.

In *The Three Signs of a Miserable Job*, Pat Lencioni notes that people want to know how their job relates to the organizational whole and to be able to measure their own progress. Help them do that. Your best people want to be held accountable.

Separate Evaluation from Compensation, in Terms of Timing

Discussions of money muddy the waters between a supervisor and an employee. Have the supervisor deal with the money portion of this well before the evaluation of work effort, and have it out of the way.

Changing the Way You Evaluate

You may evaluate annually or twice a year. Some organizations even do reviews quarterly. Never evaluate less than annually, and if you want to impress your people, do it twice a year. No matter how often you do it, here are some suggestions of how to implement a two-way evaluation system.

Plan and Consult

Before instituting such a major change as going to two-way evaluations, some planning and consultation are necessary—or you will wind up with very, very upset people. Start by establishing a staff committee (of all levels of staff) to review both the evaluation tool and the evaluation process. Discuss the importance of two-way evaluations, what they are and are not, and set the criteria for evaluation as well as the process. If you tie the evaluation process into your compensation package, talk about how that will happen and how worker evaluation of supervisors will not be held against the worker in the compensation area (there are protections against that outlined below).

Write up your new evaluation policy, and the reason it is being instituted, and transmit that to staff in writing and in meetings. I strongly encourage you to stage a role-playing exercise at this point so that people can see how the process is supposed to work. Have two staff act out the entire process.

Try the process for a year, monitoring it closely, and then evaluate and amend it. Understand that it will take time for some staff to adequately trust their supervisors to be willing to take the risk of offering criticism. It will also take time for some supervisors to be able to accept constructive criticism from their workers. Give it time, but monitor the implementation carefully. Have intermittent meetings with supervisors and workers to discuss the program and how it is going, comparing that to the original intent.

A Suggested Evaluation Process

1. The HR staff should provide both the supervisor and the worker with their copies of the evaluation form ten days prior to the evaluation's being due. Each person then fills out his or her part of the form in writing. The supervisor also at this point fills out any salary or bonus recommendation in line with the organization's compensation policy and hands it in to the appropriate person. That way, the financial part of the evaluation is done and delivered *before* the supervisor gets evaluated by the worker, reducing the chance of retribution by the supervisor if the evaluation from the worker is not perfect.
2. The supervisor and worker meet in private, exchange forms, and go over the evaluation as well as the goals that they had set at the last evaluation. They discuss the reason for each criteria rating and, in general, how they are doing as a team.
3. Both supervisor and worker now set their goals for the next evaluation period. This is best done individually and then discussed at a second meeting.
4. After meeting to discuss the goals, the supervisor may, as appropriate, inform the worker of compensation changes or bonuses.
5. It is critical that the supervisor and worker informally review the progress toward the goals two or three times during the next evaluation period. I recommend that they both put the times for such an informal review on their calendars to remind them.

Staff Recognition

An often-forgotten component of inverted-pyramid management has to do with staff recognition—celebrating and rewarding the kinds of behaviors that you want to see the most. There are virtually unlimited ways to do this, but most organizations that try this have problems that could have been avoided. The most common is to adopt another organization's program without checking with their own staff first!

Three critical rules for staff recognition programs are:

1. *The "rewards" should not be punishment.* Don't assume that what you think is a nice reward is received the same way by those whom you are trying to honor. Reward (and punishment) is a very subjective thing.

FOR EXAMPLE: Ten years or so ago, I was running a two-day retreat for a state human services department at which the Director and the fifteen "highest" level staff were participating. One of the department's training staff who specialized in working with hotels had made all the hotel and meal arrangements, and she was on-site for the two days of the retreat, ready and able to assist us if needed. The staff person, whom I will call Linda, was a very capable and pleasant person and had mentioned to me that, among many other things, in twenty years with the department she had never actually met a director. She also had reserved another training room right down the hall from our meeting room in which she would set up camp to help us if we needed her, and in which she would eat.

Following the afternoon session, the participants broke for dinner in the hotel restaurant while I remained behind in the meeting room to summarize our afternoon activities so that we could proceed without delay when we reconvened. Linda had made dinner reservations for all the participants plus me, and now I realized that since I would not be there, there would be an empty seat at the table. I saw the Director walking by in the hall and ran out to stop her, suggesting that since Linda had done such a great job on the arrangements that it might be a real treat for her to be invited to dinner with all the department senior staff. The Director agreed and said that she would set it up. I returned to my work feeling that I had really done a nice thing for Linda and that she would be very pleased by the opportunity to visit with the Director and other senior staff.

Ten minutes later, Linda stuck her head in the door and said, "Well, I *won't* be down the hall for dinner, if you need me. I have been told to eat dinner with the 'mucky mucks.'" She walked out of the room with a long face, looking completely depressed. I immediately realized that my "reward" to Linda was actually a punishment. While *I* might want to meet the people at the dinner table, the thought of spending an hour with the "big bosses" terrified Linda. It was the worst thing I could have done to her. I later apologized to her, and we still joke about the incident when we talk. ■

2. *The system must be seen by staff as fair and impartial.* There is no point to this if the staff people feel that the system is rigged and that only the "boss's favorites" will be chosen. You simply must have a system that will both actually be and, more important, *be seen as* impartial and fair.

FOR EXAMPLE: In another statewide agency, a good friend of mine took over as director, following an "Attila the Hun." My friend, whom we'll call Greg, as one of his early actions asked line staff to develop a rewards program that was fair, meaningful, and easy to administer. The results? There is a rewards review committee made up of ten line staff (the total staff of the department is over 2,000). This review committee has volunteered and also has made itself *permanently* ineligible from receiving the rewards. Each month, this committee reviews nominations for Employee of the Month, which can be submitted by peers or supervisors. Employees who are selected get a number of things: their picture in the foyer of all agency offices that month, a plaque given to them by Greg, and other "perks" that *they get to choose.* The system has worked wonders in the two years that it has been in place, but it has all the parts essential for success: peer review, impartiality, and rewards that *really* reward. ■

3. *The system must be understandable and support the mission.* You can't have a reward system that requires a degree in astrophysics to understand. You also need a reward system that rewards behavior that supports the mission. That's why soldiers get medals for valor, and police officers and firefighters get awards for saving citizens' lives; it's the kind of action that we want to encourage in those professions.

In order to do all these things well, have a group of employees from all levels of the organization study the idea of rewards and get back to you on a program. They may even tell you that staff would prefer *not* to have rewards, preferring to remain anonymous, or to have the funds that a reward program would use go into the programs instead. Do not decide from your senior management seat what is meaningful for line staff. You may well waste time, money, and morale.

Recap

In this chapter, we have reviewed the parts of top quality management for your nonprofit:

■ Living the *inverted pyramid.* Valuing your staff and remembering that by increasing the importance of your staff who are closest to the line you will improve morale and productivity. You need to live this attitude, not just put it on your table of organization. You need to be your staff's best advocate.

- Using the *coach/conductor style* of management. Remember that nei-ther the coach nor the conductor plays. You have to get your outcomes completed through the actions of others. You have to know those peo-ple and their capabilities well to have them come together and achieve a common, desired outcome.
- Understanding that all *communications* are two-way and that what someone hears is more important than what you say. If you believe, as I do, in the inverted pyramid, you need to act as a facilitator and as a supporter. That means in communications, you need to communicate in the way that your people hear best, not in the way that you feel most important.
- *Delegating* effectively, and how that is a strength—not a weakness. You need to remember that you cannot do it all and, in fact, that others can often do it better than you.
- Evaluating in the best manner: *two-way.* You and your staff should both evaluate the relationship and your contributions to it. These evaluations will improve your management skills as much as they will help your staff people.
- *Rewarding staff* for their desirable behavior. All of us like to be rewarded. Just remember to make rewards real rewards and not pun-ishments. Ask what people would like and try to give them that, not something that you would like to have.

Mr. J. Willard Marriott had it right: "Take care of your employees and they will take care of you." You need your staff to be motivated and committed. You know you can never pay them enough, so keeping the good ones takes a different kind of compensation: what they do and how you treat them. Hopefully, this chapter has provided some insights and some tools for you to apply to that end.

Questions for Discussion

1. What parts of this chapter apply to us? Let's be specific.
2. Do we value our line staff? How?
3. If we had an inverted pyramid, what would we have to change?
4. What are our styles of supervision? What do they say about our values?
5. Should we have two-way evaluations? Why or why not?
6. What about communications? Should we train our staff in this important area?

CHAPTER 8

Embracing Technology for Mission

Overview

Oh, the wired world. All of us online all the time. Constant cell phone chatter in public places, endless numbers of cable stations to click through, ".com" glued to the end of every noun, verb, and proper name, "e-" in front of way too much of the English language. Need something? Information, a friend/date/spouse, a sales venue, music, or a reservation for dinner? Go online. Need a service from a nonprofit? Want to donate or volunteer? Go online.

And, of course, that is just the beginning. Luddites aside, we can never go back to the unwired, unconnected, nontech past. You, your staff, your clients, your donors, your funders, your referral sources—in short, all the people who matter to your organization—are either online or on their way there, with fewer and fewer exceptions. Think your clientele are too poor or dispossessed to need tech? A friend of mine who runs a homeless shelter told me *fifteen years ago* about asking a new client the standard marketing inquiry that all nonprofits should ask: "How did you find out about us?" The answer from this bedraggled, unshaven man who would fulfill most people's mental image of a homeless person? "Oh, I checked you out on your Web site. I liked what I saw, so I came over." Where could a homeless man be able to check out this organization online way back then? At the library. Now, he could do it at lots of places: the public library, the Boys/Girls Club, a local church, at a job center, even at the homeless shelter itself. The tech "divide" that used to focus on income now focuses more on people and the difference between those who are comfortable online and those who are not. All online all the time is truer and truer every day.

Technology has gone from being a luxury to being a ubiquitous, necessary tool and, even more important, an expectation. The cost-benefit of tech that we waited for for so long is now well established. Quality, speed, the variety of applications, and their ease of use have all improved, and the price of each has gone down, down, down, until we have reached the point where you can get free or low-cost cell phones, software, computers, and a host of other products and services that five years ago were the mark of only the wealthy. Tech is paying off for all of us.

Tech has had an impact, of course, in the nonprofit sector as well. But more than any other part of our economy, we have lagged in seeing technology's full benefit. As this is written, much of the sector is still behind the tech curve, and many organizations are still suffering from the failure to recognize the revolution for what it is and, more important, what it can do for our mission. Part of this lack of tech-savvy is generational: Most of our senior management are members of the Baby Boom and Silent generations, and thus do not "get" tech the way later generations intuitively do. Some of it has to do with scarce resources, but that is a waning factor as costs have plummeted.

Like it or not, the world has changed. In his now classic and still wonderful book *The Lexus and the Olive Tree* (New York: Farrar, Straus and Giroux, 2000), Thomas L. Friedman notes that in the very near future, there will be only two kinds of organizations: Those that embrace technology . . . and those that do not. The first have a long life expectancy, the second next to none. I agree, and that is why this chapter is titled as it is. As I said earlier, the future of philanthropy is the successful merging of mission and technology. This does not mean that we will give up in-person service. Rather, it means that if you want to be around to do mission ten years from now, if you want to connect with people born after 1975, if you want to provide mission as effectively and efficiently as possible, tech is your friend. Tech is never a solution on its own. Remember the Jim Collins maxim from *Good to Great* that I referred to earlier: "Technology is an *accelerator* of a good idea, not a *substitute* for one." I want tech to be an accelerator of a great mission—yours.

In this chapter, I will show you many examples of how technology is helping nonprofits like yours do more service, sooner, and better. We will look at the realities of competing for donors, staff, volunteers, and people to serve online. We will examine how to adapt your organization to a tech-friendly model without breaking your budget. I will give you a technology checklist to examine now and a review and renewal process to make sure you stay appropriately up to date in using technology to the maximum mission outcome.

I know many readers (particularly those my age) hate this. Tech is still not second nature to many in our sector, and perhaps you, or some members of your staff, are tech averse. I understand, and you need to know that you are not alone. At Stanford University, which is located on the north end of Silicon Valley, the student body still breaks itself down into two groups in its slang: "Techies" are engineers, math, and hard-science majors; "fuzzies" are social science, English, art, and history majors. Now think about it: In the nonprofit world, which would predominate? Of course, the fuzzies. And there is nothing wrong with being a fuzzy. It's just that all of us fuzzies have to adapt, adjust, and get on with our lives in an increasingly techie world. We cannot do the ostrich on this one. The people who we serve depend on us to adapt so that we can continue to pursue our mission.

The "tech world" is so integral, so ubiquitous that it is no longer properly called the tech world. It is just *the world* as it is, and in nonprofits we have to deal with the world as it is. Remember, what is the job of a nonprofit steward? It is to use all the resources available to do more mission. Let's figure out the best ways to use the technology to do more mission, better, sooner, and more efficiently.

The All-Online, All-the-Time World We Live In

The second edition of *Mission-Based Management* dealt with technology for the first time. Of course, much of what I said then is out of date and has been updated, but guess what? Some of what you are about to read will be outdated as well by the time you see it. That aside, there are some valid and timeless basic concepts that you can work from as you consider the best way to enable your mission with technology.

Embracing technology will be a small step for some nonprofits and a giant leap for others. You will have "early adapters" and "late resisters." Your board may tell you that you should not spend the money on tech now and then six months later bug you about why your Web site is not awesome. So, before we get into the how, let's look at the why and perhaps get more of your staff and board on the same page about technology. Here are a few observations to consider.

The Default Location for Information about Your Organization Is Now Online All the Time

Get used to it. While still not the case for everyone, going online *first* to find out about your organization is the default for more and more people every day and absolutely dominates the preference for anyone born after 1975. Your Web site is getting more inquiries than your phone system. More people will check out your volunteer opportunities (or try to) online than will e-mail you. If you do not have the ability to take donations by credit card or PayPal on your Web site, you have lost money. Period. This is really important and no longer up for debate. We reached the tipping point in this area in about 2004 as servers got bigger, bandwidth got higher, and wireless networks took hold. And here is the other killer fact: While checking you out online is the first place people look, more and more, if they cannot find the information they want on your Web site—it is also the **last** place they look. They will not call. They will not e-mail. They will just move on to another nonprofit's Web site that is more appealing. You are, in sports terminology, "one and done."

To Keep Up with All the Changes and Opportunities in Technology You Need to Depend on Younger Staff and Board Members

Moore's Law, posited by one of the founders of Intel in 1964, states that the computing capacity of microchips will double every eighteen months at no increase in cost. Again, the tipping point for usable, cheap, online all-the-time tech hit us in about 2004 and has been going at an even more rapid pace since.

But the choices brought on by this change can be both dizzying and deafening, which can cause us to *just stop listening* after a while. This is particularly true for those of us who do not think tech first, or automatically jump online to try a new app, or download the newest version of every operating system. Thus, while it may not be our instinct to try new things, our organization still needs to be on top of all this, so what to do? Simple. Seek out, engage, recruit, employ, and then *listen* to the young.

 HANDS ON: The youngest generation (born after 1980) gets this in ways those of us born before 1980 cannot. To develop a tech-prone policy, you first need someone on your board of directors who "gets" technology from a policy standpoint—who understands how to harness tech to your mission. The younger this person is, the better because that means that he or she has had more of their lives surrounded by tech. This is also true for your staff—your younger employees will, if asked, provide you with lots of ideas on how to use the best of technology to do more and better mission, raise more funds, and communicate more efficiently. Again, the benchmark birth year here is 1980. ■

 HANDS ON: But . . . But what? But not everyone is tech savvy and tech comfortable. Thus, your tech committee (a committee every nonprofit needs that keeps up with the tech–mission bridge and writes and monitors the tech plan) should be made up of *geeks* and *nongeeks*; people who love technology and people who are still tech-resistant. This is another important balancing act for your nonprofit. You don't want to alienate, but you do need to keep up with changes in technology.

In addition to your tech team, you need a chief information officer (CIO) or IT manager of some kind. Even if you cannot afford to have someone full time in this role, you need to have someone in your organization, someone who understands—and likes—technology, and who also understands what you do, how you do it, and why. This person's job will be to match up the mission with the technology to enhance and support it. In the words of a computer-savvy friend of mine, "You need to get a higher geek quotient." I agree. One great resource for this person is *The Accidental Techie* (St. Paul, MN: Fieldstone Alliance, 2005), by Sue Bennett. It is written for the part-time nonprofit CIO and is a terrific book. ◼

The Cost-Benefit Ratio Has Tipped Permanently to the Benefit Side—But Only for Flexible Organizations

Again, Moore's Law and ruthless competition are making what was yesterday's exotic technological breakthroughs today's ubiquitous tools. In 1995, a "home page" was something foreign and somewhat geeky, and no one really knew what a URL (uniform resource locator) was. Remember when cell phones were unusual and less common than pagers? I vividly remember sitting on airplanes with my first true laptop in the late 1980s, or even with a new notebook in the early 1990s, and having people come over, look, and be amazed at the technology. Now, on many flights, the few people without laptops can't sleep because of the glow of all the laptop and PDA screens. You can get online during your flight, and nobody thinks a thing of it. What was *so cool* even five or eight years ago is *so normal* now.

E-mail, voice mail, texting, spreadsheets, fund-raising software (even customized), payroll software, and outcome measure software all have become parts of our everyday lives. They are affordable and should be viewed as essential tools, not luxuries. In some cases (think texting for those born after 1986) they are default communications tools, and the only way to reach a particular age market. In a competitive environment, you have to compete. Part of that competition is being as responsive and cost effective as your competitors, and tech can help you but you have to truly understand the ever-changing tools that tech provides. Again, listen to the young.

Of course, you cannot just buy the hardware or software and have it solve all your problems. You also have to move toward the technology, be a bit flexible, and accommodate to the new situation.

FOR EXAMPLE: I regularly look at Web sites for clients, and if I am doing a marketing or management review, I will push all the bells and whistles on the site: I'll try to donate $5 online, ask about a job, and inquire about a volunteer opening. And if there is no information on the site about those things, or if I have a problem, I'll go to the "Contact us" page, click on the "E-mail us!" link, and ask my question.

Sometimes I hear back in a day or two, sometimes a week or two, sometimes never. Hmmm. ■

Once you adopt the technology, you have to *use* it and make sure that your people have enough training and comfort with it to be getting the benefit of it. The technology will not come all the way to you. You have to be flexible enough to meet it partway.

Tech Can Get in the Way of Providing Good Mission

As you can tell, I am strongly pro-tech for mission and an advocate for your organization to use the tools that technology provides us to the maximum mission effect. However, I would be naive and would be giving you bad advice if I did not remind you that tech is just a tool and not a panacea. It will not fix a poorly managed organization that does not care about its markets, does not value line staff, does not recruit and retain good volunteers, or does not pay attention to its finances. To think so is the same as assuming that just buying a van will allow you to deliver meals on wheels or that having a receptionist guarantees prompt customer service. Tech is a tool—a wonderful, flexible, helpful, fascinating tool. But the tool is not the issue. *How well you use the tool* is the issue.

Further, technology can get in the way of good mission, usually without our even realizing it. We can get so enamored of having the newest, coolest thing or of getting tech just to keep up with everyone else that we forget that our investment in technology, just like any other mission-based investment, is supposed to result in *more mission*, not less.

 FOR EXAMPLE: When I do my training sessions on marketing and customer satisfaction, I regularly do this little exercise with the participants that demonstrates a very common example of good technology run amok. I ask the group the following question: "How many of you really dislike calling an organization and getting one of those automated systems that say something like 'Hello, welcome to XYZ organization, blah, blah, blah ...

(continued)

press one to . . . press two to . . . '? Put your hands up if these systems really tick you off." And of course nearly all and sometimes every single hand goes up. Then I ask, "Why do you dislike calling into these systems?" I get answers ranging from "impersonal" to "confusing" to "takes too long to work your way through the system" to "all I want to do is talk to a person." And they do not like having to figure out how to "type the last name of the person you want" into their phone. There is uniform, widespread, consistent dislike that borders on hatred for these systems.

And then I ask the clincher: "So, and be totally frank now, how many of your organizations use these systems?" You got it; nearly all the hands go back up! "And," I ask, "how many of you were at least partially responsible for the decision to purchase and install the system?" Again, most if not all of the hands go slowly up, accompanied by sad or embarrassed looks.

Finally, I ask the question, "Why? Why did you inflict this on your customers when you yourself despise it? What convinced you to spend money to tick off your clients and funders?" The answers usually focus on the salesperson convincing the staff that they would save money by not having to have a receptionist. So I ask, "How many of you laid off your receptionist or cut your FTE by a person?" Hardly anyone ever puts his or her hand up.

"So you irritate most people on their first contact with you and *still* do not save any money?" Silence. And I do not even deal with the fact that these systems are terribly difficult, even impossible, to use for people who have hearing problems or who themselves are technophobic. ■

 HANDS ON: Voice mail is great, but you should always have your phone answered during regular office hours by a real person. And have your people check their voice mail regularly! ■

Uses of Technology for the Mission-Based Organization

So how do we harness this huge societal change to help our mission? What is the best way to get the most out of technology? Well, it is not by going at it piecemeal—a bit here, a bit there. You would not provide services that way. You would look at the entire service array, the whole outcome as well as the pieces. I know you added tech piece by piece; everyone did. You probably got accounting software first, then e-mail, then some pagers for your staff, then your early Web site and development software, then more and more online accountability, updated Web sites, etc.

But now, as we have said ten times, tech is everywhere and you have to get your act *together* ... emphasis on *together*. You need a *plan*. More on that in a minute.

Let's look at a few uses of technology to do more mission that go beyond just the basics of finance, a Web site, and e-mail.

Education. You want your organization to be known as *the* expert, the source, the place to go for information on the issue that is the center of your mission, whether that is literacy, autism, animal abuse, or performance art. So on your Web site, develop what I call a "reading room," a place where people can find papers (in .pdf form), sites, books, and the like to educate them more about your issue, and to see your organizational opinion on the issue as well. This is a simple add-on, but one that needs to be kept current. No "set-it-and-forget-it" for information.

Volunteers. I have already told you that all nonprofits will be more dependent on "unpaid professionals over the next few years than they are now, and that you need to upgrade your volunteer recruitment, training, and management. Look at your Web site right now. If I were a potential volunteer and I came to your site to see about volunteering, could I find any or all of this information: What opportunities are available (when, where, for how long, with what skill set, etc.), online sign up, training needs, dress code, whether opportunities are available for groups? Is there discussion about how important volunteers are and a place that current volunteers can add comments about their experiences? What about a video of volunteers in action?

New employees. You need good employees more than good employees need you—you heard that in Chapter 7. But to find them, and especially those born after 1980, everything about your organization— its mission, its values, the management team, the board, the culture, the benefits, online applications, comments by current employees— *everything* needs to be online and easy to find.

 HANDS ON: Make sure that on your "Careers" page you have an e-mail sign-up for notices for future jobs. That way, even if there are no openings at the current time, a potential employee can leave his or her contact information with you. ■

Once your employee is hired, he or she can learn faster about the organization and keep up with changes by using a staff-only part of your Web site that is deep and wide with information, policies, meeting minutes, staff information, and so forth.

Transparency. In Chapter 5, we talked about this at length, so just remember that your Web site offers the ability to easily have your most recent IRS-990, your current audit, budget, and strategic plan all out there for people to see. For a complete list of transparency items that you need online see Chapter 5, page 69–70.

Development. From software to track and communicate with donors to applications that help with event planning, development has really embraced technology for the better. As I said earlier, if your Web site cannot take donations by credit card and/or PayPal, you have lost donations. Period. Remember this: Technology has brought down the cost of fund-raising, and this is key to many donors. And, while the "ask," particularly the big ask, will at least for the foreseeable future remain a face-to-face or at least voice-to-voice event, using the best tech can get you that meeting, set up that ask, keep in touch with the donor, and keep him or her focused on your mission.

That is just a sample. I know some readers are yelling at the book saying, "You forgot about . . . and it's so *cool!*" and I know you are right. I left many things out, and many more that I cannot even imagine will probably be cutting-edge or even passé by the time you read this. So let's agree: Tech has many uses for mission and many opportunities for efficiency and effectiveness.

It also has many parts that often seem to go off in different directions. I am a list person, as you probably can tell. Let's start by making a list for technology and move from there.

A Technology Checklist

Now that we have hopefully set the stage for you to look at your organization's ability to use technology in productive, cost-effective, and mission-increasing ways, let's use a checklist to help you find your way.

Have a Team

We have touched on this before, but you need a group of people to monitor your tech. Yes, technology is as important as anything else that merits a committee: development, marketing, quality assurance, finance. And, speaking of those committees, representatives of each should be on your tech team because they have technology needs and wants. So your team should be representative of committees, of ages, of geeks and nongeeks—perhaps even have a board member who is tech savvy sit in once in a while. What does the team do? Read on.

Have a Plan

There are so many parts to the impact of technology, and so many opportunities that technology brings to your mission, and as a result so many places you can spend your time and money, that you need a tech plan. There are lots and lots of samples of nonprofit technology plans online. Go do a search and see the kind of things that your peer organizations are looking at. However, in developing the plan, remember to go through the rest of this list first.

Consider the Outcomes You Want

What is the point of your technology? More mission, I hope, but that is pretty general. Before you plan to spend a lot of time and money, go through each area of your organization and look at what you want from technology. Are there easier ways for people to donate? Better methods of measuring outcomes? Better use of staff time? Improved communications with the board? Better community image? At your first tech team meeting, this list should take up most of the time. And, when it is refined and honed, it should be your backstop as you develop tech goals and objectives.

Consult the Young

Now that you know what you want, ask the intuitive experts, the people who have grown up with and used technology every day of their lives: your staff and board born after 1980. They get it in ways those born earlier cannot, and their understanding of what is out there and its potential is amazing. Ask them!

 FOR EXAMPLE: For a Boomer, I like technology a lot. I bought my first computer for my nonprofit in 1982, had the earliest Web site of any of my peers, read the tech press, tried new applications like podcasts, blogs, and video early on, and have run my own Web site for years. I think about technology a lot, not only for nonprofits but also for my business. About four years ago, I was planning to visit my techie son Ben in Denver and I told him I wanted to talk for 10 minutes with him and several friends about how to get more bang for the buck from integrating my Web site, blog, and newsletter. Ben had helped me four years earlier by designing a complete upgrade to my Web site and was familiar with my business needs, but I outlined a number of questions to him in advance and he said he would ask his business partner Dan (who I have known since he was eight) to take a look as well. I figured I would learn a little here and there, but that I had most of the big stuff nailed down already.

Make a long story short? In those 10 minutes, which stretched to 30, I got fifteen or twenty *aha!* ideas—simple, free improvements in the way I used the Web that have colored my thinking ever since. Even though I am pretty tech savvy ("for an old guy" to quote Ben), I learned a *lot* in a very short time. And Ben and Dan had talked about my site, blog, e-mail, and newsletter for about 15 whole minutes before the three of us started talking. They instantly saw what I could do to improve things. People in this age group do not need to think deeply or ponder about this stuff—it is intuitive. ■

 HANDS ON: A simple and easy use of this resource is to ask any high school- or college-aged young people you know to go to your Web site. Tell them to look at the site from the point of view of a potential user, a potential donor, and a potential volunteer. How easy was it to find the information they needed? How nice did the site look and feel? What would they change, add, delete, or improve? And when they are done with that, get their e-mail addresses and phone numbers, send them (or text them) a thank-you note, and ask them to keep thinking about ways your organization can connect better with people through technology. Try this, it works! ■

Use All Your Resources

There are tons of good resources out there that are free. First, let's talk about two organizations that have become the go-to resources online for nonprofits: Techsoup (www.techsoup.org) and Nonprofit Technology Network (www.nten.org). If you have not been to these sites, you need to, and soon. They provide great free resources, training, how-tos, and so forth. Be sure to subscribe to their newsletters as well. Great, great stuff.

Second, I have to give a bit of space to a better software option: open source. For those who have not been exposed, open source is software that often exceeds the for-pay software that it mimics. The best known example of this is the operating system Linux, developed by thousands of volunteers worldwide and updated several times an hour by those volunteers. It is so good that most major computer companies (like HP and IBM) offer Linux as an operating system alternative to Microsoft Windows or Vista.

I have used open source software for years for some basic reasons. It is nearly always better than the original program it mimics, with more great features; it is more stable, more secure; it is less bug prone and when bugs are found, they are fixed in hours; and since it is not from Microsoft, it is much less prone to hacker attack. Equally important to most nonprofits: It is free. I have used Firefox for my browser, NvU for my HTML coding, Thunderbird for my e-mail, and OpenOffice for my word processing, spreadsheet, database, and presentation software, all for years. These words are being typed on OpenOffice.org Writer. If there is an application you use, there is almost certainly an open source alternative. Go to SourceForge.net to see what is available. Proceed cautiously, read the user reviews, and talk to your tech team. But open source is a great option. And did I mention that it is free?

Focus for the Best Return

Once you know your outcomes and have figured out what your resources are, focus your efforts for the best return on your investment. For example, if you have no development software but your development staff is tech savvy and you are expanding your fund-raising efforts, that might be a place to spend some money. If your Web site is five years behind the curve, start there, but you may just want to add some things, not redesign from scratch. I have noted that the cost-benefit line for tech in society has been passed years ago, but that does not mean you should not focus your limited time and money to get the most bang for your tech buck. And remember my admonition about open source software: The off-the-shelf cost is $0, which is always a nice start if you are calculating cost benefit.

Buy What You Need, Not What Everyone Wants

When I go into a hardware store, a Best Buy, or a camping/hiking store, I want one of everything. The same thing happens to my wife in a shoe store or my daughter with purses. Wants are fine, and as we discussed in our marketing chapter, they rule. People have needs, people seek wants. But in tech, with limited budgets, you have to buy what you need, which is not necessarily what your geeks want. Some things you do need? You need lots of bandwidth to the Net, lots of storage, an internal wireless network, and good security. That said, get your plan, develop your budget from your plan, and get *what you need to do your mission better.*

Backup and Be Secure

Good security is part of any good technology plan. You need to be secure from the people who want to do bad things on your system, and most basic packages (like Norton or McAfee) and a little dose of common sense (do not open attachments on e-mails from people you do not know) will go a long way to keeping your computers and servers secure. I also recommend regular use of an open source program called Spybot-Search and Destroy that checks for malware and different bugs that attach themselves to browsers. It is great, free, and easy to use.

The most likely disaster for your technology, though, is the old-fashioned kind: fire, flood, tornado, electrical storm. You have to backup—and get that backup off site. Many organizations have their systems programmed to do regular (hourly, daily, weekly) backups. Great. Good. The more automated the better, because we all forget. But make sure that backup is either automatically or by hand taken off site. There are lots of good, constant backup services like Mozy or Carbonite, which are always on and always backing up your most important files. Check these services and their competitors out and see about automated ways to get your data off site.

That's a great list for your tech team, and your management team, to use as you think about your technology. One thing you did not see too much of in that list was your Web site—and that is because it deserves a lot more time and discussion . . . next.

Your Web Site

There are a number of great resources for Web site design, places that will give you lots of advice on ways to improve your site, what you want to use your Web site for, and options, applications, and features that you want to include. Not the least of these is TechSoup.org. It has excellent tools for improving nonprofit Web sites. There is no point in my being too specific about your site since whatever I say will be outdated by the time you read it. I do, however, want to give you a framework for your site, to make sure you have a template as you work to improve the single most important tool technology offers your organization and its mission.

You want your Web site to:

- *Clearly convey your passion for your mission.* Obviously, you want your mission statement on your site, but stopping there is doing more harm than good. Discuss what the mission means, show the outcomes, and tell the stories. Have testimonials by people who have benefited from your services, and if they cannot speak for themselves, have staff do it. On your "Careers" page, let staff talk about the rewards they get from providing mission, and on your volunteer pages, make sure there are comments from volunteers about the rich personal rewards of volunteering at your organization.

 HANDS ON: Use video. The first reaction from Boomer managers when I say this is always, "Video's expensive!" No, it is not. YouTube has brought down the standard of video to, well, cheap. Again, ask your younger staff. Most of them probably did video assignments in high school or college and are familiar with the inexpensive and easy software that will allow them to put up a number of short, personal videos on your site. A picture is absolutely worth a thousand words, but videos tell your story in ways that photographs just cannot. Use video. ■

You want your site to have your mission embedded in some form on nearly every page.

■ *Be accessible, intuitive, and easy to use.* You need to make sure that the site itself is easy to navigate and, frankly, most sites are not. You have three clicks to get from the opening page to what you want to find. More than three and people leave. So think through the mapping of your site, and do not just add stuff willy nilly. Plan it out. Add dropdown menus for large categories like "About Us" or "Services," so that people will be able to see what they are getting into on before they click.

 HANDS ON: Test, test, test. Get some staff and volunteers to look at drafts of the site as it is being developed. Ask them about language—particularly on navigation bars. Does the term "About Us" make better sense than "Who We Are" as a navigation category? Put together a list of simple tasks that are important to people using your site and then ask your test group to do them with you (silently) looking over their shoulder. For example, where they would look for a way to get a service, find out how to volunteer, locate your IRS 990 form, etc.? See what they do, and if it takes more than three clicks or if they get lost, go back and try again. ■

A Web site that is unfriendly, uninformative, confusing, or out of date is like a map that is smudged in some places but not in others—frustrating. And remember, your Web site is your first point of contact for more and more people. Make it a good experience.

■ *Be informative.* The greatest benefit that a Web site provides is that of being a deep and wide information pool at very low cost. You want much more information on your Web site than anywhere else, and you want to remember that the site will be the first (and often only) place people will go for information. I have already mentioned having a "reading room," a part of the site set aside for the best papers, books, and informative sites on the issues that are most important to your mission. You want to be the go-to place for information, particularly for people who are interested in the same issue as you. Thus, if your organization works in the field of Alzheimer's, your reading room could have a set of .pdf papers on different issues about the disease, its treatment, how to cope as a family member, new developments, etc. Part of being a life-long learning organization is having your patrons educated as well.

 HANDS ON: As I have said in earlier chapters, you want special password-protected sections on your Web site for staff and board. Use these to post as much information as you can, again organized intuitively. Ask your staff and board what they would want, but for starters, on the board site put things like contact information for all board members; dates, times, and locations of all board and committee meetings; minutes from all board and committee meetings; a deeper discussion of every service you provide; a list of key staff, with pictures and bios; your bylaws; conflict of interest policies; budgets; and audits for the past three years. For staff, put those same minutes (of the board meetings) as well as minutes of senior staff meetings, new developments in services (from your reading room), copies of all policies, all staff forms, notices of new positions, discussions of staff benefits, etc. Again, remember to ask board and staff what they want on the site, and repeat asking at least annually. ■

For **donors**, you want all the ways that they can help, and do not forget to include your transparency items: IRS 990 forms, your audits, budgets, plans, senior staff, and board bios. For **the people you serve**, you want to include short thumbnails of each service with a "For more information click here" link for a more in-depth description. You also want good current contact information for anyone wanting to talk to a staff person. For **volunteers**, you want information on why volunteering is rewarding with your organization and, of course, the when, where, why, and how of upcoming volunteer opportunities. I see more and more organizations that have separate volunteer areas of their sites as they ramp up their use and professionalism of volunteers in their organization.

- *Be a great recruiter.* If you show off your mission and values, if you embed them in some way in every area of your site, you will recruit people. Who are you recruiting? You are recruiting everyone in your organization—board, staff, volunteers, large funders, and small donors. Remember that your Web site is often your first, and sometimes only, impression point. If a 25-year-old hears from a friend that volunteering is awesome at your nonprofit, the first place she will go for more information is your Web site. Always. The same is true with a 30-year-old potential employee, a 35-year-old family member, and more and more people from 17 to 70. They will use the Web site first. And to recruit, you have to connect; and to connect, you have to use stories. People want to hear about what you do, the people, animals, environments that you save or improve. Tell the stories and invite them to come along with you on your mission journey.

 HANDS ON: Here again we get back to the power of video. But you have to use it effectively, not just pepper your site with unappealing clips. Think it through, but remember that video can tell a story better than almost anything. You can also use podcasts on your site for oral histories and stories from people you serve, but video is best. ■

- *Help with transparency.* If people start at your Web site for more information, it is pretty obvious that you want to use it to help with the transparency efforts we discussed in Chapter 5. You need a part of your site, again easily found, where you put your transparency documents. At a minimum, these should be your current and prior IRS-990 forms, your conflict of interest policy, and your most recent audit. I also encourage my clients to include a summary of their strategic plan, as well as detailed biographical information on the management team and the board of directors.

  Make sure you also discuss outcomes in ways that affect the reader. Do not just put text such as "Occupancy up 13.5 percent" as an outcome. Turn the number into a person or persons. "Last year we housed 145 more homeless individuals (38 of whom were children) than the year before." Let your work shine through the openness of your transparency efforts.

- *Be a portal for input.* In Chapter 10 on marketing, you will hear me say over and over and over "Ask, ask, ask, and then listen." When we talked about staff management in Chapter 7, I urged you to get out of your office and meet with staff—to give them more opportunities to ask you questions. The more ways people can ask, suggest, complain, point out opportunities, and have input, the better; and your Web site offers that. Make sure that for the people you serve and volunteers, there are places to comment on their experiences with you, and let your board and staff know how to find those areas and urge them to check them regularly. Link input areas in the signature line of your e-mails. "Have an idea or a comment? Let us know!" and link to that area of the site. Get as much input as possible.

Then, be ready. Some of the input may well be ugly, but if you do not offer a place for it, the unhappy people are more and more likely to go online anyway and gripe. A CEO friend of mine told me a year or two back that he sets his Google Alerts to show him every morning any posting on the Web that responds to the search string "[his company name] sucks." And when he finds the posting (usually on a blog), he tracks down the issue and either gets back to the person personally or has a high-ranking staff person do it. He seeks out input and listens.

Tell your staff what I have told mine forever: "Do we want to provide the best services ever? Yes, we do. To do that, we need to know what is broken to fix it. Remember: *Praise feeds the ego*, and we all need to be told "'Good job" on occasion. So praise feeds the ego, but *criticism feeds improvement*. Ask, ask, ask and then listen.

I cannot overemphasize how important your Web site is to your mission provision, and it will only become more important every day. Pay attention to it, keep it current, and use the checklist above to make sure you are hitting the key components of a successful mission-based site.

Keeping Current—A Review and Renewal Process

Now you are up to speed. You have done your homework, bought what you need, installed the hardware and software, and trained your staff and volunteers in its mission-based uses. They are using it, and it works! Great. So can you relax? Perhaps coast for a bit?

Nope, and you already know what is coming—you have to be at this all the time. That is why you need a tech team; that is why you need a tech plan. So, to an extent, you can delegate a bit, but you still need to keep your manager's eye on this issue. Try the following four actions.

Increase Your Geek Quotient

We touched on this earlier: You need to have an IT person either full or part time, and you need that person yesterday. Beyond just that, you also need to send your staff to tech training. Overall, you need more and more people with more and more technological savvy, and that comes naturally as you hire more and more staff who were born after 1980. Obviously, tech is too important to have just one person who can reboot the computers or install software or who knows how to deal with a jammed fax or an error message on the printer. You have a lot of tech, and it needs to work. When it does not, things tend to stop. The more people know, the more they will pay attention to technological advances and understand their implications for your organization. Make sure your techies talk to your fuzzies about what each group does. A lot.

Check Prices, Uses, and Outcomes Regularly

Set up a schedule to check on communications costs for your phones and Internet access at least annually. Have someone check for upgrades, patches, and new versions of all your software every ninety days. You do not need to buy every new version, but you do need to know that it is available. I update my accounting software about every three years, but I have the patch and improvement tool in the software set to automatically download whatever is released right away that helps operations or security.

Talk to Your Peers

We have touched on this a number of times: Do not reinvent the wheel. Use the great ideas that your peer organizations have had and adapt them to your own needs.

Read the Nonprofit Press

Every single one of the major nonprofit periodicals now has regular features on tech issues and specific articles as well. You need to get and read at least one of these periodicals anyway. Now, just make sure you read the tech columns as well. These periodicals are also online, where you can often find links to useful sites. Remember to subscribe to the newsletter at TechSoup.org. It is the best thing out there in terms of practical useful advice.

Recap

In this really important chapter, we have talked about ways to make sure that you are using technology to the maximum mission benefit. We first went over the realities of the wired world and I gave you the following observations to consider:

1. The default location for information about your organization is now online all the time.
2. To keep up with all the changes and opportunities in technology, you need to depend on younger staff and board members.
3. The cost-benefit ratio has tipped permanently to the benefit side—but only for flexible organizations.
4. Tech can get in the way of providing good mission.

Next, we went through applications of technology for nonprofit organizations, and I gave you a large number of examples. Third, we examined a checklist of technology, which was as follows:

1. Have a team.
2. Have a plan.
3. Consider the outcomes you want.
4. Consult the young.
5. Use all your resources.
6. Focus for the best return.
7. Buy what you need, not what everyone wants.
8. Back up and be secure.

Then we spent some time talking about your Web site because it is so important to your mission future. Finally, I gave you a sequence of actions that will help you keep current with the technology that can enhance your mission and cut your costs of operation. These actions are:

1. Increase your geek quotient.
2. Check prices, uses, and outcomes regularly.
3. Talk to your peers.
4. Read the nonprofit press.

One last time: The wired nonprofit can survive and prosper. The non-wired organization is doomed. An investment in technology can, if focused on mission outcomes, greatly benefit the people your organization serves. Do not let the tech wave pass you and your organization by.

Questions for Discussion

1. Who should be on our tech team?
2. What parts of our system need upgrading? How regularly should we schedule reviews of our Web site, our internal systems?
3. Are there technological applications that can improve our mission? What are they? Are there funds to pay for them from the people who purchase our services?
4. What about our Web site? What do we need to do to excel in all the areas that were listed?
5. What is the most technologically advanced nonprofit in our town? How can we learn more about how they got this way?

CHAPTER 9

Creating a Social Entrepreneur

Overview

All of us know the common wisdom that small-business entrepreneurs are the hands-on people who generate jobs, develop new products and services, and are the engine of the economy. In truth, so are many nonprofits today. I must add: All nonprofits were entrepreneurs in their start-up phase. But how about now? How about your organization? Have you been around long enough that you are no longer flexible, no longer willing to embrace and shape change, no longer willing to take chances with your organization's resources?

The term *social entrepreneur* has many, many definitions. I certainly hear the term thrown around a lot more now than when I wrote my book *Social Entrepreneurship* (Hoboken, NJ: John Wiley & Sons, Inc., 2000) some years back. To some, a social entrepreneur is an investor who only invests in companies that do social good (or do not do social harm). To others, it is a business that works in partnership with charities. Even others define it as a nonprofit that starts a for-profit business. Since you are here, reading this chapter, let me give you my definition: *A social entrepreneur is someone who takes reasonable risk on behalf of the people their organization serves.* Think about it: For-profit entrepreneurs take a risk on behalf of themselves and their *stockholders*. Social entrepreneurs take a risk on behalf of the *stakeholders*. Hence, reasonable risk taking is good mission. Focus on that adjective: *reasonable*. To get to reasonable risk, you need to add to your skill set knowledge of how to do feasibility studies and business plans. Yet another business skill that has good use in your nonprofit.

I want to you become (or get back to being) a social entrepreneur—an organization that is constantly on the lookout for how to do more and how to do it better and is willing to regularly take that reasonable risk on behalf of its clientele. This means that you will fail occasionally. But more often, you will succeed in both satisfying and mission-oriented ways that serve your community much better.

In this chapter, we'll go over ways to help your organization get comfortable with the idea of social entrepreneurism. I'll show you how to decide how much return on investment is enough, and the ten biggest mistakes people make in developing their business plan financials. We'll go over how to and how not to seek debt, which can be one of the sources of capital that you may need to expand and prosper. We'll look at ways that your organization can become a culture of new ideas, constantly seeking new thoughts from staff and board, evaluating them and trying the best out. We'll review ways to get comfortable with *prudent* risk. I don't want you to become reckless. Bungee jumping with a rope that is 20 feet longer than the drop is not a good idea. *Prudent* risk is what it's all about.

I hope that by the time you are finished with this chapter, you will be excited about the possibilities open to you if you become a social entrepreneur.

The Characteristics of the Social Entrepreneur

To me, the core of social entrepreneurism is good stewardship. Good stewards don't just rest on their laurels, they try new things, serve people in new ways, are life-long learners, and try to have their organizations be fonts of excellence. Social entrepreneurs have these characteristics:

- They are willing to take reasonable risk on behalf of the people that their organization serves.
- They are constantly looking for new ways to serve their constituencies and add value to existing services.
- They understand that all resource allocations are really stewardship investments.
- They weigh the social and financial return of each of these investments. Hint: From now on, look at your expenses as investments in mission. What should the return on that investment be?
- They understand the difference between needs and wants.
- They always keep mission first, but know that without money, there is no mission output.

These are crucial traits for you to mull over as you consider your organizational adaptation to the social entrepreneurism model. How do you, your staff, and your board view risk? As something to avoid or as something that is part of steady improvement of services to the community? What about services? Are you doing the same old thing you were five years ago or can you specifically list what the organization did to improve services last week, the week before that, and the week before that? Steady, consistent improvement in services, and the constant adding to the value of those services from the point of view of the people you serve and the people who pay for them, is an absolute necessity if you are to become and remain a social entrepreneur.

Understanding and Accepting Risk

If you and I and eight other people were to be given $20,000 today, we would do ten different things with it. Some would buy certificates of deposit, some would pay down the mortgage, some would buy a car, some would pay off other debt, and some would go on a vacation or try to win big at a casino. Why the variety? Because we all have a different willingness to take risks with money. We grew up in different eras (some of us are children of the Depression, some self-indulgent baby Boomers, others took on crushing debt to have a bigger house or better car, believing that the piper would never come to call; surprise!), we are in different places in our lives (some of us have kids to put through college or big medical costs staring us in the face), and we have different financial situations (to some $10 is a lot of money, to some $2,500 is pocket change).

But all of us take risks. It is a risk to get in your car and drive to the store. It's a risk to get married, to have a child, to take a job, to buy a house, to buy a stock, or to fly on a commercial airliner. Some risks are so small that we just accept them as part of life and stop even calling them risks. Some are so big that we do not take them. We no longer have the stomach for some of the risks that we took when we were younger. Some things we never would have ventured as a child we now do without thinking.

Risk is relative, and our willingness to take it depends on a combination of many things. In nonprofit organizations, our willingness to take risk—or be reckless—depends on the makeup of the people in charge of the organization, as well as on the organization's history and its financial condition. If, for example, there has been a history of recklessness resulting in big failures (even with another executive director/CEO), the board of your organization may be less willing to take on a risk than if you have a stellar historical record of success. Also, the board's willingness to take a financial gamble will be influenced by how much money is at stake and how financially secure you are. If you are already financially empowered, it is more likely that your board will be willing to use that empowerment for the good of the community. In a widespread economic downturn (think late 2008–early 2009) there is often a cascade of hesitation—people not wanting to take a risk, to invest, build, buy, or lend. People fear the future and their willingness to take risk plummets.

Your willingness as an organization to take risk also depends on your view of yourself as an organization. The first step is to find out what the

EXHIBIT 9.1   Internal Risk Assessment Tool

This form will help your organization assess its willingness and readiness to take risks. Below are four statements. Read all four and then decide which one best describes your view of the most appropriate role for your organization. Please note that even though your organization is a nonprofit, your staff and board can interpret the role of the organization differently.

Arm of government: Our organization gets most or all of its funds from some branch of government. As a result, we should provide only the programs that the government asks us to and is willing to pay for.

Government contractor: One or more branches of government contract with our organization to provide services. Government policy heavily influences us, but we are able to do some things outside of this source of funding.

Local charity: Our organization should provide the services that our community says that they want. We know what they want by what they fund us for, either individually, through United Way, corporate giving, or in fees for services.

Nonprofit business: Our job is to provide services to support our mission. To accomplish this we may accept funds from the government, local or state funders, corporations, individuals, insurers, or others.

I think that the description that best fits our organization's role is (check only one):

☐ **Arm of government**
☐ **Government contractor**
☐ **Local charity**
☐ **Nonprofit business**

---

people in your organization think about risk and find it out early in the process.

 HANDS ON: Try this well-tested method of finding out your risk quotient. Copy Exhibit 9.1 and hand it out to your board, senior staff, and social entrepreneur team. Let them fill it out, tally the result, and then discuss the answers. What you will find may be very interesting and will get the issue on the table.   ■

Obviously, the farther down this list of choices you go, the higher your organizational willingness to take risks. Do not assume that there is a right answer to the survey: There is only your board and staff's answer. And you need to know it now before you talk through business ideas with any seriousness. The worst thing that can happen is for you not to realize that the staff is a group of social entrepreneurs while the board really sees the organization as an arm of government, or vice versa. Ask now, and you will not only find out where people stand, you will generate discussions that will benefit you throughout the business development process.

Risk is here, risk is now, and prudent risk is part of your job as a service provider in your community.

Business Ventures

Nationally, thousands of nonprofits are turning to outside businesses to supplement and broaden their income streams. In my twenty-five years as a consultant, I have helped hundreds of nonprofits throughout the country examine their capabilities in this area and have assisted them in developing their business plans. As an executive director, I started four new businesses when our traditional funding was cut drastically.

The development of good business plans by a nonprofit is a complex enough issue to merit an entire book by itself, which is why I wrote *Social Entrepreneurism*. But here, I want to review the steps of business plan development, focus on the preparation of financials, and review the big mistakes people make in preparing their financials. Hopefully, this advice will help you avoid the big pitfalls in business development and will excite you sufficiently to begin to think entrepreneurially, but with appropriate discipline—keeping that risk reasonable.

First, a reality check: No business is going to make you independently wealthy as an organization, nor is it going to make you independent of your current major source of funding. Nearly all of my clients come to me and state that one of their main reasons for wanting a new business is to "become financially independent of the state [feds, county, foundation, United Way]." Sorry, this is not going to happen. The services that your major funders will pay for may not be provided by anyone else, and in all likelihood they will continue to be a major part of your income stream far into the future. You can, by expanding your income sources, become *less* dependent on the major funders. But independent? Not likely.

Second, remember that business income is okay and will not result in a threat to your 501(c)(3) status unless it grows to truly dwarf your charitable functions. Also, most of you will start new ventures that are related to your mission anyway. Why? Because it's what you know, and if you are a professional in education or in the arts or in substance abuse treatment, you are not going to start a Wal-Mart or an engineering firm. People take what they know and find new markets for it. You will, too, and in most cases (about 90 percent of my clients), the business that you start will result in more mission being provided, which is good.

Finally, the idea of a business is to maximize profits, and for you this is only slightly diluted (I'll address the issue in a few pages). Suffice it to say here that any profits you make will have a social use: either to fund your mission reserves or to subsidize a money-losing program. You are not just starting this to make a ton of money: There is a social, a mission, purpose.

The Steps of the Business Planning Process

Let's start the examination of the nonprofit business planning process by looking at the steps listed below. Note that this is a different process than the for-profit world uses. There, most people start with number 4, "idea generation," and that's fine for them. As a nonprofit manager, you need to do this list from start to finish, even if, in another life, you started with number 4. If you do not do these in order, you are really going to get yourself in trouble. Take them one at a time and you will do fine.

1. Establish (Reestablish) Your Mission

We've already talked at length about your mission statement and the need for it to be up to date and reflective of the organization that you want to become rather than the organization that you were in the past twenty years. If you have not already reviewed your mission with your board and staff, now is a good time. Make sure that your mission statement does not conflict with the idea of your business venture and that you all agree that a new service fits into the parameters of the mission statement.

2. Establish the "Risk Level" of Your Organization

Using Exhibit 9.1, go over your organization's willingness to take on risk with your board and senior staff. How much income do you need from this venture? How much social outcome? Talk this through with great detail and frankness. If you don't, you may wind up leading the charge up the hill and turn around to find that there is no one behind you: They thought it was too risky.

3. Establish the Mission Uses of Profit and of the Venture

Of all the steps that people miss, this is the most important. You simply have to specify what you want to do with the money you will earn and show a direct mission outcome from the new venture. If you do, people will be able to rally around the extra work (and risk) involved in the business development process. If you do not, they won't be able to focus on the outcome—they will just question why they have all the extra work "just to make money."

 FOR EXAMPLE: A number of years ago, I was asked by a large provider of services to the developmentally disabled in the Southwest to come and facilitate a session with board and staff on the development of a new business. The executive director was totally committed to starting a new venture, but it quickly became obvious that the board and staff were anything but excited about the prospect. Questions such as "Why should we try to be in business? We're not IBM!" abounded. After about 45 minutes of this, I asked the group to imagine what they would do with unrestricted funds of $10,000. After a brief pause, the ideas started flying around the room. To make a long evening's discussion short, the focus came to rest on the idea of establishing a "scholarship" for three people with disabilities to send them to summer camp each year, something that the state would not fund.

I then asked the group, "Where are we going to get the money for that?" They immediately chastised me with comments like, "We can't get it, and you said just to imagine what we would do." I said, "Okay, but what if a business, one that employed people with disabilities in the community, was able to *net* $10,000 in two or three years, and then its ongoing profits were used to support the scholarship? Would you support the idea of a new business then?"

"Yes!" was the answer, with great enthusiasm. The group had gone from staunch resistance to avid support simply because they could now wrap their heads around a tangible mission outcome.

Postscript: The organization started a swimming pool cleaning service three months later, with developmentally disabled persons on the crews. Three years later it had broken even, profited almost $15,000, and profited $12,000 per year for the next five years. Each year, when they awarded the scholarships, they reminded everyone that this was money spun off from their business. ■

Establish the uses of your profit—specifically. For example, name the program that will be subsidized by the profit and list the amount you need per year and by when to accomplish your social goal. Then, when you finish your business plan, you can look back and see if your business meets your goals for social outcome.

4. Idea Generation

Only when you have done numbers 1 through 3 should you seriously consider what it is that you and your organization can do to earn extra income and provide new services. In developing ideas, use your staff and volunteers. They almost certainly have thought about what the needs are in the community and how you could meet them. They just may, however, never have had the forum in which to voice them.

 HANDS ON: Get your staff together for a brainstorming session with a facilitator. Explain the need for a business and the social outcome that the business will meet. Then ask for ideas (remember, in brainstorming every idea is a good one). In a minute or two, the ideas will start to flow. If there are problems in getting the group started, use the questions that follow:

1. What is your organization's primary mission as a nonprofit organization?
2. What are your organization's core competencies?
3. What are the markets (the groups of people) you want to target?
4. What do these markets really want?
5. How do those wants match up with your competencies?

When you have your list, develop some criteria against which to weigh each idea. For example, you might want to prioritize businesses that can be started up in fewer than six months, with no more than $10,000 invested, and have a direct social impact. The combination of criteria will be up to you, but by establishing what is important now, you can fairly weigh all your potential business ideas and not get the people whose ideas do not get followed up on mad at you. ■

Feasibility Study

There are two steps to establishing feasibility, and they represent two different kinds of feasibility studies: preliminary and final. In the preliminary stage, you take three to five pages and review the business, its markets in general, and what kind of services are being provided in this market. In the final feasibility study, you go into much greater detail about the market you want to serve, a definition of the service you want to provide, why the market wants this service, how you will provide it, the barriers to success and how you will overcome them, and preliminary financials.

The emphasis in the feasibility study phase is: "Can we do this?" "Do we have (or can we get) the resources to accomplish this?" and "Does it meet our social outcome goals?" If you do your homework and complete the feasibility study well, the majority of the work in your business plan will be done.

Do not, however, automatically proceed to the next stage without considering the key question: "Is this business feasible?" In some cases it will not be, and then your choice is to rework the idea or wait for conditions to improve. For example, if you are considering a recycling business, you might have to wait until the market for recycled goods rebounds to a certain level. Or if you are in a highly leveraged business (e.g., buying, renovating, and reselling low-income housing), you perhaps could not afford to start the business if mortgage interest rates were high.

Remember my maxim of "reasonable risk." The idea of a feasibility study is twofold: to focus you on what the business is and to see if it is feasible. Some businesses will not be and that is okay! Whatever you do, however, do not throw out the idea or the work that you have done. Most ideas that make it to this point are good ideas, but many are just waiting for a market to move under them. Think about recycling: It is a great idea, a terrific business—when the price of the recycled goods is high enough. When that price is down, recycling loses its appeal.

 FOR EXAMPLE: By now, almost everyone has heard the story of the development of Post-its—the re-stickable notes from 3M—and how the developer had to battle against the odds to get his case heard, and how the product is the single most successful product 3M has ever launched. What you may not know is the part of the story about the glue that is used on Post-its. It is a glue that "failed" all the tests that the chemists put it through. Prior to Post-its, 3M's criterion for adhesives was that they stick to something and hold things together. This glue failed that test but was not discarded, and thus was available when the new product idea was presented. The chemists simply kept the formula in case an unanticipated condition developed, which it certainly did. ■

It may for you, too. Don't throw away your work.

Marketing Plan

The marketing plan portion of a business plan is crucial. Here, all the questions that need to be asked are the same ones we will discuss in detail in

Chapter 10: Who are the markets? What do they want? How do we know? How do we let them know we are here? You want your business to be market driven, not service driven, and that means that you will probably have to change the method of service delivery a number of times from your original concept through the business planning process as you ask the markets what they want.

Business Plan

Now that you have done all the preliminary work and found that your business is feasible, why go on and write an entire plan? It's a lot more work, and you probably want to get going. You like the idea you've come up with and want the mission benefits it will hopefully spin off. Well, sorry. Remember that the entire business development process is designed to take something inherently risky and reduce (but never eliminate) the risk to a reasonable level for your organization. To do that, you have to write the plan! Here are three specific reasons:

1. Writing a business plan forces you to take an objective, critical, unemotional look at your business project in its entirety.
2. The finished product is an operating tool that, if properly used, will help you manage your business and work toward its success.
3. The completed business plan is your means of communicating your ideas to others and provides the basis for your financing proposal.

Over half of all new businesses fail within the first two years of operation, and over 90 percent fail within the first ten years. A major reason for these failures is the lack of planning. If you have a well-written business plan that takes into account all the variables involved in starting a new business and is based on reality, you can move your venture on the road to success.

Implementation

Once the plan is written, reviewed, and adopted, the final step—and certainly not the easiest—is to go and set up and run the business. Obviously, only through the implementation of the plan can you hope to achieve the social outcomes you desire, as well as the new income streams that are so important to your financial empowerment.

Remember, the most successful entrepreneurs fail the first few times before they hit it big. I do not want you to be like them. I want you to develop a sound business plan based on good research and valid marketing and succeed, and in a big way, the first time out. With a solid business plan, you should be taking only prudent risks, not the "leap off the cliff" that so many small businesspeople refer to.

A business plan consists of several parts. The most important components are:

- *A cover letter identifying the business plan as the property of your organization.* This cover letter includes your name, address, and contact information and the month and the year that the plan is written or revised. One paragraph states in simple terms who the business plan belongs to and the limitations on its distribution. (1 page)
- *A table of contents.* (1 page)
- *A summary of the plan with a brief paragraph about your organization.* A four-line description of the product or service; a four-line description of the market; a brief paragraph on production and one on distribution, if needed; and, a short paragraph on the financing requirements. (2 to 4 pages)
- *A description of your organization and its business with the following subheadings.* (4 to 6 pages):
  - The organization
  - The product or service
  - The target consumer
  - The consumer's need for the product or service
  - The sales strategy
- *A description of the market for your product or service,* including information on the competition and cost price comparisons between competitors and your organization. (4 to 8 pages)
- A marketing plan that includes information on:
  - The markets
  - Customers
  - Competitors
  - The macroenvironment:
    - Demography
    - Economy
    - Technology
    - Government
    - Culture
  - How each of these areas affects the marketing and selling of your product or service
  - Evaluation of potential pitfalls
- The financial plan with sources and applications of cash and capital and:

- An equipment list
- A balance sheet
- Break-even analysis
- Cash flow estimates by month for the first year, by the quarter for the second and third years, projected income and expenses for the first three years, and notes of explanation for each of the estimates. (8 to 10 pages)
  - Other reports and statements that can be included in this section (but are not appropriate for all plans) are:
    - Historical financial reports for your organization, such as balance sheets for the past three years and income statements for the past three years
    - A current audit report
    - An annual report if one is available
  - An appendix with:
    - Management resumes
    - Your organizational marketing materials and Web site URL
    - Other pertinent material about your organization and its work
    - Letters of endorsement
    - Copies of signed contracts for business if you have them

How Much "Return on Investment" Do You Need?

Before we get to the financials in your plan, let's take a short break and look at a key issue that will be shown (or disproven) when you develop the numbers for your plan. How much return should we get on our investment, our risk? The answer? It depends.

 FOR EXAMPLE: A nonprofit organization in Colorado was developing a business plan for a janitorial service that would employ some of its clients—people with developmental disabilities. In completing the plan, the staff and board found that they could go two ways. First, they could clean upscale offices with crews made up of both workers with disabilities and those without. If they proceeded this way, they would make about 25 percent return on their investment due to high prices and high profits. Or they could clean factory and warehouse space using crews with a much higher proportion of people with disabilities. If they did this, however, they would make less money. The quandary: Should they earn more dollars and employ fewer people with disabilities, or employ more and make less? ■

FOR EXAMPLE: A performing arts nonprofit in Connecticut decided to offer children's theater classes to optimize staff and volunteer talents and to take advantage of the theater building in late afternoon when it was empty. The center knew from its financial projections that it could make some money, but its dilemma was whether to charge a high fee—say, $120—for the lessons, turning a larger profit, or charge less—$40—thus making the class affordable to more youngsters but receiving very low returns on the investment. ■

What should these organizations do? How much return on investment (ROI) is enough for an organization that is going into a new venture? Are there any benchmarks or ratios that should be followed? Is there such a thing as making too much money? How can you ensure that the staff and board of your organization are getting the most from your limited resources? These questions are among the most commonly asked by nonprofit staff and board members as they examine the feasibility of new ventures, and rightly so.

Analyzing ROI is not as simple for a nonprofit as it is for a for-profit organization. A for-profit invests in a business or a piece of equipment or a new employee, and it is concerned with traditional financial ROI: How long will it take for me to recover my investment and how much profit will I make?

A nonprofit making the same investment should also be concerned about *financial return* but has to add to that an analysis of *mission return*. There will always be services that you need to provide since no one else is doing them, or no one is willing to pay for them but that are very mission-rich, even if they are money-poor. That's okay, but if that is all you do, you'll be out of business. We'll look more at this in depth in Chapter 11 on financial empowerment.

Here, I want you to keep in mind what I've said a few times already: When your nonprofit makes any expenditure, it's really an *investment in mission*. If you believe that, then you should look for a return on that investment, some combination of financial return and mission return.

For the purposes of this chapter, let's assume you are looking at ventures or services that do, in fact, make money and spin that profit off to the remainder of the organization. Hint: If you're like most nonprofits, you already do that (at least I hope you do) with one key service. It's called your development or fund-raising department. If fund-raising (which does no mission) does not make a profit, it is a bad investment. If it does make a profit, it can contribute funds to doing more mission. That's the return you are looking for.

Since nonprofits don't just look at financial return, the two organizations in the examples above had to consider not only their earnings but also the social impact of its new venture: jobs for people with disabilities or arts for kids. Having more of one meant having less of the other (although that is not true in all cases). This twin return need makes the analysis more complicated, though still fairly straightforward. Let's look at the way the performing arts organization described in the second example analyzed its two returns.

Before starting the theater classes, the organization staff and board discussed the purpose of the venture. They set goals for the classes and made sure that these goals supported the mission (either financially or in service units). Suppose, for example, that the main goal was to expand appreciation for the theater throughout the community, starting with its youngest members, while at the same time not losing money. To accomplish this goal, it would be of the greatest importance to keep tuition low so that the most possible children could attend. If, however, the main goal was to contribute $15,000 a year in related profits to a fund for renovating the theater in three years, the profits become paramount, and tuition may need to be higher (although not so high that no one comes to the classes). In this case, cash return is a higher priority than social return.

It is important to note that putting a higher priority on cash than social return is not only acceptable, in certain cases it is *essential*, even for the most compassionate nonprofit staff or board member. As we've noted repeatedly, don't associate profits with bad things; making money in one area can help subsidize another area of service that will never pay for itself. Again, think about your fund-raising staff: You *want* them to make a profit each and every year.

Next, the staff and board developed feasibility studies and a business plan. These documents gave them a good handle on the total investment, including cash, staff time, board time, and volunteer time. They were thus able to make a true comparison of the cost and benefit of various outcomes.

As in any investment decision (and that is exactly what this is), there are options. Our theater group, for example, could start the class with a high price and profit, start with a lower price and profit, leave the money in the bank, or try a different tack altogether. Let's examine how they might view each option.

Assume a cash cost of $25,000 to start the class and a total staff and an investment of volunteer time equivalent to $5,000. Look at the table on the following page to see the results of three options.

Obviously, the last option—leaving the money in the bank—is the least risky, but it also offers no return in service units and in visibility. The decision between the first two options (high or low tuition) is tougher and will depend on the goals the board and staff set earlier: Do they want cash or

Option One—High Tuition

Start-up cost—CASH	$25,000
Start-up cost—TIME	$ 5,000
TOTAL COST	$30,000
Profit per year	$ 2,500
Students per year	100 (service units)

Cash return on investment in year one: $2,500/$30,000 or 8.3%

Invested cost per service unit $30,000/100 or $300 each

Option Two—Lower Tuition

Start-up cost—CASH	$25,000
Start-up cost—TIME	$ 5,000
TOTAL COST	$30,000
Profit per year	$ 500
Students per year	225 (service units)

Cash return on investment in year one: $500/$30,000 or 1.6%

Investment cost per service unit: $30,000/225 or $133.33 each

Option Three—Leave Funds in Bank at 7%

Start-up cost—CASH	$25,000
Start-up cost—TIME	$0
TOTAL COST	$25,000
Net income	$1,750 ($25,000 at 7%)
Students per year	0 (service units)

service? And if their goal is to have $15,000 a year in profit for the capital fund, are the outcomes of any of the options good enough? Probably not.

One flaw in this analysis is that we can't consistently quantify the risk associated with the business. Is the risk of failure (and of losing some or all of your investment) high or low? You will need to make some estimates of risk, include these estimates in your analysis, and weigh them in your decision-making process.

The other intangible to consider is the benefit to your organization from exposure. For example, if your museum is offering classes, a low fee will (usually) bring more people into the museum and, therefore, provide more exposure for the museum. Greater exposure translates into more potential contributions, visibility, public awareness, and overall goodwill.

Good management is basically resource allocation—making the best use of what you have and committing resources where they will do the most good. By setting and sticking to your goals, carefully accounting for all your costs, and reviewing your options fairly, you and your board can make the best decision possible with the information available regarding your new business. No manager can ask for more than that.

Preparing Your Business Financials

Now that we've examined your two returns, let's look at how to generate the numbers for your business plan. Too many of my clients focus on the markets, on the service, or on the product and forget the key parts of the financials. Remember, no money, no mission, so we want to get this part right!

There are three steps to go through in developing your financial information. They are listed below.

Assemble Your Financial Data

In the early stages of product or service selection and feasibility analysis, you should have gathered most of the information you need to prepare your business plan. Your work now is to refine and organize that information, check the accuracy of your estimates, and replace as many estimates as you can with firm figures. For example, for the purpose of your feasibility study, you may have estimated that your rent payment would be $600 per month. In your actual business plan, you may state that you are leasing property at 1124 East Church Street for $675 per month.

Following is a description and listing of the information you need.

SALES TARGETS   In order to make reasonable financial projections, you need to predict as accurately as possible what your volume of business will be. There are two major constraints here: the market and the assets (like money, skill, and time) that can be put into the enterprise. One way to approach these constraints is to estimate, based on your market research, what the potential market for your product or service is if you have restraints on money, skills, or time. The next factor is your internal constraints. This information allows you to estimate with some confidence what your potential sales will be. You should project sales for at least a three-year period.

Be careful not to project growth that cannot be sustained by the market. For example, if you are selling janitorial services in a community of 10,000 people with only twenty-five business establishments, there are only a limited number of the businesses that may be willing to buy your services. This is true even if you provide top-quality service and beat the price of all the competition. You simply cannot sell any more. Conversely, in a big city, there is an unlimited market for janitorial service at the quality and price you offer. But if your potential workforce is limited to about ten employees, it makes it difficult for you to reach your entire potential market.

Finally, remember that there is a relationship between price and sales. In general, lower prices mean more sales, *but only to a point*. There is a point at which no matter how low you price your service, no one will buy it. For example, if you clean swimming pools, you can have only as many customers as there are pools: Even if you give services away, you will have no additional customers. So, in your sales projections, remember to consider the impact of price and of the competition.

PRICING INFORMATION   Pricing is the art of finding the price that your market will pay that will cover your production costs and provide a reasonable return on your investment. By using the information you gathered in your marketing research, you can determine the going price or *price range* for products or services that are similar to yours. Next, set a target for the amount of profit you wish to make during the first three years of operation. This information is used to set the price after you analyze the various costs involved in your operation.

As I have said repeatedly, nearly all nonprofits are trained to *underprice* their services, and thus they do. Do not assume that you will compete solely on price. Perhaps you can do what your competition does better, faster, or with less turnaround time. Consider both the fixed costs and the variable costs in your pricing mix, as well as your profit and your competition. Remember, you will have the tendency to underprice: fight it!

START-UP COSTS

Capital Items   These are the one-time purchase items that you need to operate your business. This category includes the purchase of land, buildings, equipment, and furniture. These are the assets that continue to benefit your business operation. Items like inventory and supplies that are *used up* in the course of conducting business are expenses. With the exception of land, you depreciate your long-term assets. Depreciation is simply an accounting method of distributing capital costs to the expense of the business operation. Some nonprofits do not bother with depreciation because they do not pay taxes and cannot take advantage of depreciation as a business expense deduction. However, depreciation gives you a more accurate picture of the cost of running your business. Large-ticket items should routinely be depreciated even if the business is a nonprofit; otherwise, you never recover your full costs. For your larger expenses, review one or two financing options even if you plan at this point to pay cash. Borrowing or leasing might be more advantageous, and you need this information to test the financing options.

Other Initial Costs   In addition to capital items, you have other costs related to getting your business started that are not reflected in your operating expenses. Items such as legal fees, costs incurred to set up an accounting system, licenses, and introductory advertising are included in this section.

OPERATING EXPENSES

Fixed Costs   These are the expenses that you pay regardless of whether you sell any product or service. They are sometimes called *indirect costs* or *overhead*. These expenses include items like rent, heat and electricity, and salaries. Most of your fixed or indirect costs change at different levels of sales or production. For example, if you operate a mail-order nursery, you produce a certain limited number of plants to sell from one greenhouse. If you wish to sell more, you need two greenhouses. This action increases your capital costs and fixed costs. If you anticipate growth during the first three years of operation, you need to estimate your fixed costs at various sales levels and identify the levels where your fixed and capital costs increase.

Variable Costs   These are expenses that vary directly with the number of items or services you sell. Variable costs are also called *direct costs*. These costs vary depending on the type of business. If you manufacture a product, then all of the material costs are considered variable costs. If your product is made by workers who are paid only for contracted work, then their wages are part of the variable costs. If, however, your workers are salaried, you must pay them regardless of whether there is work to do. This makes salary expense a fixed cost.

Analyze the Financial Data You Gather

After you organize the critical financial data, you are in a position to analyze the information to help you make decisions about financing and pricing your product or service. There are specific types of analysis you need to perform. Each of these is described in the sections that follow.

START-UP COSTS AND WORKING CAPITAL NEEDS   *Start-up costs* are those costs you have to get the business up and running. Licensing, land, building, equipment, raw materials, and training are all start-up costs.

Your *working capital* is the money you need to operate your business during its start-up phase, and then, when the business is operational, this money becomes what you run the business on between the time you deliver a service or manufacture a product and the time you get paid. Your working capital needs are not fixed. For instance, if you make 1,000 widgets a month and you get paid in thirty days for those widgets, you need to have enough working capital to pay for the direct costs of the widgets plus your operating costs (overhead) for the same period. But what if your customer suddenly decides to pay you in forty-five days? Now your working capital needs go up by 50 percent. As noted before, more businesses go out of business making money than losing money, because they forget that fast growth starves businesses of working capital—of cash. (For more on working capital and some hands-on estimation forms, see Chapter 11.)

BREAKEVEN ANALYSIS   Breakeven analysis provides you with a sales objective that is expressed in either the number of dollars or units of production at which your business is neither making a profit nor losing money. The breakeven point is the point where sales income is equal to fixed costs plus variable costs for a certain period of time. Breakeven analysis is a technique used to analyze your cost information. The technique helps you to decide how much you have to charge at various levels of sales or how much you have to sell at various prices in order to get a return equal to your expenses. Breakeven is calculated by the following formula:

$$\frac{\text{Fixed costs}}{\left(\text{Unit selling price} - \text{Variable costs per unit}\right)}$$

You may find that to charge a competitive price, you have to produce an unrealistic number of sales to achieve a profit. In this case, you need to reexamine your cost assumptions to see if expenses can be reduced.

How important is breakeven? See my list of the ten biggest mistakes people make on their financials later in this chapter. Breakeven is there, and it's there because it is important.

PRO FORMA PROFIT-AND-LOSS STATEMENT   This statement is a projection of your income and expenses. Like the breakeven analysis, it provides a further check on the soundness of your venture. Most business plans project income and expense statements for at least three years. I recommend that you project income and expenses for a three-year period, the first year by month and the next two quarterly. However, the farther you move from present day, the less meaningful your numbers become. To develop your profit-and-loss statement, simply use the figures from your operating expenses form for fixed expenses. Subtract your expenses from your income to show your pretax profit, add taxes if you anticipate incorporating your business as a for-profit enterprise, and subtract any profit sharing or bonuses. The final figure is your retained earnings or fund balance.

PRO FORMA CASH FLOW ANALYSIS   Your cash flow is probably the most important analysis for internal management of your new business, just as it is for your nonprofit. It is the document that banks are most interested in because it indicates your ability to pay back your debt. The cash flow analysis shows how much cash is needed, when it is needed, and where it comes from. After you develop the cash flow analysis, use it as a check on how your business is doing. If you spend more or take in less cash than you anticipate, you may run into trouble. Variation from your cash flow projection helps you see early on if you are likely to run into cash problems. This analysis gives you a chance to take action and correct the flow of cash before you run into a serious shortage. Do your cash flow by month for the first year and quarterly for the next two. This will give you the most realistic view of your cash situation, and then you can design a credit policy to get you over temporary shortfalls, but *only* if they are temporary.

Prepare the Financial Data to Incorporate It into Your Formal Business Plan

The financial section of your business plan should include the following five displays.

PRO FORMA SOURCES AND APPLICATIONS OF FUNDS   This statement identifies where you intend to secure the funds you need to begin your business and how you intend to spend the money. In order to prepare this document, you must first look at your start-up costs and cash flow analysis to determine how much money you need to start the operation and how much working capital you need to carry the business until it generates its own revenue. Next, identify where you anticipate getting your money (your fund sources) in one column. In the second column, list the ways you intend to spend or apply the resources that are available.

THE FINANCIAL CONDITION OF THE OWNER   Be sure you include descriptive statements about the financial condition of the organization initiating the new business in this section of your business plan if you are going outside your organization for loans. This includes any information you believe reassures the bank that the financial position of the "parent" nonprofit organization is sound. It also includes your financial statements for at least three years, audited if possible, and a copy of your annual report if available.

PRO FORMA BALANCE SHEET AND PROFIT AND LOSS STATEMENTS   This statement is prepared to show the anticipated financial condition of your business to bankers and others who wish to help you finance your venture. Many times, this statement is completed for three-year periods. I suggest that the first year be month-by-month, and the second two years presented quarter-by-quarter, just like your P&L. The first balance sheet shows where the business is on the first day of business and the second a month later. You already prepared your pro forma profit and loss statement for your own analysis of the potential profitability of your business in the future.

BREAKEVEN ANALYSIS   Include a short section that indicates the number of units you must sell at the asking price in order to break even. If you can find any information about the business you are entering that indicates typical sales for your demography or any other information that shows costs and anticipated sales based on sound information, be sure to include it.

PRO FORMA CASH FLOW   Include a pro forma cash flow projection for at least three years. The first year is a month-by-month projection. The following years can be done on a quarterly basis. Remember, this is the most important document for your banker. Compile the information with care because it provides you with an invaluable measure of how your business is doing.

Working with these financials will give you a much better idea of how your business will operate, let you have a clearer idea of the risks you will run, and make the policy decisions for the senior management and board much more prudent.

The Ten Biggest Mistakes People Make on Their Financial Projections

Now that we have looked at how to prepare your business plan financials, let's see what not to do. In working with hundreds of nonprofits developing plans to start or acquire businesses, I have seen a lot of great plans and a bunch of so-so ones. It seems to me that nonprofits are quicker to "get" the marketing concept, to understand the idea of meeting market wants than they are to do really good, indeed, useful, financial statements.

I have a week's worth of theories as to why this is, but perhaps the most salient is that all of us in the nonprofit sector have been trained (by our funding streams) since we were right out of school how to do financials that *don't* cover all of our costs, how to rationalize expenditures that may or may not be related to the program, how to double up, maximize match, make something out of nothing. This accounting alchemy is difficult to overcome in developing a business plan, and it leads to serious business planning problems that I see repeated over and over again.

In order to help you perhaps avoid some of those common and often fatal (to the business) mistakes, I have developed my top-ten list below. Note that the list is in reverse order—the *most* common business mistake is number 1, at the end.

10. *Many People Do Not Read Financial Projections after They Are Prepared*
     Now, why would you spend the time putting together financials and not read them? Well, lots of people do, and mostly because they are unreadable—they are too long, too weighted down with appendices, too arcane to actually read through. Solution: Have an objective outsider

read, edit, and improve your plan before you send it to the board. The same solution will help you with the next two items.

9. *Financial Projections Do Not Support the Stated Goals of the Business*

As I have said repeatedly, the point of your nonprofit's going into business is to (a) do more mission by having the business be part of the mission; (b) earn money from an unrelated business to then use to buy more mission by supporting another program; or (c) a combination of the two. The trouble with financials for a new business is that too often decision makers get so excited about the business that they forget about the point—the overall mission. If, for example, the new business's financial projections show a profit of $15,000 per year for the second through the fourth year, that may be great. But if the point of the entire exercise is to get a $30,000 per year boost to support a key program, the numbers are not meeting the goals. We have already talked about this a bit, but it bears repeating.

8. *Numbers in the Profit-and-Loss Statement, Cash Flow Analysis, and Balance Sheet Do Not Jibe*

This is, yet again, a surprisingly common problem. People put together different financials at different times, the sources and applications one week, the profit-and-loss (P&L) statement the next, the cash flow after that. They then revise each one a number of times, but do not remember to cross-check the numbers and wind up with a lot of mistakes. For example, if in revising and fine-tuning your numbers, you merely change the interest rate on a loan from 8.0 to 7.75 percent, that changes the interest rate shown in the P&Ls, the debt service shown in the cash flow, any calculation that you may do of the cost of capital, and the display of liabilities in the opening balance sheet. If you change one or two and not the others, your numbers no longer jibe, and someone reviewing your plan—particularly a banker who may be considering lending you money—may rethink your business acumen.

Understand that, in my experience, the numbers are not usually off just by a quarter of a percent. I see things like the Sources and Applications noting the purchase of $250,000 of factory equipment and *no* depreciation in the P&L, or a loan for $300,000 in the balance sheet and the appropriate interest line in the P&L but no debt service payments shown in the cash flow. Little things like that. Little things that can sneak up and bite you. The solution? Just as with numbers 10 and 9, have an objective outsider look at your numbers and make sure that they work with each other.

7. *People Do Not Do a Cash Flow Analysis or Create Just One Cash Flow Analysis Each Year*

P&Ls are nice, balance sheets are "cool," breakeven is important, but you live and die by cash flow. When I do training on this subject I make all the participants write this down:

$$CASH = OXYGEN$$

Then we talk about how long one can live without oxygen, and how this translates to your organization. You've got to know your cash situation and see cash shortfalls coming. The solution is to have cash flow projections for six months out. Yet agencies that I work with repeatedly don't do them, or do them only on an annual basis. Particularly in a business start-up, doing a yearly cash flow analysis instead of a monthly (or biweekly) one is a recipe for disaster. In truth, it would be better to not have one, because a yearly projection too often provides dangerously out-of-touch information. An annual cash flow predicts the cash at the beginning and end of the year only, with nothing about the status in the middle. It would be comparable to assuming that temperatures are cold year-round if you measured the temperature only on January 1 and December 31.

Do cash flow projections—and do them on a monthly or biweekly basis.

6. *People Do Not Allow an Adequate Number of Days for Accounts Receivable*

Unless you are a retail business, always assume that people are going to pay you as late as is possible. Then add seven days for the mail or for the bank to release your electronic transfer. Then add fifteen more for bureaucratic mess-ups and an extra twenty-one days if you get your funds from the federal government. If you assume you will get paid too soon, you will not set aside enough working capital to get you through. Receivables are part of your cash flow estimation process.

 HANDS ON: Think of this scenario: You ask a customer, "How fast do you pay?" and he honestly tells you, "Thirty days." So, on April 8, you provide a service and bill him, expecting to get paid thirty days later—May 8. But by May 18 no payment has arrived and you call the customer. "Where's our payment?" you ask. He responds, "Like I told you, we pay in thirty days. That hasn't passed yet."

What didn't you do? You didn't ask: "Thirty days from when? From when we do the work, or from when you get the bill, or from when you post your payables, or from the end of the month, or, or, or?" In this case, the customer posted its payables at the end of the month: April 30, not April 8. Thus, thirty days became fifty-two—and your nonprofit had to float that difference. ■

5. *People Do Not Understand the Concept of Breakeven Analysis*

Breakeven is *very* important to good business planning for nonprofits, and yet few managers and board members really understand how to compute it and, more important, what the numbers really mean. First, breakeven is computed by the following formula:

$$\frac{\text{Fixed costs}}{(\text{Price} - \text{Variable cost})}$$

This calculates the units of service or number of widgets you need to sell to break even *in a particular time frame.* For instance, if you were selling widgets for $10 that had a variable cost of $4 and you needed to pay off a fixed cost of $3,000 per month, you would need to sell 500 widgets [$3,000/($10 − $4)] *per month* not to lose money *that month*. The value of this projection is to allow you to see how much sales volume is needed to stop losing money, and then to calculate how many months it will take for you to get up to that sales volume. Unfortunately, many people take breakeven to mean the volume of sales that will let you start to make money for the *life of the business*, and it is anything but that. Thus, they make incorrect and overly optimistic assumptions about the business and assume that the money will start to roll in long before it really will.

4. *People Do Not Understand Murphy's Law*

Here's a news flash: Stuff breaks, people get sick, machines get stuck, storms occur, airline flights get canceled, and customers change their minds or get fired or lose their income stream. Mr. Murphy and his Law show up all the time. To paraphrase the crude but accurate bumper sticker, "Stuff Happens." If you do not allow for things not to go as planned, you will be very unhappy. In terms of your financials, that means not cutting your working capital so close and your cash so thin that any one of a hundred things could put you under. I recently saw a business plan that had projections of $250,000 income per year and a net profit of $34 each year. And on the basis of these projections, these folks were prepared to borrow $200,000 over ten years. I did my best to talk them out of it.

For-profit businesses have a technical term for their Murphy Money. It's called "Contingency Funds." You need such a fund as well.

3. *People Do Not Start New Businesses with Enough Cash Reserves*

This mistake is a combination of nearly all the items that have preceded it. People don't do or understand breakeven, so they do not reserve enough cash. They don't do a cash flow analysis, so they do not know how much cash they really need. They don't allow for a lengthy enough receivable time, so they do not reserve enough cash. They forget about Mr. Murphy and don't give themselves a cash cushion. Sounds like I'm repeating myself.

If you doubt me, remember this: More businesses go out of business making money than losing it. That's right. How? They get starved for cash and close down.

2. *People Price Their Product or Service Too Low*

This is a big-league mistake, and easy to understand given nonprofits' training in getting paid for work at less than costs. In a new business, you must (a) charge enough to pay all your expenses or (b) have very deep pockets. I have heard people tell me in their business plans on more than one occasion that they will compete based on price *before* they know what their costs are! You would think they were an airline, the way they talk about cutting costs—and we all know how financially healthy our airlines are.

If you think you can compete on price, great—but read on before you think you can.

1. *People Do Not Take into Account All Costs When Preparing Financial Projections*

This is so common it must be a communicable disease. I have lost track of the number of nonprofit executives who do not add their time into the overhead of the new business even though they will be spending 25 percent of their time on it for the first six months. Or there are those who leave out rent as an expense "since our building is paid for." Let me put it this way: If your competition is charging for it, you should be. Or let me put it another way: If you are not accounting for all your costs, you are probably losing money on each sale and you will *not* make it up in volume.

Be brutal in this area. Compare your business P&Ls to your own organizational books. Are all the same line items there? If not, why? Are the additional things that are different accounted for? Is there a realistic number for depreciation, administration, rent, utilities, support services, accounting, and bad debts? If you are manufacturing, is there a contingency for wasted raw materials? Put everything in, or you do not have a realistic view of what is really going on.

So there they are: The ten big mistakes that you can avoid if you try. They are easier to make than you might imagine.

Creating a Climate of New Ideas

One of the most important things that you need to do if you want to develop or enhance your social entrepreneurism is to develop a climate of endless new ideas, one in which suggestions are encouraged, ideas are fairly weighed, and the best ones implemented.

In line with our theory of the inverted pyramid of management, this means *everyone's* ideas—board staff, management, and line. You need these ideas to stay fresh, to see new methods of providing service, and to keep in line with the changes in your many markets' wants.

To create this climate of ideas, you must constantly be asking. Do at least these things:

1. *Talk to all staff—particularly managers—about the need to use people's ideas.* Let all staff know that ideas are welcome, valued, and will be evaluated fairly and objectively. Let them know that no idea is too small, and that all suggestions—even those that are not used—are appreciated. As John Chambers, the CEO of Cisco, says, "Every idea is a good idea, until we find the best idea." I love that. And as a manager, you're paying for all of your staff's brains. Use them. Ask for ideas.

2. *Create a number of ways for people to offer ideas.* Have something better than just a suggestion box. Ask for ideas at staff meetings. Have an idea wiki on the staff portion of your Web site to encourage input and ideas. Make a new idea or process a reward item on people's evaluations and a time during the evaluation for discussion of new ideas. The freer people feel, and the more opportunities they have to offer their thoughts, the better.

3. *Develop an objective review system.* People need to know that their ideas will be reviewed impartially. For small suggestions, the managers can probably do this; for larger ideas, you perhaps can adopt the criteria you developed in your business development process to weigh varying suggestions.

4. *Close the loop—get back to people.* Let anyone who puts forth a suggestion know what happened to his or her idea—it was implemented, it will be implemented, or it cannot be implemented and why. And *always* thank people for their ideas.

5. *Consider a reward/recognition system.* Regardless of whether you do this on a systematic basis, if someone makes a suggestion, or does a great deal of work on a particular idea, at least recognize him or her publicly and consider rewarding him or her financially. If you feel the need to systematize this, just make sure the reward is a reward, not a punishment. (For more on reward systems, see Chapter 7.)

You need your staff to use all their synapses and neurons on your organization's behalf all the time. Creating a climate in which new ideas are valued, recognized, and encouraged will not only make you able to be more entrepreneurial, it will also keep you flexible.

Recap

Life is full of risk and all of us learn to accommodate a certain level of risk every day. It is no different for mission-based managers. The skills that you have learned in this book will help make it easier for you to take risk on behalf of your clientele. Building a better board, a stronger staff, becoming market oriented, having strong controls, and becoming financially empowered all build your ability to evaluate and take risks. Some of these skills increase your strengths, some reduce unnecessary risks, and others build an important financial cushion—all of which leads us to the skills you have been learning in this chapter: how to be more entrepreneurial for the benefit of your community.

I hope that in this chapter I have given you food for thought on how to become better risk takers and more entrepreneurial. We have reviewed how to assess and take risk and how to accept its presence in your organization. We have looked at new sources of income and have reviewed the steps necessary to start an outside business venture.

The next decade is a risky one for you and for your organization. You need to meet those risks with an ability to think and act like an entrepreneur.*

Questions for Discussion

1. Do we meet the characteristics of a social entrepreneur? How?
2. Are there business ideas that would make both mission and money sense for us?
3. How do we look at expenditures now? As investments in mission? How can we be better at this and communicate it to our staff?
4. What risks are we taking now? How can we incorporate the idea of good risk into our culture more?

---

*For much more on this subject, see my book *Social Entrepreneurship* (John Wiley & Sons, Inc., 2000).

Developing a Bias for Marketing

Overview

This chapter is central to your success. If you don't know who you are serving, if you don't know what they want, if you don't know how to ask them how to improve, if you don't know how to let people know that you are around—how can you stay in business? You cannot. You need to adopt a culture of marketing, and this chapter will show you how. In the following pages, we'll talk through the benefits of marketing, and then go through each of the seven key steps in the marketing process, which are:

1. Identifying your target markets
2. Assessing what the market wants
3. Developing and redeveloping the product or service
4. Pricing
5. Promotion
6. Distribution
7. Evaluation

After that, we'll look at the best ways to ask your markets what they want, and then show you the ways to evaluate your marketing efforts. By the end of the chapter, you'll have a new understanding of who your markets *really* are, what they *really* want, and how to satisfy their wants.

There is no question in my mind that, of all the business skills you can put to work for your mission, marketing is the most applicable in the most areas. If done properly, consistently, and with an eye to innovation and improvement, you can use marketing to recruit and retain better employees, make your board happier, generate more good community buzz, raise more funds, and have more satisfied mission recipients as well as funders who not only return to fund you in future years but who refer other funders to you.

Sound good? I thought so. Remember, though, that marketing is not the equivalent of fund-raising, it is not just promotion, it is not just sales. It's marketing, broader in scope and in impact than any small part of the whole. Let's get started.

Why Market?

Marketing is essential, integral to your success, and yet, in many ways, foreign to nonprofits. Let's start this critical component with a short quiz:

- You are a nonprofit, so you don't have to worry about marketing, right? *Wrong.*
- The people who you serve are your primary markets, right? *Only partly.*

Successful nonprofits know that their continued success, even their continued existence, depends on living, breathing, eating, and sleeping this slogan:

EVERYTHING THAT EVERYONE HERE DOES EVERY DAY IS MARKETING.

Every employee and volunteer. At home, at work, at the grocery store—24/7/365. This means that the way the phone is answered, the way the staff dress, the way the trash is picked up and the lawn is cut, the quality of your Web site, the knowledge of the board, to say nothing of how services are provided. All these activities go into the marketing mix. You have to assume that every interaction with a client, patron, donor, funder, neighbor, friend, stranger, relative, or politician—even those who you are totally unaware of—have an impact on some part of your organization: a decision to come to you for services, a decision to refer someone else to you, a decision to donate, or a decision to fund.

As I said above, this maxim is not just applicable to management, or to service provision staff, but to every employee and volunteer who is associated with your organization. Remember the story I told in Chapter 6 about the new board member who attended the cocktail party? She had two ways of presenting her new experience—one positive, one less so. It is important that everyone understand that his or her role in the entire enterprise is essential and part of your team marketing effort.

 FOR EXAMPLE: During the late 1990 buildup to the first Gulf War, Americans saw interviews with dozens of young military personnel on television. Often the young men and women were asked, "What are you doing here?" Regardless of their job—cook, truck driver, munitions handler, mechanic—they answered, "Kicking Saddam's butt out of Kuwait!" No matter how menial their task in the huge war machine, these service men and women had been taught that their small component was critical to the larger task at hand. I remember hearing a dockworker who spent his 105-degree days offloading cargo at one of the ports saying, "Hey, no one eats, moves, or fights without supplies, and no supplies get to nobody [sic] without me. That means I'm winning the war!" And he meant it. You want to work on *that* type of ownership with your staff and the understanding that what they do *does* affect the whole, even if on the surface there is not a direct impact on your services or your funding. Everyone matters. ■

You'll also get resistance from some staff who say something like this: "But I'm just a [receptionist, social worker, janitor, teacher, accountant, IT specialist], I'm not a marketer. I don't sell anything and don't want to." When you hear this, just smile and say that you agree that they won't be selling. But even so, tell the staff that everything they do matters to the future of the organization.

In the discussion on staff management, I talked about the fact that the lowest paid people in your organization are the most important: They are the ones who have the most direct contact with your clientele and the public and the most impact on your marketing potential, directly or indirectly. These people need to be involved in your marketing, in the planning and execution of your marketing plan. They need to understand their critical role in the marketing of, and therefore the future of, your organization and its mission.

Marketing Basics

Marketing is so often considered a "dirty" word in nonprofits. It is unseemly, and after all, you are not in *sales*, right? Wrong. You need to attend to your markets (and there are more of those than you think), find out what they want, and give it to them within the limits of your resources.

Let's start by looking at the basic marketing flowchart shown in Exhibit 10.1. As you can see, the entire process starts not with developing a product or service and then trying to sell it, but instead with choosing your target markets. Now, what do we do in our organizations? Usually, we say, "We're here to provide arts (medical, educational, etc.) services, and we know how to provide them. So we'll let you know when we are open and y'all come!" This is known as *product-driven marketing:* We believe in our product (or service) and that it will sell itself. If we build it they will come. Or not.

Let's go through these parts of the marketing diagram one box at a time.

EXHIBIT 10.1 Marketing Flowchart

Identifying Your Target Markets

Fact: The nonprofit industry is the only industry in the world that regularly gets together in groups to berate and complain about its best customers. Think about it. Your best customer is the group or groups that send you the most money. For most readers, that is some branch of local, state, or the federal government. Do you see them as customers? If you are like 99 percent of nonprofit managers, you see them (at least some of the time, admit it) as the *enemy*. This, to say the least, is a self-defeating viewpoint. You and your staff and board need to start thinking of your largest funders as your best customers, and then start treating them that way.

But before we discuss how you can do that, I need to realign your thinking about who your markets really are. Stop and think for a minute. Who *are* your markets and how can you identify them? Look at Exhibit 10.2 for a start in breaking down the concept that the only market you have that counts is the people you serve. They *are* the most important market, but they are *not the only market.*

I have divided the nonprofit marketing mix into three main categories:

1. *The payer markets.* These are the people who send you money. They may be the federal, state, or local government; donors; foundations; users; or others. Each of these should be considered a different market segment. For example, if you get money from three different state programs, each program should be assessed as a different market segment. I also include in the payer markets a box for "referrers." These are the critical people who send other people your way. They might be mental health counselors, social workers, friends, physicians, or ministers, but without their referrals you would be in trouble. You need these people. Their referrals translate into mission out and income in.

EXHIBIT 10.2   The Markets of Your Nonprofit

Internal	Service
• Board and Staff	Service A
Payer	Client Type 1
• Government	Client Type 2
• Foundation	Service B
• Membership	Client Type 1
• United Way	Client Type 2
• Donation	Referrers
• User Fees	

2. *The service markets.* These are the people who you serve. Think about how many different markets are represented here: each different program you provide multiplied by each different age, socioeconomic, and gender cohort you provide those services to. For example, if you provide family planning services, the way you provide them to married couples is a great deal different than how you would provide the same basic service to single teenage boys and girls. You have lots of different service markets.

3. *The internal markets.* These are two different markets: *staff* and *volunteers*. The brutal truth that we've covered in prior chapters is that you need good, solid staff *more than they need you*. The same is true for your volunteers, both governing and nongoverning. They are, in the truest sense, essential markets, ones that you have to attend to if you want to do any mission at all.

Each of these markets warrants special attention. You need your payer markets: no money, no mission. If you accept the payer markets as truly being an important customer (regardless of whether you like it) then you need to figure out how to keep them as your customer. You need your service markets to be happy and satisfied, otherwise you are not doing good, high-quality mission. If you run out of service markets, you have just run out of a reason for existing. You need your board, nongoverning volunteers, and staff, and you need them to be qualified and motivated; they are the key resources available to plan for and provide your mission. You are also *competing* for each and every one of these markets, just the way Dell competes with Apple, or Delta competes with United. The payers, the service recipients, and the staff and board all have choices, and those choices are only going to increase in the coming years. Without your paying constant attention to those markets, the choice they make may very well be to choose to not have anything to do with your organization.

HANDS ON: To get a handle on your organization's many markets, do this: Sit down with a chart that looks something like the one shown in Exhibit 10.3 and put all of your markets into it. The key here is to try to distinguish (segment) markets to ensure that you give each the attention that it deserves. Note that I have included only one or two "wants" for each market. In reality, there will be many. You need to ask. Also, note that there are different wants for the special education *districts* (payers) and the special education *administrators* (referrers). This is not unusual. The paying side wants one thing and the program side another.

Before we go further, I want to give you one overriding caution about markets and market segmentation. Do not ever fall into what I call the "census" trap, saying that your main market is the 590,400 people who live in your county. It is not. Your market is never *everyone*. It is the people between ages 12 and 90 who enjoy live classical music and have the ability to pay and attend concerts if you are a symphony orchestra; it is (primarily) women between 12 and 50 who are sexually active if you are a family planning organization; but it is *not* everyone. This extends to the way we will implement our marketing activities; we can't expect everyone to take our next survey developed online on Sur-veyMonkey.com. What about the people who don't have or use computers?

No market is everyone, so why do we assume it is? We were trained to think of our markets by the federal government in this style as a result of what is called "capitation funding," wherein an organization's government grant each year was based on the service area's population. This was poor training, but you can begin to relearn if you apply this chart to your many markets. And if you do this for your organization, I guarantee that you will be stunned as to how many markets and market segments you have. Don't panic. You've taken an important first step: You know who your markets *really* are, and now you can decide which merit the most immediate attention and which can be lower on the priority scale. ■

Assess the Market Wants

Note that I said "wants," not "needs." Professionals tell people what they need. People buy what they want.

EXHIBIT 10.3   Market Wants

Category	Market	Wants
Payers	Special education districts	Low cost, accountability
	State department of rehabilitation	Good bookkeeping, timely filing
	Private payers	Low cost, prompt billing
Staff	Speech therapists	Career growth
	Physical therapists	Varied patients
	Teachers	Continuing education
	Administrators	Stability, retirement
Service	Children 0–3 with perceived disabilities	Happy, loving staff
	Children 3–5 who need physical or cognitive testing	Happy, fun place
	Parents of children 0–3 in the above programs	Safe place that helps their child
Referral	Special education administrators	High-quality services
	Pediatricians and family practitioners	Highly educated staff
	Disability-specific parents' support groups	Inclusion

 FOR EXAMPLE: Statistics tell us that one in eight American adults is in need of substance abuse treatment—mostly for alcohol, but some for harder drugs. If we assume that a third of those people need inpatient care, that is still more than 8.3 million adults in need of treatment. There are not one-tenth that many treatment beds available in the country, and many of them are empty. Why? Because as anyone who has struggled with addiction or who is related to someone with an addiction will tell you, people will not seek services for their addiction until they *want* it. Do they *need* help? Sure, and we can prove it to them medically. Heck, everyone in their zip code knows they *need* help. But until they *want* treatment, there is no point in even trying. Here is a second example for anyone with kids, nieces, nephews, or grandchildren under the age of 12. How many of your children *need* additional toys? More video games? And do you buy them more? Yeah, I thought so. ■

With this background, we now need to establish ways to find out what all of these markets we've identified *want*. There are a variety of ways to do this, and they all start with a basic discipline that has just three letters:

A-S-K

It is really very simple. You ask people what they want; why they came to you; what made them happy or not so happy about your services; whether they will return, and if so, why, and if not, why not; and how you can improve services to meet their wants. By developing a discipline of asking, by getting everyone in the organization in the habit of market research through asking, you will learn extremely important things, many of which will completely astound you.

How do you ask? You can ask formally through surveys or focus groups. You can also ask informally every chance you get. You should, at the very least, establish some kind of baseline of employee and consumer satisfaction through a formal survey. You can then remeasure that satisfaction every twelve to eighteen months. You should also ask everyone who seeks or utilizes your services in any way how he or she came to you: Was it a referral from a friend? Did he see the ad in the paper? Did she hear about you from her doctor (or minister or art teacher)? You need to know these things and evaluate trends over time.

There are a variety of ways of asking. Surveys and focus groups often sound very technical, complex, and expensive. Not always so. They are essential tools for you as you develop your asking skills, so let's look at them in some detail.

SURVEYS Many organizations wrongly assume that establishing baseline survey data is very expensive and the purview of only expensive marketing firms like Harris Polls or Gallup. And certainly, polls and surveys *can* be expensive, sometimes prohibitively so. But let's focus on the five important components of a good survey, and then you will need to decide whether you can provide or find the expertise in-house, online, from an expert volunteer, or whether you need to go outside of the organization for help.

1. Surveys need to be *focused* around a central theme. Do not ask a referral source the same things you would ask an employee, and also do not ask the employee ten questions about job satisfaction if your main survey goal is to find out what the staff wants in terms of noncash compensation.
2. Your survey needs to *ask the right questions*—ones that will generate the information you need. In deciding what questions to ask, be frugal. What do you really want to know? Is it about customer satisfaction in general or their satisfaction with a particular program? Target your questions.
3. You need to *ask the questions right*. There is a great deal of difference in the responses you will get depending on how you ask the question. I can generate a huge difference in responses about a particular program if I ask the question "On a scale of 1 to 5, how much did you like the

program?" as opposed to asking "Did the program appeal to you or not?"

4. Surveys need to be *short enough* to have people fill them in. As a rule, if it looks like it will take more than four minutes and the respondent is filling out the survey only out of kindness, it won't happen. (You can have longer surveys filled in if you are compensating them: giving them money, a lunch, a free coupon for a pizza, etc.)
5. To make the whole exercise worth it, you have to survey enough people to have a *representative sample.* If you are a church and you want to survey your congregation's attitude toward a new church building, asking three people out of a congregation of 600 will not tell you what you need to know. However, not making a move until you have surveyed the other 597 members is foolish and suffers from the curve of diminishing returns.

As you can see, many of these issues are technical, and thus most organizations get some help in setting up their surveying. There are some excellent written resources on surveying, and these can be easily found online. A second source is the marketing department of your local university, where you might get adopted as a student project. Also, the marketing professor might be willing to help you pro bono or for a much lower fee than a proprietary marketing firm.

For some surveys, the online option is terrific. I use SurveyMonkey.com (as do many of my client organizations), which, for many surveys, is free. There are other services online as well, but the key is that you can construct your survey quickly and with great flexibility. You can distribute it without paper; as people fill out the survey, the results are tabulated instantly and without any input errors; and you can read, report, and show the results instantly. Each year, I have an ongoing survey of training client satisfaction, and the link to the survey results is shown in the training area of my Web site. Thus, potential customers can see what other customers said, in detail, in real time. Think about this for your organization for, say, a volunteer satisfaction survey with the results posted on your volunteer information pages.

Surveys also allow for one use that no other form of asking does: trend analysis. If you ask the same questions cycle after cycle (and thus you need to get the questions right the first time), you can see trends that can really help you manage your services, your staff, and your mission better. You will know that 75 percent of your staff the last three years were completely satisfied with their jobs, but this year the number dropped to 70 percent, and thus some more in-depth analysis needs to be done as to why. You'll be able to tell a funder that each year your client satisfaction number has gone up and how much. Trend analysis is a great use of survey data.

Surveys are excellent information-gathering tools, but get some help with your first one, and don't do just one. Do them regularly, and compare and analyze the data you receive.

FOCUS GROUPS   Focus groups are great. While they do not generate the kind of objective data that surveys do, the subjective information gathered on feelings, reactions, impressions, and opinions is invaluable. At their core, focus groups are sessions of one to two hours with a *focused* set of questions posed to ten to fifteen people who represent a market or homogeneous group. A focus group is almost always run by an outside facilitator, and I urge you to find a local facilitator who is experienced with focus groups because the quality of the facilitator makes or breaks these sessions. The great benefit of a focus group is that a talented facilitator can follow up on ideas and answers generated by the group, investigating leads that you could never expand on in a formal survey. For instance, a facilitator might ask, "What kind of service improvements could we make for kids?" and a participant might give an excellent idea. Right then and there, the facilitator can pose the new idea to the rest of the group, gathering on-the-spot reactions and modifications that can lead to earlier and ultimately more successful implementation. When looking for a facilitator, look for the talent in group facilitation first and the knowledge of your program second. Once you retain the facilitator, he or she needs to get up to speed on all aspects of the issues your focus group will be discussing, including jargon and potentially controversial issues.

You also need to hold separate groups for separate issues, even though it is more time consuming and costly. For example, don't expect a group of lower-income service recipients to be as forthcoming if they are mixed in with affluent donors, or staff to share openly in the same group as funders. You also need to focus your questions. You just can't ask everyone everything you might want to know. People wear down after about two hours, so don't wring them dry.

THE DISCIPLINE OF ASKING AND LISTENING   Asking people what they want is in itself an image enhancer for your organization. I have facilitated more than one hundred focus groups in the past ten years, and our firm has surveyed at least 15,000 people. During those activities, one of the comments we hear most often is "Thanks for asking! No one ever has before."

That is both a terrible indictment and an amazing opportunity. Remember that, by asking, you get valuable information *and* make people feel better about your organization, all in one action. A twofer!

However, there are several other important points to keep in mind about asking. If you ask, you *must* listen. And you may not hear things that make you happy, especially at first. You will almost certainly hear criticisms of your programs, your management style, your philosophy of service. Take them as opportunities to improve, not as personal assaults on your capabilities and character. And, if you listen, you need to respond, both orally and in writing. Thank people for offering their insights, perhaps in a memo to all who participated in a survey or in a personal note to those who took the time to offer their reactions in a focus group. In that correspondence, close the loop with them and let them in on what you are doing with their ideas. You can put the main ideas that came out of the survey/focus groups into four categories as follows:

1. Things that are suggested that you will be able to do right away
2. Things that you will have to work on over the near term
3. Things you will need to defer to future years
4. Suggestions that are inappropriate or impossible

Tell people all of those things. If the ideas are going into a strategic plan, say so. If they are being passed on to your main funding source, let that be known. If they are going to be used to plan a major capital campaign, a new program for a specific group, an additional site, or any tangible outcome, let people know. Be forthright—do not promise what you cannot deliver on, but *do* get back to people.

What can you learn by asking? Wonderful things.

 FOR EXAMPLE: A few years ago, my firm helped a rural primary care health center with a community perception survey and focus groups. I facilitated a number of focus groups: two of current patients, one of former patients, and one of community officials. I found several common complaints/suggestions during these sessions. These are listed below, with the actions that the health center took to respond.

- *"Your center looks run down, inside and out."* The center found that the grounds maintenance service was not doing the job. Over time, the appearance of the facility had declined and the staff had not noticed. But the patients, who only came in once or twice a year, noticed the difference. The clinic changed maintenance contractors with an emphasis on trash removal and neatness. Inside, a new coat of paint and more staff emphasis on picking up and neat work spaces resulted in a much higher satisfaction rating in this area the following year: Total cost: $500 in painting.

(continued)

(*continued*)

- *"Your receptionist is rude."* This feeling was prevalent among *former* patients, but a fact that the administrator had never noticed because when he was treated, he did not enter through the normal patient reception lines. The receptionist was given sensitivity training. That did not help much, so she was transferred to a different clerical job. Total cost: $100 for the training.
- *"Your toys are dirty—I worry about the kids catching a 'bug' when they play with them."* In fact, the toys were cleaned every night; they were just old. The center bought new toys each year and had the staff clean them in front of the patients every day. Total cost: $200 per year. ■

After these items and a few others were resolved, the center got back to all those interviewed, with particular emphasis on the former patients, noting the changes—new toys, new receptionist, better maintenance—that had resulted from the information gathered at the focus groups. *Every single former patient returned* within the next six months for an office visit. The patients liked the practitioners, and the practitioners had not thought that they cared about these nonmedical but still important issues. The center never would have known why patients were leaving if they had not asked.

Ask, listen, act, respond! It works.

Develop and Redevelop the Product or Service

Only now that you know who your markets are and what your markets want, can you, to varying extents, modify your service array or develop a new service. Some readers will be hamstrung by service definitions dictated by their funding source: "You must provide inpatient 28-day residential rehabilitation" or "You must have each child tested in an approved setting every 18 months" or whatever guideline you must follow. But you need to try to match your services to your markets and their wants as closely as possible, noting that those wants will change over time.

This is an excellent place to note the conflict represented in the preceding paragraph: The funder wants you to provide a service in a particular way, regardless of whether the recipient wants it that way. Look carefully at what is going on—to meet a payer's want (service provided within specific guidelines), you may have to give the service market's want a lower priority. This is an excellent example of the conflicts that you need to try to resolve and the balance that you need to try to achieve. It is tough, and no one should misunderstand that. Often, a program that is wildly successful in one community catches the eye of a funder who wants to have it replicated elsewhere. Too often, the success was a result of a confluence of events in that initial community—a key staff person or volunteer, a community event that precipitated demand for the program—and not because of the fundamental attractiveness of the program itself. In his book, *Reinventing Government* (Boston: Addison-Wesley, 1992), David Osborne recounts the story of a woman in the Bronx who organized a tenants' group to run their low-income housing unit and turned it around. The group worked out all sorts of ideas and methods to reduce crime, increase occupancy, and improve tenants' lives. But Osborne, who advocates similar empowerment programs elsewhere in the country, also found that without the key leader, all of the other items, no matter how admirable, were not used.

In marketing terms, if enough (or the right) people did not *want* it to happen enough to *work* for it, it won't happen, and in many cases your organization will take funds to try to replicate a program before there is a demand for the program. This is *very* hard work. In these cases, you also need to ask, and ask regularly, to see if you can refit, improve, and customize the program to meet the wants that exist in your community now rather than in some other community three years ago.

You must also make sure that you have *listened*, and that *all* of the staff is on board and prepared for the changes the market wants.

 FOR EXAMPLE: A few years ago, my firm was asked to assist a number of community substance abuse rehabilitation providers with assistance in broadening their markets. In discussing this project with the providers, it was clear that they wanted to move beyond the Medicaid-eligible client to, as they put it, "serve the executive covered by Blue Cross." The reasons for this market shift were understandable and valid: The providers could recoup $320 per day from Blue Cross for a service for which they were then getting $165 per day from Medicaid. But were they ready to provide the services? They said they were, and many had in fact upgraded their physical plant markedly.

I asked them if their staff were also ready to serve this different clientele, noting that business executives, even ones with substance abuse problems, have significantly different expectations than their traditional clientele: those eligible for Medicaid. I was assured that the staffs were ready for this change. I doubted it.

(continued)

(*continued*)

So we checked. We had a woman on our staff call each of the agencies in question and ask for help for her husband, who was portrayed as an alcoholic who worked for a large firm and had Blue Cross coverage. She also called the community hospitals that had competing substance abuse programs in each community. In every single case, the community rehab center staff blew it. The receptionist did not have any knowledge of Blue Cross. She referred the "patient" to a staff person who was either equally limited in knowledge or never called back. There was never any follow-up to the call in writing or by phone. Conversely, every single hospital had its act together. The caller talked with a knowledgeable and sympathetic nurse immediately in each case. The nurse followed up by phone and with solid marketing material in the mail.

I returned to a meeting of the community providers armed with this information, and they, frankly, didn't accept it as valid. So I asked them to exchange business cards with another provider, take a break, and go call in pretending to be a person seeking care. They returned 15 minutes later and reported their experiences, which were uniformly awful.

They and their staff were not yet ready to serve the market that they had targeted. They were not ready to meet the market wants because they had not asked the market what they wanted: They had *assumed* that they knew, and in marketing, assuming that you know what the market wants is not only egotistical and arrogant, it is suicide. ■

Ask, but also *listen* to the answers.

Price the Service

There are so many variables in pricing, most of which you do not control, that I won't take a lot of space discussing pricing here. Also, there are many excellent resources in pricing strategy. Suffice it to say that most nonprofits underprice their services through either the training they have gotten from funders throughout their careers (funders don't want to reimburse all of their costs) or naiveté, or both. However, learning how to price, to say nothing of what providing an individual unit of service *actually costs* to provide, is a critical skill to develop in any organization. Knowing what your costs are and which programs are making money, which are losing money, and which are breaking even is a key component of any plan for financial empowerment (see Chapter 11).

I do, however, at least need to cover a few key points. Pricing is both an art and a science. Price development is fluid, not static. It exists in a world where there are many dynamics occurring. Pricing is composed of the following four components:

FIXED COSTS Fixed costs are the costs that you normally think of as "overhead." Technically, they are the costs that are fixed whether "sales" rise or fall. So, for example, in a school, the administrative costs and building and maintenance are fixed costs, because they won't change if the enrollment (the sales) goes from 70 to 90 (or 70 to 50). The crux of charging a fixed-cost component is the issue of how quickly you want to recover these costs: over how many sales. For example, if you tried to recover the entire fixed cost of a Nissan factory in one auto, the price would be a little steep. Nissan tries to recover that cost over millions of cars. But if it adds too low a charge for the fixed-cost component in each car's price, and does not sell enough, it loses money on its fixed costs.

VARIABLE COSTS Variable costs are the costs that vary as the sales vary. In manufacturing, they include the raw materials for the product, the unit costs of labor, and the energy to produce the product. In my school example, they would be the costs directly associated with each student: food, supplies, linens, and differing energy costs (for a residential school). As the enrollment increases, these costs increase.

PROFIT Yes, profit is okay. A nonprofit can have a profit, and nowhere in any regulation or law does it say that you can't. It is just your funding sources that say you shouldn't. The profit you make will help you pay off debt and put money aside. This critical issue will be discussed further in Chapter 11, "Financial Empowerment," but for our purposes here, let's just note that you need a profit, and the component of price attributable to the profit will depend on how quickly you want to recover your initial investment and how much the market will bear. The profit margin will usually be some small percentage (probably 2 to 6 percent) of the price.

COMPETITION AND MARKET CONDITIONS The competition has much to do with what your price is. If you price out your item (e.g., tuition at our hypothetical school) and find, in comparing your tuition to the competition's, that yours is 20 percent higher, what will that mean? It may mean that you will lose *some* students to the lower-priced school. Conversely, it may mean that you will gain some students who want to go to only the "elite" (read: expensive) school.

Obviously, this is a very fluid situation. In the case of the school, let's imagine a teacher's union arriving, and a contract signed guaranteeing increases in salary for the next five years. What just happened to fixed costs? They went up. What if three graduates get full scholarships to Harvard or if the test scores for seniors are tops in the state or if the football team is nationally ranked? Demand for enrollment will increase. In one case, your price (tuition) *needs* to go up due to cost increases; in the other, the price (and the profit) *can* go up due to market conditions.

Don't fall into the trap of assuming that you can just underprice everyone and that that will make people come to your organization. First, it's just not smart (which is not to say that people do not do it all the time). If you just keep cutting prices, and have prices less than your costs, you will soon be out of business unless you have very deep pockets and can outlast your competition. All one has to do is look at the suicidal price wars that the major airlines constantly engage in to see that. A second good example is auto rebates. They do encourage sales, but at a loss to the automakers. I can think of a dozen examples of my nonprofit clients in business development coming to me and saying that they planned to compete on price without knowing whether they could do so and still make money. As noted earlier, there are a number of good resources on pricing, and your auditor may also have ideas on this.

One final take-away for pricing: Remember, *it's never about the cost; it's always about the value.* If cost ruled with all customers, we wouldn't have Ritz-Carleton or Whole Foods or Lexus or Neiman-Marcus. For some customers, cost may be 99 percent of value, but there's always something else. Think downscale to Fairfield Inn or Wal-Mart. Low cost, sure, but if nothing they sold worked, they would not have customers. So it isn't just about cost. What value can you add to your services? And who gets to decide what's valuable? Not you. No, the customer decides what's valuable and to figure that out, you have to ask. See how all this is interrelated?

Promote the Service

There are dozens of ways to promote your services: on your Web site, word of mouth, referrals, traditional or online advertising, personal contact, presentations to community groups, flyers put under windshield wipers, and, of course, the classic two-fold six-panel brochure. How you promote your service will depend on your budget, your service, and the people you are trying to inform that you are there. But no matter what your status, think about this: With all of the different *payer* markets and all of the different *referral* markets you have, to say nothing of all of the different *service* markets you are trying to attract and retain, does one brochure with a short history of your organization and a picture of your building really get your point across? Of course it doesn't. Yet that is what many nonprofits still have: a brochure that talks about the organization's genesis; lists its services, often in jargon; and sometimes does not even include a phone number. Worse, many organization's Web sites are just electronic representations of these outdated pieces of paper.

My question is: Who really cares about a picture of your building? No one cares but the architect and the builder. Who cares about your history? Hardly anyone cares, except those who were there at the time. Can one short brochure or one bland Web site really attract people with all sorts of different wants to your organization? Can it really explain how your organization can meet the wants of funders, donors, referrers, or service recipients? Of course not.

Promotion, whether in person, online, or on paper, must *never sell the program*. Rather, it must *attempt to solve the customer's problem*. If I am the parent of a developmentally disabled child, do I care how long you've been in business? No. I want good evaluation and educational opportunities for my son or daughter. I want you to recognize me as a customer. I want to feel that you are sympathetic to my feelings and that you will provide only the best services on the planet to my child. I want to know how much it is going to cost me. So your marketing material must say those things clearly and in straightforward prose. Show me the benefit that I will receive by sending my child to your organization.

Remember the number one rule of promotion and sales: *Don't sell the product—solve the customer's problem*. You need to let the potential users of your service, the potential funders, staff, and board (in other words, all of your many markets) know what benefit they will gain from using your services or donating you money. Don't just tell them who you are or what you do. Make the connection between what you do and how it will help them. Wording such as "XYZ agency provides substance abuse rehabilitation services" is much less compelling than "If you or a loved one have a problem with substance abuse, the staff at XYZ can help put them on the road to a more productive, less dependent life." The first sentence talks about services (in jargon), whereas the second promises benefits.

The other major flaw in most nonprofits' promotion comes from falling into the "census trap" discussed earlier in this chapter in the Hands On activity. Organizations that wrongly assume that their market is the entire population often also assume that the entire population needs to know about their organization, and these organizations waste a great deal of time and money trying to achieve that goal.

 FOR EXAMPLE: A client of mine, a rehabilitation facility specializing in head injury patients, recently bemoaned the fact that it had done a public awareness survey and only 0.6 percent of the area's population recognized the organization's name

(*continued*)

(*continued*)

and knew what general services were provided. Both the executive director and the board were adamant about spending money (a great deal of money) on a public awareness campaign that would, in their words, "solve this problem."

"What problem?" I asked.

"Not enough people know about us!" was their startled answer.

"So? Do patients self-refer?"

"No," they replied.

"Do you get 5 percent or more of your money in small donations from the general public?"

"No," they replied.

"Where do your referrals come from?"

"From area neurologists and surgeons," they said.

"What percentage of those physicians know about your programs in detail?"

"We don't know," was their answer.

"Find out, and forget about the public. They don't need to know about you (nor do they want to, for that matter). You need to focus your efforts on your referral sources." ■

This example is a classic one of misunderstanding the target market, as well as the market wants.

Provide (Distribute) the Service

Once you have developed the service, you need to provide it. Here you have lots of choices and are probably doing an excellent job in being flexible, but let's review the options. Just like solving a mystery, writing a story, or preparing a book report, the key parameters of service provision to meet a market wants are who, what, when, where, and why.

- *Who provides the service.* You can't just have someone who is knowledgeable in the service area; you need someone who can "connect" with the service recipient. Someone who doesn't speak Spanish is not going to be an optimal provider in a largely Hispanic neighborhood. Someone who acts very "square" probably will not be the best with kids in a youth ministry.
- *What service is provided.* You've already established this through the previous steps.

- *Where the service is provided.* Your clientele need easy access to the extent possible. Is the place you provide service convenient? Is there adequate parking, sufficient security? In the past few years, more and more hospitals are providing off-site radiology and therapy sites that are closer to where their patients live. This helps the patients avoid having to come to the central hospital where parking is often difficult; security is sometimes inadequate, especially after dark; and patients must walk long distances from their car to their service site.

- *When the service is provided.* A family planning seminar for teenagers is pointless if held at your office on weekdays: The kids should be in school. The flexible *when* is a key component of market sensitivity in today's predominantly two-income and or single-parent families. People seek services at odd hours and they value time-saving convenience over many other considerations. Thus Domino's Pizza thrives, Toys R Us stays open around-the-clock during the pre-Christmas period, and 24-hour convenience stores are solid franchise investments. Be convenient and you will increase both market share and market satisfaction.

- *Why. Don't forget the why. Why is this particular service being provided?* To educate, to prevent, to entertain, to cure, to soothe, to enlighten? The *why* becomes a key component of the provision mix, and it should always be close at hand.

Evaluate the Marketing Effort

As mentioned earlier, you need to know how you are doing. Getting baseline information is a good start, but steady and consistent asking is essential. Are your staff happier than they were last year? Are you getting better quorums than you were two years ago? Is attendance or occupancy up or down? Are more people responding to advertising or to referrals? You need to ask, regularly and consistently.

Also, be cognizant of the fact that the wants and needs of the markets are constantly changing. Thus, you may need to change with them. The only way to accurately assess the changes is by asking and tracking the answers over time.

Asking Does Make a Difference

I spend a lot of my time speaking to state or national nonprofit associations, and I regularly point out to them that their best customers are their biggest funders. There is usually uncomfortable silence. I then ask them, "When was the last time any of you went to your state [federal, county] project officer and asked, 'How can I make your job easier?' " There is either silence or laughter. I then point out that this is basic marketing. After these sessions, I am often asked, "What difference will it make if we ask bureau-crats how we can make their life easier? They have no control over our money."

This is an understandable question, and in response I want to offer two examples of what a difference such a simple, no-cost technique *can* make.

 FOR EXAMPLE: As I told you earlier, in the early 1980s I was the executive director of a health systems agency, a nonprofit formed as a result of federal law, and almost 100 percent federally funded. We did health care planning and regulation for a specific geo-graphic area. Our federal contacts were in Chicago, at the Federal Regional Office Building.

Shortly after I became executive director, I had to go to Chicago for a meeting and I made it a point to meet not only with my federal program officer, who was nominally my key con-tact, but also with the woman who was our grants administration officer, the person who processed our budget, vouchers, and grant checks. This woman, whose name was Betty, worked in a win-dowless office in the midst of a vast, drab, government building, but she was warm, personable, and obviously pleased to have been visited. "I rarely get to meet the people at the agencies," she said. "In fact, I think it's been three years since I got face-to-face with someone from the field." I said that I was glad to meet her, and that I hoped that our staff would process all of the forms for her correctly, but if we messed up, I wanted her to call me right away. Betty responded appreciatively, noting that everyone usually denies filling in the forms wrong or complains about their length, instead of offering to cooperate. I told her I just would think of her as my best customer. She laughed and we parted friends. The next time I was in Chicago, and the next and the next, I stuck my head in Betty's office and said hello. That was the total extent of my "marketing" with her.

Two years later, ten days before our 200-page grant applica-tion for federal funds was due, our financial manager quit on three days' notice and left the financial part of the application incom-plete. I did my best to fill it out and get it in on time, and I beat the deadline by twelve hours.

Three weeks later, I found out that I had not done a very good job. Betty called me at work on a Thursday afternoon to let me know that a number of figures were wrong and that she could not submit our application to Washington the next day at 5:00 P.M. unless they were redone. My heart went through my shoes. How could I rework all those figures and still get them in to her in 24 hours? Betty said, "Stay cool. Just put me on hold, pull out pages 23 through 27 of the financial section, go make a copy of them, and get back on the phone." I obediently did so. Betty said, "Okay, see line 27c, column 2? You have $356,798 there now. Change it to $398,558." And so it went. Betty had done my work for me. She had spent the previous evening redoing over 100 calculations and essentially saved my organization. I filled out a new form and overnighted it (this was the era before faxes) to Chicago. We got the grant. ■

I have always believed that because I treated Betty like a friend and a customer rather than as a bureaucratic enemy, she went the extra mile for me. There was no serious cost to this, it was just good marketing.

 FOR EXAMPLE: A few years ago I did a number of focus groups for a residential school that worked with behavior-disordered teens. One of the groups was with a primary referral source: juvenile delinquent officers (JDOs). The session was spent assessing what the school was doing well, not so well, and what it could do better. At the end of the session, I posed the question "What can the school do to make your job easier?" After a long silence, one JDO said, "Interesting question, and one I've never heard before. But one thing does come to mind. You know the admission verification form (J-345A) that you need to fill out after you admit a child that we refer to you? Well, my supervisor is all over me to get those in, because then we get our federal match. Your people are getting those to me in 45 to 60 days, and they're only one page long. Could you get them to us in 21 days, maybe?" The other five JDOs in that session concurred with the need for these forms to be turned in sooner.

I said, "How would seven days be?" "*Terrific!*" they replied, "Oh, and thanks for asking."

"Keep letting us know what we can do," I said.

I returned to the school to report on the session and brought up the request. "No problem," said the staff. "We didn't realize they needed the form in a hurry. We'll get them out the same day, as part of the admission protocol." They started implementing the change that day.

(continued)

(continued)

The next year, the referrals from those six JDOs were up 15 percent, and at this writing, seven years later, they continue to climb, and those six people constitute the highest referral group for the school.

The lesson here is twofold. First, by asking, we made a very positive impression. By responding, we made an even bigger one. It was a small thing—a minor question, a no-cost response—but it paid huge long-term rewards. ■

Do not assume that people who work in a bureaucracy are necessarily mired in it. Choices have to be made: where pilot money goes, or lapse funds, or the most interesting research is run, and on and on. If you meet the wants of the funders, the funders will help you meet yours.

Recap

Marketing is an excellent example of the topic that was broached in Chapter 1: that the business world has a lot to offer the nonprofit world in terms of techniques and expertise. As a mission-based manager, you want to tap that experience in surveying, market identification, promotion, and pricing, all in an effort to do more mission more efficiently and effectively.

You market every day. Your staff need to understand this and that they are a critical part of the marketing team. If you don't market aggressively, if you don't work to keep your market share, you may have none in ten years.

In this chapter, we have covered several issues that are central to the improvement of your organization:

- The fact that everything you do every day is marketing.
- The fact that your markets are much more numerous and diverse than you may have previously thought.
- The real process of marketing.
- The ways to ask what your markets want.
- The ways to develop a discipline of asking.
- The methods to ensure that your marketing efforts are on track.
- Examples of organizations that have profited by asking and by giving even their governmental funders what they want.

Hopefully, you have found ideas that you can incorporate into your organization as you go about building a culture of marketing, a tradition of asking, and an organizational appreciation for your markets, their diversity, and their changing demands.

The importance of continuing marketing cannot be overstressed. It needs to become part of your culture, and should also become an integral component of your staff training and continuing education program—for everyone in the organization.*

Questions for Discussion

1. Who are our markets? Within those, who are our target markets?
2. What do our markets want? How do we know? How often should we ask our target markets? In surveys, focus groups?
3. How do we ramp up our informal asking? Should we look at staff training in this area?
4. What about customer service/satisfaction training for staff? Can we instill the idea that everyone (even our funders) are customers, and that everyone is on the marketing team?

---

*For much more on this subject, see my book *Mission-Based Marketing* (Hoboken, NJ: John Wiley & Sons, 2002).

CHAPTER 11

Financial Empowerment

Overview

A refresher: What's the first rule of nonprofits? That's right: MISSION, MISSION, and more MISSION.

We talked about this at length in Chapter 4 and learned that everything you do, every resource you allocate, every action you take should result in more or better mission being provided. Mission first. But then, what's the second rule? Easy. It concerns the *enabler* of all mission: money. The second rule of nonprofits is this:

NO MONEY, NO MISSION.

Mission *is* first, and money is a close second. Money should never ever be first, but without it, you can't provide mission. So, again, it's a balancing act. Too much mission (and spending all your money) leads to no mission at all; your organization closes. Too much money and not enough mission and you become, well, just a business. You have to factor into your zeal to provide more and better mission the reality that there is only so much money to work with. The fact that your organization is a nonprofit does not mean that the rules of economics are suspended. You still need working capital to grow, still need to make money to have the money to innovate, still pay back debt from profits, just like any other organization.

Chapter 9 focused on using the business model to provide more services while making money to provide even more services. The purpose of this chapter is to show you how to use financial skills and concepts from the business world to make sure that the money you receive from all sources goes to do more mission and, most important, more mission that you want to do, not the mission that your traditional funders limit you to.

Imagine having funds that you can both depend on and that you can spend without approval from anyone other than your own board of directors. Imagine having a great idea or noting a terrible problem in your community and being able to attack it head on, this year, this *month,* without having to go to a foundation or your state capital or to Washington, D.C., for a lengthy review and then denial. Sound great? You bet. This is the reality for many nonprofits today, the ones that have worked toward financial *empowerment* and away from the traditional dependency (and thus subservience) model discussed at length in Chapter 2. Successful nonprofits, those that will flourish over the next ten years rather than wither, will be those who are financially empowered.

Here's the hard truth: If you want to be around doing good service in ten years, you had better work toward financially empowering your organization, starting today.

Here's the good news: You don't have to be big to do this; small nonprofits can be just as empowered as large ones, and often remain more flexible, a key ability of a social entrepreneur. Also, you don't have to have been around since 1932—many start-ups are positioning themselves for financial empowerment from day one.

Here's the bad news: If you are like the vast majority of nonprofits, you are anything but empowered; you are regularly teetering on the brink of financial disaster, you have little or no operating reserves, and your cash flow is too often a trickle in and a river out. For you (and this includes most nonprofit managers) the road to financial empowerment will not be short or smooth. But, you *can* do it; in fact, you must if you are to do your job at all.

In this chapter, we will cover the issues that will allow you to start your plan toward becoming a financially empowered organization. For those who are already working in an organization that is financially stable, these discussions hopefully will reinforce your good habits and perhaps provide an insight or two to help you improve further. In the following pages, you'll learn about the eight characteristics that exist in financially empowered organizations. You'll learn which of the many numbers you can review mean something important, how to communicate about finances inside your organization, and how to estimate the capital needs that you will have from expansion in the next decade.

Then we'll concentrate on how to keep what you've earned, how to find and work with a lender, and how to use your empowerment to benefit your mission, your clientele, and your community. By the time you finish this chapter, you will know what you need to do to become and remain financially empowered.

What Makes a Financially Empowered Nonprofit

I define a financially empowered nonprofit organization by the following eight characteristics, which I break out further into three subgroups:

measurable (having quantified outcomes), *management* (requiring some change in policy or attitude), and *mission* (things that directly impact or enhance your ability to do mission). Let's look at the eight in a little bit of detail.

Measurable

1. *The organization has more revenue than expenses in at least seven out of ten years.* Right out of the chute in Chapter 1, I provided you with my Three Core Philosophies of Nonprofits. The third of these was "Not for profit does not mean no profit." To review: Nowhere in any state or federal law or regulation does it say that just because you are a nonprofit, you must lose money. Remember, you are formed for purposes that are primarily charitable, and thus "not for-profit." No one in Congress ever said you had to lose money or just break even to qualify for your 501(c)(3). In fact, the Internal Revenue Service (IRS) code says "that the profits of the [501(c)] organization shall not inure to the benefit of..." proving that profits are legal in the IRS's eyes. The point? Making money is good for mission.

   On a practical level, we all know that an organization that loses money each year will eventually fold—it's just a question of how long it will take. I contend, however, that each of you should evaluate having an organizational goal of making money nearly every year to allow you to continue to provide high-quality services in the years to come. Why? For many of the reasons we discussed in Chapter 2: little real new government funding coupled with higher demand for services at the same time that there is more competition for everything. You need a profit—yes, a profit—to give you some maneuvering room, to give you the working capital to try new ways of providing service or to expand to help more people. Note: Remember in Chapter 1, I also noted that this does not mean that every service has to be profitable, just the organization as a whole. Some services will always lose money. That's why you have a development department, and it *better* make money.

2. *The organization has a cash operating reserve of at least ninety days.* So many nonprofits go from financial crisis to crisis, and I see organization after organization struggling to make rent and payroll every month. Why? The most common answer is that "we just never seem to be able to get ahead." Trust me, "getting ahead" never just happens. It is planned. It is the result of careful discipline. A comfort reserve is not only stress reducing on senior management, it is also a turnover reducer, a morale booster for both staff and board. As you become financially empowered, you should strive to have funds in an accessible interest-bearing account

equal to at least ninety days' operations. For some organizations, ninety days would be far too little; while some funders do not allow grantees to keep more, for most readers having more cash reserves than they do today would be a good thing on many levels.

3. *The organization gets at least 5 percent of its annual operating income from its endowment.* Endowment? Yes, endowment. They are not just for the big organizations, the ones that have been around for decades. I have a client organization that is only five years old, grosses only $250,000 a year, but annually gets between $5,000 and $7,000 from its $125,000 restricted fund. Endowments for nonprofits are the best way you can get and maintain a source of income that is steady and inviolate. You cannot, like a for-profit, sell stock or even usually issue debt (although that is changing). You can, however, use your 501(c)(3) designation to secure long-term funds in a restricted account or subsidiary corporation (more about this later).

4. *The organization has sources of revenue from nontraditional, nongovernmental funds: It has business income.* More and more nonprofits are developing a business that supports its mission without drawing its revenues from traditional sources. This means risk. We discussed business development at length in Chapter 9 and won't go into all of it again here. Suffice it to say that organizations that do meet this test have done one of the things we need to do: expanded their universe of income streams. Don't assume for a moment that these entrepreneurial organizations are swimming in cash and now independent of their traditional funders; they aren't and never will be. But they do have a source of funds that is no longer dependent on bureaucratic or political whims, and that is a strength in and of itself.

Management

5. *The organization shares its financial information widely and practices bottom-up budgeting.* John Chambers, of Cisco Systems (the people who build the stuff that runs the Internet), says this about his huge organization: "No one of us is as smart as all of us." This wisdom requires him to share information about the company with all of his staff. For you, the empowerment benefit comes from training all your staff how to read financials in general, then how to read *your* financials, and then to see them regularly. You need to get staff more involved in budgeting and spending those budgets. This is, by far, the most threatening criterion of empowerment for most organization's management teams, and we'll spend considerable time later in the chapter on these techniques.

6. *The organization is appropriately leveraged.* Leverage, which is defined as borrowing against an asset, allows many nonprofits to do more mission sooner. It is not for every organization, however, and certainly not for every situation. The ironclad rule is: **Never borrow unless you are making money or plan to shortly.** Thus, borrowing is a way to do more mission, not a way to bail out past poor management decisions. And, as odd as it may seem, your organization can have *too little* debt! We will discuss more on borrowing later in this chapter.

Mission

7. *The organization supports its mission directly by establishing and using a rapid-response mission reserve.* More reserves, you ask? Where does all this extra money come from? First, it is not extra. You need all your money, but putting aside a mission reserve allows you the ability to respond to local needs as they occur, not when someone far away with control of the dollars finally recognizes the problem. This is the ultimate result of financial empowerment.

 HANDS ON: Empower staff to do what you need done here. The absolute best way to use this is to decide on your amount of reserves (you can start today with $500 or $1,000), and then solicit ideas from staff to spend that amount (or some part of it) on *direct service.* Once all the ideas are in, convene a group of line staff members and let them decide which idea(s) should be funded. The key here is to let your line staff make the decision, not you. You get much more motivation and ownership if you let them spend the money. ■

8. *The organization is financially flexible enough to accommodate changes in the service delivery patterns.* Far too many nonprofits have all of their limited assets in their buildings and none in cash. Thus, when an opportunity arises, they cannot take advantage of it. And their mission capability suffers. Financial flexibility may mean having access to cash quickly through a line of credit, or it may mean looking at more leasing and less owning. Or it may mean a larger than 90-day cash reserve. Whatever it takes, if you are going to be a social entrepreneur, you have to let your finances empower you to do so.

As we move through the rest of the chapter, we'll examine some techniques to become empowered, some of which are basic good financial management and some of which are a bit more entrepreneurial.

Something should be emphasized here and now. Becoming empowered is not easy, and it is not the result of a single action in a single year. It is a long-term strategy that combines a commitment to financial well-being by all members of the board and staff, a setting of reasonable goals in each year, savings, reexamining the budgeting process, fund-raising, and usually some corporate restructuring. It is a multiyear (and in some cases decade-long) task. But it can happen in almost any organization with the will to make it happen. So let's get started.

Numbers That Mean Something (and Those That Don't)

While it is important to have more and more diverse income, and to spend less through bottoms-up budgeting, it is also a staff responsibility to manage what you have well. This means knowing where your money comes from, where it goes, what causes income and expenses to go up or down, and in general to understand the finances of the organization. Many managers think they know their organization when they really don't. For example, I know of ten large organizations in which the executive wants to know the cash flow (cash in over cash out for the day) but never asks to see a cash projection. So what if cash flow is positive or negative today? For a capable manager, it's the *trend,* the projection into the future, the analysis of a long period of the past that is important, not so much the present. These execs think that they are in control because they know how much money is in their organization's wallet. They aren't.

On the other hand, Robert Crandall, the former CEO of American Airlines, ran a multibillion-dollar corporation with hundreds of thousands of employees, billions in assets, and operations in forty countries. Was it possible for him to know what was going on everywhere? Of course not. But Crandall did need to know what was important, the numbers that did mean something, and every day, seven days a week for the nearly fifteen years that he was CEO, he got a sheet with ten numbers on it: the ten key numbers that helped him run the airline. What were they? He never told, but in an interview with him, he noted that the ten numbers changed over the years as the priorities of the airline changed. Why just ten numbers and not twelve or twenty? Crandall noted that that is all anyone can really, usefully keep track of and that he set the number as a discipline for himself. If there was something off from the goal or standard in a particular number, he investigated, pursued, prodded, and demanded answers. If not, he left it alone.

A number of points should be noted here. First, Crandall, who was a very successful leader, realized that his job was too complex to spend all his time with a spreadsheet, but that didn't mean he should *ignore the numbers.* Ignoring the numbers is a key mistake that managers who were not initially trained in business (which includes nearly every reader of this book) make: "I'll leave those to others who really *like* to deal with numbers." This is a big mistake, and one that can be fatal. Remember, while the subject of the chapter is financial empowerment, the point of the exercise is *mission*. If you, as a mission-based manager, do not take the time to learn how to most effectively use your financial resources, you are short-changing your organization and the people you serve. Second, Crandall realized that he would lose the big picture if he drowned in detail (pardon the mixed metaphor). Therefore, he limited his daily (and I assume weekly and monthly) numbers to a critical few.

Crandall made his own job easier by setting benchmarks and goals. If the number he got was good in relation to the benchmark, he moved on; if not, he asked questions. This is called putting your numbers in context. This is a critical tool of the successful manager and it will make your job a lot easier. Instead of just getting a report with a bunch of numbers, whether it be a budget, an expense report, a report on occupancy, or new donors, always put it in the context of the past and the goal. So what if you had $450,453.67 in income last year? Was the budget (the context) that you should have had $440,000 in income or $500,000? If your occupancy is 78 percent, is that good or bad? It depends on the context, which for occupancy could both be a goal or the trend from the past three months. Here's the rule: Numbers by themselves can be *interesting*. Numbers in context are *useful*.

So what numbers do you need to know? The choice will, obviously, depend on your organization. Most, if not all, readers will be in organizations that cannot produce daily numbers of any great accuracy. But that does not mean that they cannot produce numbers at all, or on a more regular basis than just monthly. Again, what you need to know depends on your organization, but let me at least propose some general areas that you need to have information on. You will see that most of these numbers are either trends or numbers weighed against a goal or an industry norm. This is important to give you perspective, to give you context. Also, later in the chapter, we will discuss internal reporting, and there will be some actual sample forms for you to consider.

Cash

I make everyone in my training sessions write this down: **CASH = OXYGEN**. Without oxygen, you die. Without cash, your organization dies even faster. You need to have reasonably accurate cash flow projections for six months in advance, and you need to see these every two weeks (have them updated after each payroll). This can be done most efficiently on a spreadsheet, and most good accounting software can also produce them or export them to the spreadsheet easily. Having a good cash flow projection is essential to your organizational well-being in that you know when you will be cash rich and when cash poor. Daily cash in and out is fine, but it is the trends and future projections that you need to focus on most.

Income

If you have income-sensitive numbers that you can see, read them regularly. For example, if you are a museum and your income is heavily dependent on the number of people through the turnstiles each day or week, take a look at that number and compare it to a month ago, a year ago, and any goals that you may have. If you are a school and get reimbursed on a basis of student days, what was your attendance last week? If you are a managed care hospital, you probably want to know your inpatient occupancy, and hope, unlike fifteen years ago, that your beds are *empty,* not full. If you are a church, what was your count of parishioners this week, and what was in the collection plate?

Payables

Payables is the amount that you owe people in the short term. Particularly if you don't write the checks yourself, you need to know the trend in this area. What is the amount of payables that you have (usually recorded monthly) versus a month ago or compared to average monthly expenditures? For example, if your average expenditures per month are $100,000 and your payables are $150,000, you are not paying your bills in thirty days. Worse, if that payables number is climbing while your expenditures are staying the same, you are falling further and further behind, something you *really* want to avoid. Keep on top of your payables and ask questions about making sure you are keeping current and not incurring late fees. You should also see, with your monthly reports, a listing of any and all accounts that are late: usually thirty days past due. Find out why these are late and do your best to get them paid. If they are going to be very late, call the business or person you owe and explain why, as well as your plan for repayment.

Receivables

This is the other side of the coin. Particularly in organizations in which primary customers (government, foundations, insurance) often play such a huge part in your income stream, you need to stay on top of what you are owed. It is very easy for organizations to pay you late if you let them. You need to understand your funders' systems, know how they work, and be a pleasant bug in their ear to get paid sooner rather than later. You need to know how "old" your receivables are and have a policy of when you personally get involved to get a late payment sent. Again, if your income is $100,000 per month and your receivables are $140,000 month after month, or are growing in relation to income, you are getting paid late and it is getting later. Watch this number as a trend and take action as needed.

Expenses

Usually, expenses are recorded and fully accounted for once a month on a monthly statement. I assume that you see the statement the minute it comes out, but do not be content with just the overall statement. You should see the income and expense statement compared to your budget for the month and your year-to-date statement compared with the budget for the year to date. Only by having these comparisons can you ask reasonable questions about expenditures, make staff justify any changes in the budget, and generally stay on top of this key area. Again, this is a once-a-month set of numbers, but many managers just look at the bottom line and don't examine the statement against their previous goal as embodied in the budget.

Remember, too, that your highest expense, unless you are very unusual, is your payroll. You want to keep a handle on how much your people are costing, because cutting people is the most painful thing you will ever have to do as a manager.

Finally, keep in mind that expenses are really investments in mission. We talked about this in Chapter 9, and you need to know your expenses to be able to calculate the return on that investment, not only in financial terms but also in mission.

Balance Sheet and Ratios

Balance sheets are financial snapshots of your organization at the end of each month (assuming that you generate balance sheets monthly). They show your assets (what you own or what you are owed), your liabilities (what you owe or are obligated to over the short and long term), and your fund balance (assets minus liabilities). For many nonfinancial managers, balance sheets are often confusing. However, balance sheets can be used to generate important numbers that help you manage financial ratios. Like so many other tools, ratios are often misused and too often misunderstood.

A financial ratio is a comparison of two factors on your balance sheet (or on your balance sheet and your income and expense statement) that allow you to get a common denominator viewpoint on your organization's financial position.

There are literally hundreds of such ratios, but you do not need to deal with more than a few key ones. Like everything else, which ratios you need will depend on your organization: Talk to your CPA or financial expert on your board about which ones are most important to you and how to use them. Examples include:

- *Profit margin.* Net revenue (profit) divided by total income. Is the percentage of profit high enough?
- *Current ratio.* Current assets divided by current liabilities: This is a measure of how much liquidity you have—can you pay off your current obligations with cash and current receivables? The number should always be higher than 1.0 and probably your goal should be between 1.5 and 3.0 (not including your endowment). Much higher means that you are probably sitting on too much cash.
- *Debt-to-fund balance.* The total debt divided by your fund balance. This number measures the ability of your organization to take on more debt if you need to and monitors your debt against your net worth. You don't want this too high or you will get over-leveraged and interest costs will begin to eat you up.

As I noted, there are lots more of these than bear discussion here since the specific ones that will help you may be very obscure. See your CPA and your banker. Talk with them about which ratios will give you the best help in monitoring your finances.

Administrative Costs

I truly hate having to talk about this, since administrative costs, commonly called admin costs, are far, far too much a concern in our field, particularly to large funders. Funders want to have a way of measuring good management from one nonprofit to another, and they've decided that this is the metric that tells all. It doesn't actually tell them anything from nonprofit to nonprofit, and the enforcement of arbitrary "good" and "bad" admin percentages has done great damage to the sector. Most nonprofits I interact with are *under*administered, not overadministered. And, for what it's worth, I challenge any foundation to show me that it can administer *its* organizations for 12 percent a year. I've been in lots of foundation offices, and I bet they can't come close.

My feelings on this aside, you need to keep track of your admin costs, and report them on your IRS 990. Funders want to see this, and what funders want ... In truth, looking at your organization's administrative load *over time* (Is it going up, going down, staying steady?) can help you manage your own organization better. Just don't waste time comparing your admin load to another nonprofit down the street. You won't learn a thing.

To decide what goes in your admin percentage, sit down with your CPA and come up with your contributors to administrative costs. You have to do this anyway for your 990, so make good use of the numbers. Then keep those contributors steady. Don't add and subtract them at will.

Nonfinancial Indicators

Not all of the numbers you need to see have to do with money. There are other items that bear regular scrutiny that are indicative of whether or not you are succeeding with your mission, your people, and your stewardship. For example, the number of units of service provided per FTE staff person, the number of people on waiting lists for service, the average turnover of staff per quarter or per year, the number of people seeking service for the first time, or the number of people who return repeatedly all could be important to you. Now that you understand that even a nonfinancial manager needs to pay attention to the numbers, don't limit those numbers to the ones with dollar signs in front of them.

Profit and Loss

You need to know what you are earning and losing, and this is so important an area that I've broken it out separately.

Knowing What You Earn (and Lose)

As you have read repeatedly in this book, it's okay for a nonprofit to make money. Not just that, it is essential that you make money seven out of ten years to maintain and improve your ability to help your community. To do that, you have to know what programs and what parts of your organization make money and what parts lose money and, in both cases, how much money is involved. It is fine to have some programs that are subsidized by others: There are things that nonprofits do that will never be fully reimbursed, and as we've discussed before, that's fine if they are mission-rich. But you *have* to balance those programs with profitable ones, or you will be out of business.

The problem for most nonprofits, especially those who get government reimbursement, is that they are trained to manipulate the numbers, and this training leads them to take shortcuts in actual accounting so that they do not know their real costs of operation for anything. I'm not talking about anything immoral or illegal, just about "cost shifting," a very common practice in our sector.

FOR EXAMPLE: A nonprofit mental health agency in the South received federal funds for one of its programs. For the past five years, this particular program has allowed for a 15 percent over-head charge (for all administrative support) in addition to rent, utilities, and actual documentable costs. Whether the actual time spent on the project by the administration was 9 percent or 19 percent, the "charge" was 15 percent, the allowable maximum. If it was higher, the administrator would just say, "That's the most we can get reimbursed." If the actual administrative cost was lower, the administrator would rationalize. "We can get the reimburse-ment, and we need it to cover underpayments elsewhere." In truth, probably no one in the agency ever checked the real costs of administration by watching them for a three- or six-month period. Thus, they never really knew the real costs. As time went by, the agency began an internal accounting method that charged each program for administrative time. The percentage: 15 percent of the amount that they had all gotten used to as their overhead cost. But was it really 15 percent? Almost certainly not, and definitely not on every program. ■

You need to know your real costs of doing business. If you are like most organizations, you probably are pretty good at recording income by program and in doing estimating and accounting of direct costs for an individual pro-gram: the costs of the people, supplies, transportation, and equipment used each day, week, or month. But it is in overhead, administration, rent, depre-ciation, and utilities that many organizations grossly under- or overestimate their expenses.

HANDS ON: Time sheets are a start in teaching your staff where their time is *really* spent. I admit that they are no fun, particularly when staff have never used them before. To make a point with administrative staff about how important accurate accounting is, try this. Ask your administrative team to estimate how many hours in the coming week they will spend on different tasks. You should ask them to break their roles out by program where possible, and then by administrative task: budgeting, marketing, evaluation, fund-raising, and so on. Develop categories that make sense for your organization and then let staff fill in their hour estimates in advance.

Now collect their estimates and have them do it for real, in 15-minute intervals for that week. Have them carry their time sheet with them all day and stop intermittently (at least at lunch and at the end of the day). If your staff are like most of us, they will find serious differences between their estimates and reality. Use this to underscore the fact that a standard organization-wide percentage is not the best way to account for overhead and administrative costs. ■

Once you know your real administrative costs, you can really begin to examine which programs are profitable and which are not. Why? Are you going to simply cut out the "losers" and keep the "winners"? Of course not. There will always be programs that you need to provide that will lose money, and it is naive to think otherwise. But knowing which programs are making money and which are losing (and how much each year) is part of both the management and policy-setting mix. If, for example, a program that is a high priority in your needs assessment or strategic plan is losing money, you will probably be more willing to subsidize a large amount than with a program that has outlived its mission-based usefulness. Alternatively, decisions about where to put your marketing dollars will be a mix on where the most net income can be generated (to subsidize other programs) and how much mission will be accomplished. Thus, the profitability of a program is not, and never should be, the only issue. But it *is* an issue, and one that your management team needs to consider.

Spending Less through Bottoms-Up Budgeting

I will start with the assumption that you have an organizational budget. If you don't, STOP READING AND GO DEVELOP ONE. Now that you are back, let's discuss why bottoms-up budgeting saves money, because, if it is appropriately implemented, it *always* does, even in the best-run organizations.

The term *bottoms-up budgeting* comes from the idea that people at the bottom of the traditional organizational chart (those nearest the provision of service) make the best decisions about resource needs and use. As you already know, in my ideal organization, these people would be nearest the top of the chart, just below the recipients of service. But no matter. The people who need to develop and then monitor your budget are the people who are as close to the provision of service as possible. These people know more than you ever can about what their real needs are, how to spend money most effectively, and how to monitor outcomes best. Why? Because it affects their lives on an hour-to-hour basis.

The Components of Bottoms-Up Budgeting

You cannot just make a major change in your budgeting process by going to your line managers and staff and saying, "Here, write the budget" and expect it to work. You have to do the whole process, and that includes some things you may not care much for. Bottoms-up budgeting has some important components:

- *Training and orientation.* Many of the staff that will be included in the budgeting process will have never seen the budget, much less understand how it was generated. You need to walk them through the budget and help them to understand where your income comes from and its limitations, as well as the history of your expense numbers and how they have been developed in the past.
- *Delegating both budget responsibility and authority.* In using this process of budgeting, the entire point is to pass the responsibility and authority for the budget development and implementation to other than senior staff. But note that I said responsibility *and* authority. If you just ask your staff to help you develop the budget but then micromanage its implementation, you are no better off (and arguably worse) than you are now. What you want is for staff to have ownership and input into the budget development process. Once the budget is reviewed by senior staff and adopted by the board, the line items in the budget should, within programs, be authorized and approved by the line managers within those programs. Thus, if your board has authorized a $5,000 line item for supplies for one of your programs, you as an executive should have no real oversight into what supplies are bought, or when or from whom, as long as the program meets any bidding requirements and stays within its $5,000 per year. For some readers, this will require changes in procedure for payment approval and rethinking their control systems. That is probably overdue for many organizations, and this is a good time to look at these areas. Remember, it's key to give authority with responsibility.
- *Risk taking and risk reward.* This system will not work without the added component of risk and reward. Staff who are monitoring budgets must be at risk for their implementation. Thus, their evaluation should, in part, incorporate their budget management skills. More important, if staff come in under budget on the expense side or overbudget on the income side (for those programs that can impact on their income

statements), they should be rewarded. My recommendation is that, when a program beats its budget, it should get to keep half of the "net." In other words, if you are a private school and your preschool staff cut their expenses by $40,000 under budget, they get to keep $20,000 (at no penalty on next year's budget) to do with as they see fit: buy extra equipment, fund training, allocate funds for a part-time aide, and so on. This reward system is absolutely essential—otherwise, the staff do not have the incentive to look for bargains or cut their costs. Any less than half of the savings and your incentive levels really start to drop. Don't be greedy as an administrator. Remember, you just got some "free" savings, too. Share the wealth and there will be more. Get greedy now and the source of those savings will dry up.

- *Regular feedback and reporting.* The only way that your staff can monitor how they are doing is by regular reporting back to them from your accounting people. The best format is to have a monthly statement that shows actual income and expenses versus budgeted for the current month and year to date. These should be done for each program, and the administrator in charge of overseeing that program should go over the statement with the line staff and manager but only question lines in which there are large discrepancies—perhaps 10 percent in a monthly line and 5 percent in a year-to-date line. This communications flow will help everyone be more comfortable with the delegation of responsibilities and ensure that no program area staff have concerns or questions that are not answered.

If you do this kind of budgeting, you will see results, 10 to 15 percent savings in nonpersonnel lines, and even personnel cuts in some cases. I would not, however, suggest that you implement this wholesale if you have had a traditional top-down approach. Try this next year in the one or two programs with the highest likelihood of success, orient all staff to the new approach, and at the end of the year publicize the results and expand the program.

Don't expect all staff to welcome this idea. Again, here, we have change on the march. Perhaps your biggest surprise will be that those staff who always gripe about not having enough say will resist having control over their budget.

 FOR EXAMPLE: A few years ago, a good friend of mine took the job of headmaster at a large residential school on the East Coast. His predecessor had been at the school for twenty years and had
(continued)

(continued)

been the penultimate autocrat. For the first full year my friend was there, he listened to staff griping about management making ridiculous decisions and how the allocation of resources was just plain stupid. In his second year at the school (the first in which he was responsible for budget planning) my friend called all the program heads into his office and told them that they were going to make the allocations of resources based on the budget mark (amount) that had been received from state funders. He told them that the first year they would only have to allocate the purchases of equipment, books, and classroom supplies. This meant that the managers, who had previously been given these allocations and could just sit back and gripe about not getting enough, now had to come to a consensus on how to divvy up the school's entire allocation for each line item.

The program heads *hated* the job and found it was much tougher than they had ever imagined. Four days later, they came back to the headmaster and asked that he take back the responsibilities he had delegated to them. He refused, saying that it was crucial for them to have the ownership and understanding of the budget dilemma and the allocation of resources. ■

Resistance to change aside, this process works. If you can come in underbudget for the next three years and have enough discipline to then set the funds aside, you are well on your way to a culture of financial empowerment.

Reporting Inside the Organization

One of the key areas where empowered organizations excel is in the area of internal reporting. In external financial reporting, what you do is dictated by your funders, by your auditor, and in some cases by tradition. But internally, you can be much more flexible and creative.

Internal reporting means getting the right numbers to the staff and board. All organizations are different, and what you report and who you report it to will vary with your management style, your organizational policies, your organizational history, your size, and whether you have a collective bargaining unit (a union), but no matter what your shape and size, there is one key tenet of internal financial reporting:

GIVE PEOPLE THE INFORMATION THEY NEED IN THE WAY THAT THEY WANT TO SEE IT AS OFTEN AS THEY NEED IT.

Why should you be flexible in your reporting? Why not just give everyone the monthly profit and loss statements and perhaps a cash flow projection? Let's look at the different groups you need to report to. As you review this list, ask yourself: Do all these people need the same information on the same schedule?

- BOARD—All
- BOARD—Finance committee
- BOARD—Treasurer and Chairperson
- STAFF—CEO
- STAFF—Senior management
- STAFF—Midmanagement
- STAFF—Service providers

Of course, they need different numbers in different forms at different times. And with today's accounting and reporting software, giving each of these groups what it needs in the way it wants as often as it needs it is neither time consuming nor expensive.

In the next few pages we will review some sample ideas of the kinds of information these different groups might want in your organization, as well as look at some sample formats that transmit this information the most efficiently. Understand that these lists are starting points for you, not all-inclusive—because they cannot be. You will need to find the mix of reports and the types of formats that work best for your organization and to do that you need to return to our most basic marketing technique: Ask!

Ask the people in these groups what information they need, how often they need it, and why they need it. Ask whether they want their reports in numerical form, on a spreadsheet, in graphs, or interpreted in writing. Or do they want some combination of these? Once you have established what people want and how much they need, remember to ask them regularly if the information is working. If it is, great. If it is not, amend it. Remember, this kind of information targeting is cheap in both time and money, particularly if it gets the information that people need in their hands promptly. If you gave each of twenty people a half hour a month by saving them from wading through unnecessary data, that's 120 person hours per year or *three weeks* of staff time saved. This is not an unusual savings obtained by targeting your information.

There is, however, information that is *off limits,* information that should not be generally shared. Briefly, this information includes salaries, perks, retirement, and medical information, as well as information on individual contracts and contractors. Additionally, you should never send out inaccurate, indecipherable, or misleading numbers, reports, charts, or graphs. For excellent examples of just such inaccurate or misleading information, look at charts and graphs included in many advertisements and much of the press.

With all of that as background, let's examine when you do send information and who gets what. Let's start with some premises.

1. *The more your people really understand how your organization's finances run, the better.* If your organization is like most, few if any of your staff outside of your central management team understand how your finances work. Most of your staff assume that the money comes from the state (feds, city, foundations), that you have lots of it, and that you are just stingy in giving it out. They probably have no real understanding of how long it takes you to get paid, the reporting requirements that you have to go through, or the true nature of your balance sheet. In truth, most of them have probably never seen a balance sheet and would not know how to read one if they saw it—through no fault of their own.

   If you plan to include staff in budgeting, give them responsibility for their areas of budgeting, value them as individuals: Let them see the numbers that help them do their job. I work with dozens of organizations in which no staff but the executive director and comptroller/financial manager ever see the budget or the monthly profit-and-loss statements or know how much over or under their budget line they are. They don't know where they are in relation to their budget—how much they have left to spend in any line item. But consistently in these organizations, the exec will tell me that his staff are involved in the budget process and have spending authority. How can they when they haven't a clue about where the money came from, is, or will be going?

2. *The more people participate in the budget development process and are held accountable for its implementation, the better.* We've already discussed how you save money by including staff in the budgeting process. Letting line staff develop and be responsible for the budget in their area saves money. But for staff members at any level to be involved meaningfully in the budget development and budget implementation process, they have to have the information they need at the time they need it in a format that they can understand and use.

3. *A little knowledge—especially in the financial area—is a very dangerous thing.* Imagine (and this may not be too much of a stretch for those readers who have had this very thing happen in their organization) a staff member who makes $35,000 per year being given a copy of your organization's balance sheet and reading things like "Total Assets $1,450,000" or "Cash and Securities $267,560." To a person unfamiliar with financial terminology, that could sound as if you have bags of money hidden in your office somewhere. Without the context (that perhaps 90 percent of

your total assets are fixed [buildings] or that most of the cash and securities are in restricted funds), this person will be justifiably upset with the fact that the staff got only a 2 percent raise last year or that needed programs have been cut.

What is the moral? If you are going to hand out financial information, *train* your people in how to use it and what it means. If possible, have an outsider (who will be seen as neutral) come in and go over what a balance sheet is and explain an asset, a liability, a fund balance, a restricted account, a fixed versus liquid asset, and how your cash flow really works. Have the trainer explain how your income streams are set up, how staff can influence them, how growth may actually mean less cash in the organization's hands instead of more, and how an organization should configure itself for financial strength. This training is not only important for the development of the staff involved but it is a key preventative against a general uprising over resources.

Now let's look at who needs what.

Staff

CEO   The CEO of your organization will need a variety of information. Again, what the CEO wants is a decision he or she will have to make, but at the least, the CEO should see the following:

- *Cash flow projection.* The cash flow projection should be for the coming six months shown by payroll or by the 1st and 15th of each month. It should have a rolling net cash line to show the total cash situation. This is a key piece of information that too few people have.
- *Monthly/annual statements versus budget—overall and by department area.* This statement should show the actual income and expense in the previous month and for the fiscal year to date versus the budget for the same period. Problem discrepancies should be investigated.
- *Working capital projections.* How much is the expansion of the organization going to cost? How much should we set aside for a new program? These numbers tell that. We will go over how to project these key pieces of information later in the chapter.
- *Receivables (aging).* How long has it been since your major funder paid you? How much are you owed now versus a month ago and a year ago? This item is important for the CEO to know as he or she interacts with your funders.
- *Occupancy/utilization.* If you have a "capacity" number or a census, show it versus a month or a year ago. For example, if you have residential beds, what is the percentage of occupancy in each program?

If you have a capacity of ticket sales, what percentage was sold? Or what is your count of patrons last week, or the number of students or parishioners? Trends here are key.

■ *Cost of capital*. How much is the cost of the capital you have? For most, this will be a calculation of the overall cost of any debt reduced by your cash invested and adjusted for your working capital "losses." Talk to your CPA about how to calculate this, but watch the number carefully from quarter to quarter. You don't want it to rise too steeply.

How often and in what format should you provide this information? Look at the samples of a CEO Data Sheet (Exhibit 11.1), a Statement of Income and Expenses (Exhibit 11.2), and a Cash Flow Projection (Exhibit 11.3). Note the simplicity of the executive director's sheet, the combination of numbers and charts. Some people like their information this way. If so, give it to them!

SENIOR MANAGERS   What senior managers want and need depends on the areas that they supervise. They will need at least:

■ Organizational cash flow
■ Overall agency statements of income and expense versus budget
■ Similar statements for each department they supervise
■ Budgeting information
■ Occupancy/utilization figures for the areas they supervise

SERVICE STAFF   Service provision staff need information, too. If you agree with my philosophy of information being a good thing and of staff becoming involved in the budgeting process, then they need at least:

■ Organizational cash flow
■ Statements of income and expense versus budget for their area of work

Board of Directors

Does the board of directors need the same information as the staff? No, most of the board should focus on policy and have no need to see the nitty gritty. They are, however, fiduciaries and responsible for supervising the appropriate utilization of your financial resources. The board members need:

■ Information that they can use efficiently
■ Information that makes sense
■ Information without jargon
■ Information that is not out of date

EXHIBIT 11.1   CEO Data Sheet

	Current Month	Last Month	Last Year	Budget or Goal
Revenue	144,533	142,456	132,677	144,000
Occupancy (unit 1)	87.0%	88.0%	90.0%	95.0%
Number of hours billable (outpatient)	2,435	2,490	2,680	2,750
Staff turnover (12 months)	24.0%	26.0%	45.0%	12.0%
Receivables (in days)	43.5	45.0	55.0	40.0
Payables (in days)	32.1	32.0	34.1	30.0
Current ratio	0.50	0.56	0.76	0.45
Cash reserve (in days)	47.6	45.6	32.1	90.0

Cash Flow Summary

	Month 1	Month 2	Month 3	Month 4	Month 5	Month 6
Total receipts	144,000	144,150	149,400	134,080	120,575	265,625
Total disbursements	133,271	132,831	134,861	180,541	133,371	216,611
Net cash flow	10,729	11,319	14,539	(46,461)	(12,796)	49,014
Ending cash balance	34,289	45,608	60,147	13,686	890	49,904

EXHIBIT 11.2   Statement of Income and Expenses

Line Item	Monthly Actual	Monthly Budget	Monthly Variance	% of Budget	YTD Actual	YTD Budget	YTD Variance	% of Budget
Income								
State program	55,400	53,000	2,400	4.5%	310,045	321,000	(10,955)	–3.4%
Medicaid	65,443	61,000	4,443	7.3%	422,449	415,000	7,449	1.8%
United Way	5,000	10,000	(5,000)	–50.0%	30,000	60,000	(30,000)	–50.0%
Fees	18,440	19,500	(1,060)	–5.4%	114,598	124,600	(10,002)	–8.0%
Donations	250	500	(250)	–50.0%	10,500	3,000	7,500	250.0%
Total Income	144,533	144,000	533	0.4%	887,592	(887,592)	(36,008)	4.1%
Expenses								
Salaries	105,800	107,900	(2,100)	–1.9%	623,980	602,300	21,680	3.6%
Fringes	9,522	9,711	(189)	–1.9%	56,158	54,207	1,951	3.6%
Occupancy	2,500	2,500	0	0.0%	15,000	15,000	0	0.0%
Insurance	8,000	8,000	0	0.0%	8,000	8,000	0	0.0%
Utilities	1,244	1,200	44	3.7%	7,698	7,400	298	4.0%
Telephone	857	900	(33)	–3.7%	4,680	5,400	(720)	–13.3%
Depreciation	6,588	6,588	0	0.0%	39,528	39,528	0	0.0%
Supplies	2,240	2,500	(260)	–10.4%	12,679	15,000	(2,321)	–15.5%
Travel	1,243	1,500	(257)	–17.1%	11,340	9,000	2,340	26.0%
Total Expense	138,004	140,799	(2,795)	–2.0%	779,063	755,835	23,228	3.1%
Net:	6,529	3,201	3,328		108,529	(1,643,427)	(59,236)	

EXHIBIT 11.3   Cash Flow Projection

	Month 1	Month 2	Month 3	Month 4	Month 5	Month 6
Receipts						
State program	53,000	53,000	53,000	53,000	53,000	53,000
Medicaid	61,000	61,000	61,000	0	0	183,000
United Way	10,000	10,000	10,000	10,000	10,000	10,000
Fees	19,500	19,500	24,500	18,500	17,450	19,500
Debt received	0	0	0	40,000	40,000	0
Donations	500	650	900	12,580	125	125
Total Receipts	**144,000**	**144,150**	**149,400**	**134,080**	**120,575**	**265,625**
Disbursements						
Salaries	107,900	107,900	107,900	107,900	107,900	107,900
Fringes	9,711	9,711	9,711	9,711	9,711	9,711
Occupancy	2,500	2,500	2,500	2,500	2,500	2,500
Insurance	0	0	0	48,000	0	0
Utilities	1,200	800	850	950	1,450	1,650
Telephone	900	900	900	900	900	900
Debt service paid	7,960	7,960	7,960	7,960	7,960	88,000
Supplies	2,500	2,500	2,500	2,500	2,500	2,500
Travel	600	560	2,540	120	450	3,450
Total Disbursements	**133,271**	**132,831**	**134,861**	**180,541**	**133,371**	**216,611**
Net Cash Flow	**10,729**	**11,319**	**14,539**	**(46,461)**	**(12,796)**	**49,014**
Ending Cash Balance	**34,289**	**45,608**	**60,147**	**13,686**	**890**	**49,904**
Starting Cash	23,560					

Let's look at the differing needs of different parts of the board, from the people who need the most and the most detailed information to those who need just the overviews.

BOARD (TREASURER AND CHAIRPERSON)   These two people need to *understand* how the money flows in your organization—how it is earned and how it is spent. They need to be able to articulately advocate for your financial needs in front of a funder, as well as to give the other board members some peace of mind that someone understands your arcane finances. Thus, they need to see at least:

- Organizational cash flows
- Statements of income and expense versus budget
- Critical information about new or crisis programs
- To be involved early in the budget development process
- Early information on major changes in funding streams (a rate change, a foundation award)

BOARD (FINANCE COMMITTEE)   The finance committee is the key oversight group of the board and should have at least:

- Organizational cash flows
- Occupancy/utilization figures
- Statements of income and expense versus budget each month
- Budget projections
- Working capital projections
- Close involvement in budgeting prior to the budget's going to the board

BOARD (GENERAL)   These people need to be the least involved in the financial oversight, if there is a strong finance committee, and if the treasurer really understands how the numbers run. They need:

- Summary information on cash and income and expenses
- Audited statements from your CPA
- Management letter from your CPA
- Organizational cash flows

See Exhibit 11.4 for an example of a Board of Directors Summary Report.

Remember with the board that you can put all the financial information, not just the report summaries, online in the board area of your Web site so that those board members who want more detail can easily get it.

Again, the key to all of this is to give people what they want in the format they can best use, and to train, train, train in the information's use

EXHIBIT 11.4 Board of Directors Summary Report

Income and Expense Line Item	Monthly Actual	Monthly Budget	Monthly Variance	% of Budget	YTD Actual	YTD Budget
Total income	144,533	144,000	533	0.4%	887,592	923,600
Total expense	138,004	140,799	(2,795)	–2.0%	779,063	755,835
Net	6,529	3,201	3,328		108,529	167,765

Cash Flow Summary

	Month 1	Month 2	Month 3	Month 4	Month 5	Month 6
Total receipts	144,000	144,150	149,400	134,080	120,575	265,625
Total disbursements	133,271	132,831	134,861	180,541	133,371	216,611
Net cash flow	10,729	11,319	14,539	(46,461)	(12,796)	49,014
Ending cash balance	34,289	45,608	60,147	13,686	890	49,904

	Current Month	Last Month	Last Year	Budget or Goal
Revenue	144,533	142,456	132,677	144,000
Occupancy (unit 1)	87.0%	88.0%	90.0%	95.0%
Number of hours billable (outpatient)	2,435	2,490	2,680	2,750
Staff turnover (12 months)	24.0%	26.0%	45.0%	12.0%
Receivables (in days)	43.5	45.0	55.0	40.0
Payables (in days)	32.1	32.0	34.1	30.0
Current ratio	0.50	0.56	0.76	0.45

and meaning. Good information is critical to financial empowerment in your organization. Don't force fit your people's needs to one format. Scrimping of the time and software to make flexible reports will only cost you big time in both the near and long term.

Finally, remember to ask at least annually whether the information is still working. People's needs and wants change, as does the key information the organization produces. For example, a particular program that was running in the black last year may be a loss center this year and need more senior-level attention. Or you may have received some kind of accreditation and need to monitor a new data set. Ask and amend as necessary, but no less than once a year.

Planning for Your Future Cash and Capital Needs

One last part of constructing a financially empowered organization: planning for your future cash and capital needs. This is an area in which many organizations (for-profit and nonprofit) fall flat on their faces because they forget that growth costs money. You need cash for new programs and cash for growth. Unfortunately, it is not just the cash that you will spend on equipment or on a new building or on people. It is the cash that will be lost in the mail: working capital.

Working capital is the money you need to operate on between the time you manufacture a product or provide a service and the time you get paid. The more business you do, the more working capital you need. The longer it takes people to pay you, the more working capital you need. A simple example is this: If one of your programs is currently reimbursed at cost for $120,000 per year, and if the funder of that program pays you in sixty days, you need two months' working capital ($20,000) just to carry your receivable for that program. Now suppose the program doubles in size—presto—you need $40,000. Or perhaps the funder now decides to pay in 90 days—your working capital needs just went up by 50 percent. This is why so many rapidly growing organizations are starved for cash—it all gets sucked up into their working capital. Exhibit 11.5 is a working capital needs worksheet.

You will see a format for estimating your working capital needs that I recommend you use every year. The first column shows the current income per year, the second column shows the projected income, and the third column shows the days to get paid. If you subtract the projected income from the current income and multiply that times the days to get paid and then divide by 365, you'll get the new cash needed next year for the growth in that program. If, as in this example, you do it for all your programs, you'll get a better idea of your working capital needs for the entire organization. If

EXHIBIT 11.5 Working Capital Needs Worksheet

Programs	Start-Up Costs	Current Budget	Next Year Budget	Days Payable Currently	Days Payable Next Year	Cash Need
Residential	0	440,000	480,000	95	100	10,959
Day	0	327,500	410,000	56	56	12,658
Outreach	0	457,000	395,000	55	55	(9,342)
Hot lunch	0	110,000	115,000	45	45	616
Prevention (new)	45,000	0	197,000	0	65	80,082
					Total New Cash Needed	**$94,973**

the number is very large, you may need to start working with your banker to borrow funds to cover the cash shortfall.

The second part of the format has to do with the new program working capital needs. Here you have the development costs (the "up-front" costs) and the working capital costs, which are the income per year times the days to payment divided by 365. Here you see the agency needs $80,082 just to open the new program that will bring in only $197,000 per year!

Do these calculations. They are part of your better understanding of how your organization works, how the cash really flows, and how to do business in an enlightened and empowered manner.

Keeping What You Earn

I wish I had a magic potion to give you to avoid what is still a major problem for many nonprofits in this country: being punished for being financially responsible. However, many funders, from the government to foundations to the United Way, still have the feeling that if you do not use up what you said you were going to spend on a project or a service, they deserve the money back. Worse, some funders still feel that if you have any money, you do not need theirs.

So if you do become empowered, and you have reserves for mission, or for simple financial stability, how do you keep it? How can you do what I suggest and make money seven out of ten years and not get punished? There are a number of ways, and these work solely or in some combination for most of our clients. However, I must caution you: In some states, the government is extremely aggressive about coming after "excess funds." They have an overdose of what I see as "what is yours is ours" (discussed in Chapter 2). Thus, for some readers, there may be little protection today. You may need to start now to lobby for some commonsense regulation that allows you to set aside your earnings in the future.

Here are some techniques that have worked.

1. *Avoid "use it or lose it": Contract rather than grant.* When negotiating with a funder, contract for a specific set of services rather than accepting a cash grant. Negotiate into the contract wording that says that you will provide X services for $Y at Z level of quality, and that any excess is yours to keep, not theirs to recapture. Please understand that this means that if you don't keep your budget under control and you spend more than $Y, you eat the losses: You can't go back to the funder to ask for an increased contract unless it changes the scope of services that it wants.

2. *Put income-producing ventures and/or property into separate corporations.* In Chapter 9, we discussed earned income ventures. If you

start having large enough net revenue from these ventures, it may be beneficial to place them in a new nonprofit subsidiary to harbor their assets. Many nonprofits have their property (buildings, vehicles, equipment) in just such a second corporation and lease it at fair market rates to the primary corporation since the funders will reimburse rent but not depreciation or interest on debts. Please understand that corporate restructuring is a tool, not a panacea. You will probably have to have a related, uncontrolled corporation hold your assets to qualify for reimbursement and thus, technically, will lose control of your assets. Check your funders' regulations on related-party transactions before setting up a second corporation to house assets (other than a foundation).

3. *Have restricted accounts.* Set up accounts that are restricted in use for specific items (e.g., a depreciation account, a capital fund account, etc.). Funders are more likely to attempt to go after general revenue than targeted, restricted funds. Have a board resolution to restrict the funds and have your accountant show them that way in the audit.

4. *Set up a foundation.* Later in the chapter, we will examine the need for an endowment. The most common method to house this money is in a second 501(c)(3) that people loosely term a foundation. (Note: You do *not* want to be a foundation in the technical sense with the IRS. If you file your own paperwork for your new 501(c)(3), do not check the line that says "Private Foundation.") A foundation corporation will allow you to keep the money that you raise out of your current 501(c)(3) and will be a marketing tool for donors, some of whom will be concerned that their donation will just get eaten up in operating expenses.

 HANDS ON: Note that even though your endowment funds will be off the balance sheet of your nonprofit, they won't be hidden in any sense (nor should they be). Your audit will contain a notation titled "Related Party Transactions" or "Related Entities," and your auditor will spell out the relationship your nonprofit has with its endowment. ▪

5. *Work with your funders.* Try to work with your funders to help them see the cost of growth (in working capital), the cost of future capital expenditures, and the need for financial stability and a quick reaction fund for your mission. Explain to them that you are not just hoarding the money; you are managing your resources to the best mission outcome possible.

You can't be financially empowered if you lose everything you have gained. Try these ideas to retain your earnings.

Does Your Board Prohibit Debt?

As I work with nonprofit organizations around the country, I regularly see organizations that have board-generated policies prohibiting the organization from taking on any debt. Often these policies are many years old and may have resulted from abuses by former staff, from former board members' concerns about major funding cuts, or from a feeling that this policy reduces the board's risk and exposure.

When I ask each organization's board about the policy, the conversation usually goes something like this:

Board: We cannot take on debt because our funding is only approved annually. If our funding were cut, we would be unable to pay a loan back.

Peter: How many of you have lifetime guarantees of employment? (No hands go up.) How many of you live in a house that you paid cash for? (No hands go up.) Okay, so you took on a debt, a risk, even though your major source of income (your salary) may be ended at any time?

Board: But that's different. We are individuals. Our board job entails responsibility for an entire organization, and we must be prudent.

True. But nonprofit organizations are also business, and business is risk. The real issue here is how much risk your organization is willing to take on behalf of the people you serve. Understand that I am not talking about highly leveraged, sub-prime loan craziness. This is not the "Real Estate with No Money Down" commercial you see on television.

What is important to understand is that, in some instances, taking on debt to expand a service, build a building, or purchase equipment may be a *good* risk to take on behalf of the people you serve. Each organization is different, as is each situation, but I strongly recommend that you consider *all* your options in planning your future and carrying a prudent amount of debt is one avenue many highly successful businesses (both for-profit and nonprofit) use to grow and serve their customers better.

Working with Lenders

As a CEO or CFO (chief financial officer), you may think that your most important working relationship is with your board president, with your key governmental or foundation funding source, or with another key staff person. But sooner or later, your most key business relationship is going to be with your banker. The problem is that if you are like most nonprofit staff you have little or no relationship with a bank, other than having a checking account and perhaps a certificate of deposit or money market account.

Why is this a problem? There are a number of reasons, the most important of which are:

- At some point as your organization grows, you will need to borrow.
- The lending decision process excludes you.
- Most bankers don't understand nonprofit finances, and all bankers fear what they don't understand.

Let's look at each of these in more detail.

1. *You will need to borrow.* Sooner or later, you will almost certainly need a loan, either to cover cash flow (when your major governmental funding check is late and you have to make payroll) or to cover the advance costs on a new contract.

   Nearly all organizations need some form of debt at some point, and your credit rating (how lenders look at you) is influenced in no small part by how well those lenders know you and how promptly you have repaid any past debt. But commercial banking is, oddly enough, a personal business, and your personal relationship with a single person in a single bank will go a long way toward improving your "creditworthiness."

   Nothing, of course, can help you like a solid balance sheet and profitable (net revenue over expenses) operations, but you will find that even with good numbers, no one will want to take a risk on your organization until they know you and understand your organization (more on this later).

2. *The borrowing process excludes you.* Second, when you go in for that loan, you will (let us hope) have prepared your numbers, showing the need for the debt, the term (length) of the loan you need, and how you plan to pay it back (where the funds will come from, over and above your normal day-to-day expenses). You will give this information to your banker, and the banker will ask you a number of questions and then say, "Thanks for coming. I'll get you the answer in a week."

   What happens now? The banker prepares whatever forms and applications are necessary and takes the application before a loan committee, made up of people who probably don't know you, who have only a superficial understanding of your organization, and whose job it is to minimize the bank's risk (in other words, figure out all the reasons they can to turn your loan down).

Your only advocate, aside from the material you prepared, is your banker. If you have not kept your banker up to date on your organization, your activities, and your plans, the odds are that the bank (particularly in the current environment) will not take a risk on you and your loan may be reduced, be made very expensive (a high interest rate or loan fee), or denied altogether. So you need your banker solidly in your corner, and later I will show you how to do so.

3. *Banks don't understand nonprofits.* The third issue is one that makes the first and second tougher to resolve: Banks and bankers often don't understand how nonprofits work. To a banker, not knowing about something is risky, and risk to bankers is like acid rain to industrialists—something they would rather avoid thinking about, thank you very much.

Look at it from the banker's point of view:

You get most of your money from one source—government—and every-one "knows" that this source is, at best, unpredictable and, in any event, only guaranteed for one year at a time. You (the executive director) are probably not a trained manager, and your organization prides itself on giving services away and does not collect very well from those who are supposed to pay. You are overseen by a citizens' committee of well-wishers and do-gooders, staffed by a bunch of program zealots. Who is watching the store, and why should I lend my bank's money? I mean, you are a nonprofit, and loans are only repaid from profits!

Sound exaggerated? It's not. I have heard every single one of these arguments from well-educated, well-meaning bankers, referring to nonprofit organizations that were (despite the banker's prejudice) very well run. And just think about the bank's willingness to take risk after the 2008–2009 financial meltdown. They went from too high a willingness to take risk to no willingness at all. So having an advocate inside the bank (your banker) is even more important than ever.

The problem is one of education as much as it is internal operations, but you do have an uphill battle with most lending institutions, no matter how much they love what you do and no matter how much they have given you in donations or staff time in the past.

There are a number of things that you can do to beat these problems and to develop or improve your relationships with your lenders. Here are the steps to take:

1. *Fix up your finances.* First, get your internal house in order. No business, for-profit or nonprofit, is going to be given a loan if its financial house is outside of the metrics the bank wants. Make sure your internal act is

together before you go the bank. Regular statements, an annual audit, and good cash and receivable controls are all essential. So are many of the things we've talked about in this chapter: making money, knowing which programs make money and which lose, tracking your productivity, being aware of trends in your field. In short, be businesslike while pursuing your mission.

2. *Seek a banker, get to know him or her.* Once your house is cleaned up, and if you don't already have one, go down and meet a real commercial banker. As noted earlier, banking is, at its heart, a personal business. The banker will want to know lots of information about your organization and will also be keenly interested in *you*—your background, your attitude, your management skills.

   Meet with this person regularly, every six months (one good time to go in is just after your annual audit comes back, then on a six-month basis). Talk business—your industry, your past six months of operations, your high and low points. Let the banker see that you know your organization from a business point of view.

3. *Give the banker lots of information.* As we said before, what people don't understand, they fear. This information should include at least the following: your monthly statements; your audit; your newsletter; copies of all major grant awards, certifications, and so on; and all news releases and newspaper articles on your organization *and* your field. Keep your name regularly on your banker's desk. The more he or she knows, the better off you are.

Invite the banker to visit your program site(s) once a year. If you have multiple programs at many locations, pick a different one each time. Invite the banker to a board meeting, particularly the one that includes discussion of your budget. Let him or her see you in action. If you have an open house, or ribbon cutting, or press conference, send the banker an invitation.

When you are developing your strategic plan, invite your banker to sit in on the financial parts of the discussion or at least review the numbers. The same for a business plan, a capital spending plan, and so on. Such a consultation will have lots of benefits. First, you will receive excellent advice and ideas. Second, you'll know what to expect from your banker if any part of the plan requires debt. Equally important, your banker will be similarly forewarned about your requests and you will give the banker more "ownership" in your organization.

The idea is to develop a long-term relationship that benefits your organization and the bank. It is an ongoing process, a discipline, but one that will pay off enormously when you need it most. Remember, the banks want "good" business. You want to be a good business that does good things. By working together, you can both accomplish your goals.

Finding the Right Bank

Now you know why a good relationship with a banker is so important to your organization. But there's more to it than that. The banker with whom you work will only rarely be the owner. Bankers are employees of the bank and must abide by its policies, processes, priorities, and, of course, its prejudices. These may very well affect your banker's ability to meet your needs and thus may preclude your wanting to invest a lot of time fostering a relationship that, as far as you are concerned, is a one-way street running the wrong way.

So what should you do? Well, first, let's get our perspectives straight. You are the *customer*. I know that's hard to believe, given the way some banks treat you, but it's the truth. Remember, the bank is *selling* you money. In fact, the bank is almost certainly selling *your* money (your checking deposits) to *other* people for short periods of time. Unfortunately, some bankers tend to forget this with small businesses or with nonprofits, and it is up to you to remind them politely of the fact.

Still, you want to find the bank with the best set of services and the best possible attitude toward your organization. Just as with anything you buy, it is prudent to shop around for a bank, even if you have been using one to your satisfaction for some time (some would say, *particularly* if you have been with one bank for a long time). But what is the best way to compare? Here are the steps to take.

1. *Start at the top.* Find someone who knows the CEO of each of the three or four (or more) banks that you wish to check out. Have that person (let's call him Mike) phone the CEO (let's call her Jan) and inform her of your interest (let's call you Joe). Have Mike say, "Jan? This is Mike. I heard that Joe's organization is looking around for a new bank, and I thought you might want to give him a call, since I know you're always looking for some new customers. He's got an annual budget of around $1.5 million. Just thought you'd like to know."

    Now what has Mike done? He's done his friend Jan a favor, and he has not taken any risk by declaring you a good risk. Proving that is your job.

    Now you wait and see how far down the organizational chart you dribble. If Jan or her first vice president calls you back and invites you to lunch at the bank to explain the bank's services, you know the bank is interested and will probably treat you pretty well (assuming its prices are competitive). If, on the other hand, you are never called back, or your call is returned by a junior loan officer with $2,500 in personal loan approval authorization, then you have a good idea about what that bank thinks of nonprofits in general and of yours in particular.

2. *Remember that you are the customer.* For the banks that call back, you need to take the next step: shop prices and services. Always ask what services are available for a commercial account. Are there checking fees? What minimum balance waives such fees? Do balances in checking over a minimum earn interest? How much? Are investment services (CDs, money market accounts) available? What types of loans does the bank make? What collateral do they want? Who makes the decisions?

Also ask for comparative interest rates and terms on lines of credit, equipment loans, and receivable loans.

 HANDS ON: Banks will often tell you that your loan is "two over prime." The question to ask is, "Whose prime, and what is it today?" Some banks use New York prime, and some use their own (often inflated over New York by 1 or 2 percent). You need to know the rate so that you can make a valid comparison. ■

Ask the bank for small-business references, as well as references on other social service clients. (Be prepared for a shocked look. Bankers are rarely asked to give references.) Then check out the references. Ask the reference person at least the following questions:

- Who is your contact in the bank? How is your relationship with that person? Do you think your contact person values your business with the bank?
- How long have you been a customer? Why did you choose this bank? What services of the bank do you use? Are they of high quality? Were loans easy to apply for or a major hassle?
- If there were periods during which you had a downturn, did the bank stand by you or get nervous? How did your banker act toward you in hard times?
- Do you feel that your banker understands your business? What has your banker done to show interest in your organization?
- (Explain a little about your organization.) Would you recommend your bank (and banker) to me? Any advice on how to deal with your banker?

  Weigh the financial information along with the reference checking and then make your move. If you are bringing a major account to the bank (over $1 million in payroll in most towns, less with smaller banks), negotiate for the waiving of fees. Once you choose your bank, stick with it unless service declines or prices jump dramatically. You should build a long-term business relationship with the bank and the banker. Jumping from bank to bank is bad business, unless you are poorly treated over a period of time.

Note, however, that many banks are being bought and sold these days. If your bank is acquired by a new owner, this should lead to a reevaluation on your part of whether the bank still sees you as a priority customer. You should also reevaluate whenever you are assigned to a new loan officer.

Finding a good bank, one that values you for your economic contribution to the community as well as for your mission, is one of the best management moves you can make. It takes some time, but you will reap the benefits over and over in the coming months and years.

Creating an Endowment

Wouldn't it be nice to have a cash machine, one that churns out money every year—regardless of whether the government funds you or donors give to you—one that you could depend on, not have to advocate or beg for? There is such a cash machine: It is called an endowment, and lots of your peer organizations have one—even organizations that are very new and very small.

My rule for endowments is this: You need a large enough endowment to have *at least* 5 percent of your total annual income come from the endowment's earnings. That means if your endowment earns 5 percent return each year, it needs to be the same size as your annual budget. If it earns 10 percent, it needs to be half the size of your annual budget.

Why do you need to do this? For a number of reasons. First, it's good fund-raising marketing: You need a steady source of income, and sophisticated donors know this. If you just ask for money with no endowment, you can ask only for operating or special funds. If you create an endowment (usually in a separate 501(c)(3) foundation), you can attract larger funds from people who know that their gift will keep on giving. Second, you need the steady income, income that is free of the need to lobby, the need to beg. And don't stop at 5 percent. That's the *minimum*. If you can have 20 percent of your income per year from the endowment, great! Just think of all the additional things you can do. Third, you have the resource of your 501(c)(3) status, which allows you to take financial contributions. Use it, and not just for current operations. Show some long-term vision and save for the future.

I am not an expert in development and fund-raising. Thus, I will not even attempt to tell you how to go about this. I would merely lead you astray. There are, however, a number of excellent texts on the subject. Make it part of your long-term planning to put aside funds in a restricted fund or in a foundation established so that you get the income, but do not touch the principal. This is the toughest part: the discipline of not touching sources of funds when you have done without for so long. Learn how, and your organization will really benefit.

Using Your Empowerment

Getting to the point where you feel you are financially empowered will continue to be a tough, long-haul job. So why do it? Why raise the expectations of your staff, board, and, yes, yourself to do this work now for the benefit of others in five, ten, or even fifteen years? For a number of reasons. First, it's your job. You are not just a senior staff person for this year's work; you also are building a better organization for the long term, at least you are supposed to be. I hope you buy property for the long haul, with an eye to minimal maintenance and hopefully to appreciated resale value. I hope that you buy computers and software with the capability to upgrade easily and inexpensively and that you buy vehicles based on utilization and on repair and resale records. If you are doing this, you are investing in the future. When you spend money and time on a strategic plan, you are investing in the future. And, when you train staff, or start a marketing plan, you are counting on a future reward for your investment.

Imagine if you or your predecessor had started financial empowerment planning for the organization ten years ago. Just think what you could do with that money now! The second reason to become financially empowered is that it is good mission. Only by becoming less dependent on your key funders will you and your organization be able to meet the needs of your community quickly and with the skill and knowledge that you alone possess. Your ability to do good mission and thus the value that your community places on your organization will both rise. If the mission is the reason for your existence, financially empowering your organization is a key component, and one that you need to start on—today.

One other caution: It is key in empowerment planning that you bring all the staff, board, and funders in on the plans early, if possible. You need to educate your staff and funders to the fact that having money is okay, and the fact that you have some funds now and are putting other funds aside is not an indication that you have given up on the mission and are hoarding. You need to let them know that these funds that you are setting aside are targeted for mission, for long-term income, and for financial stability. As noted above when we discussed keeping what you earn, work with your funders and staff on the front end to let them have input, and it will pay off here.

Recap

If only doing all of these things could be included in your next one-year plan! But there is much to be done, and some of it takes a great deal of time, no matter how good your intentions or how great your financial or service needs. But by reading this chapter, you've made a start on the long road.

We have covered a lot of ground in this chapter and have started you on the road to empowering your organization financially. Now you know the eight characteristics of financial empowerment. You know how to use numbers to your benefit and how to pick those numbers that mean something to you and those that don't. You have been exposed to methods of using financial and nonfinancial indicators to tell how your organization is doing and how to give different people in your organization the numbers that they want and need to do their job.

Finally, I have shown you some ways to predict future financial needs so that you can plan well in advance and not get caught short.

Again, no money, no mission. Financial empowerment will take your organization from being a creature of the 1970s to being a thriving, contributing member of your community in the twenty-first century.

Questions for Discussion

1. What parts of this chapter apply to us?
2. How do we do in relation to the eight characteristics of empowerment? Where can we do better?
3. What can we do to improve our internal reporting? What information do people need to see when? Can our software accommodate different reports?
4. How do we feel about spending the time and money training our staff to understand our financials? Do we want to share them? Why or why not?
5. How do we get started on an endowment? How soon can we get something in place?

CHAPTER 12

A Vision for the Future

Overview

Nonprofits that succeed, that thrive, that are going to be providers of the best mission over the next decade, all know where they are going. A vision for what you want your organization to be and a road map of how you want to get from here to there is absolutely essential if you are to be a good steward of your nonprofit's resources. This chapter will give you some hands-on ideas of how to plan and how to use both the planning process and the plan itself as a tool for the benefit of the organization.

In this chapter, you will read about the nine distinct phases of the planning process, and I will provide some detailed ideas on how to use that process to your best benefit. We will review the four reasons why you should develop and maintain a plan, examine some varying philosophies of planning, and I will offer recommendations on how often you should plan, how inclusive the planning process should be, and how to go about evaluating the planning process and the plan's implementation status.

After that, we will look at various types of plans, define some important terms in the planning process, and look at outcomes that you can expect from a good planning process and plan. I will also describe a variety of uses for your plan once you have it completed. We will look at some barriers to planning, and I will include an outline for your plan to help you get started.

By the time you finish with this chapter, you should have a better understanding of the task you need to tackle. If you are new to planning, reading this chapter will help you get acquainted with the need for planning and how to do it. If you are an experienced planner, you will probably pick up a nugget or two for how to do your next plan even better.

The Phases of Planning

Good planning comes in several phases. The following phase list is fairly complete, and we will review each phase in some detail. However, I want to make several points about the list as a whole. First, the sequence listed is just that: a sequence. While it allows for a great deal of flexibility in how you actually do the planning, I urge you to do your planning in this order. In my quarter century as a consultant, I have helped well over seventy-five nonprofits of all types and sizes develop their planning processes and their plans, and this sequence has been tried and tested: It works. While there may be a certain overlap, for example, with Data Gathering starting about the same time as the Retreat and extending into the time of Drafting Goals and Objectives, the basic sequence should be preserved.

The phases of planning that I suggest are:

1. Preparedness
2. The retreat
3. Data gathering
4. Drafting goals and objectives
5. Outside comment
6. Final draft and adoption
7. Implementation
8. Evaluation
9. Go to step one and start over

We will go through each phase in some detail, but first we need to discuss some philosophies, decide on which type of plan you intend to develop, provide some definitions, and look at the outcomes of planning that you can expect.

Why Plan?

Too few organizations that I consult with have a strategic plan. The excuses are many, and we will discuss them in more detail near the end of this chapter, but the most prevalent concern is "with rapidly changing circumstances I don't want to be stuck with some plan that is totally out of date." I agree. But the planning horizons that we will talk about are not overly long (three to five years), and the key to strategic planning is one of strategy, not of tactics. The issues that you should be considering in a strategic plan need to be planned for and should not be greatly changed within the planning cycle. Also, your planning process should be ongoing, so that if some major change is initiated in your field, you can adapt the plan to it. I would also argue that few, if any, major changes in service delivery or funding patterns show up for work at 8 A.M. one morning unannounced. Usually, major changes are researched, discussed, rumored, and debated for months or even years before they are enacted. Thus, in the part of the planning process during which you look at the environment, you will be able to predict most of these changes in advance.

Still, organizations resist. Many people tell me that they cannot plan when things are chaotic or in times of organizational trouble. They contend that so much is up for grabs that it does not make any sense to plan for the future. I disagree. When things are at their most unknown, what do you need to show you the way, to help you make choices, to guide you back from the abyss? Your mission? Yes. Your values? Yes. And your strategies—the decisions you have made on what is most important, which service markets are your priorities, and what your organizational core competencies are and what they are not. If you have those three things (mission, values, and strategy), you can get through a lot of disorder, change, and disruption. And, if you have the first two but not the third, in a chaotic environment, developing the strategy can point you in a clear direction, stopping you from feeling like you are fumbling around in the dark.

And when things change (and they always do) good plans actually help you remain flexible because, like good marketing, they keep you and your organization focused on what is important. They assist you in not wasting resources and not getting tied down in fruitless or out-of-date services, and keep your staff and board up-to-date on the realities of the world in which you are working. Finally, the well-run planning process is often a wake-up call for board and staff members who still think they are working in 2003, and this enlightenment makes later change less difficult for them.

With that in mind, let's examine the four reasons that you should expend the time, money, energy, and political capital to develop a plan.

1. Without a Plan, the Only Way You Get Where You Are Going Is by Accident: What Your Organization Does Is Too Important to Occur by Accident

Yogi Berra said it even better: "If you don't know where you are going, you will wind up somewhere else."

 FOR EXAMPLE: Let's look at the planning process through the metaphor of a family vacation. If you and your family are getting ready to go on vacation, once you know you have the time off and want to go together (preparedness) you will certainly get together as a family and decide where you are going (the retreat). Let's assume that you decide to drive to San Francisco and stay for a week. You have to first set the long-term goal of getting there.

(*continued*)

(continued)

Your strategy is to go by car. To achieve your goal you may check out some options for things to do online, buy a road map, make sure you have sufficient funds, and review the condition of your vehicle (data gathering), and plan your route, program your GPS, and set your itinerary (set goals and objectives). You will check the conditions en route and in San Francisco—things like the weather, roads, tolls, and fuel and hotel costs (assess the environment)—and probably call some friends who have been to San Francisco recently for ideas and feedback (gather outside comment). You will investigate their suggestions online, look at reviews, and make your decisions about how to use your time. You then finalize your plans, get packed, and leave (implement). If between home and San Francisco, you find that a road is under construction, there is a place you had not heard about, or there are other sights that you want to see, you may vary either or both of your route or your timetable.

Congratulations. You have just done strategic planning. The important thing to remember here, however, is what you *did not* do. You did not just pack up, drive to the first corner, and say, "Where are we going?" and then go to the next intersection and say, "Which way?" and the next and the next. That would be an interesting vacation indeed.

But in your organization, when you do not have a plan, when you act only in reaction to events, when you go from only one funded program to the next or one community need to the next, you wind up in some very strange and sometimes dangerous places, just the way you would on your vacation if you chose each turn at random. Planning allows you to see where you are going and to transmit that information to the people who are going with you: your staff, board, funders, community, and, most important, the people you serve.

2. A Strategic Plan Allows All Other Planning (Budgets, Staffing, Fund-Raising) to Be Coordinated

When you have a good, current strategic plan, you can coordinate the activities of your organization better by using the strategic plan and its overall goals as a backstop for decisions. You can discuss management, program, and policy choices in light of the priority goals of your plan. You can ask questions about whether a particular item in the budget supports the long-range plan. For example, if in your strategic plan you have a five-year goal to build a new building and you need to have 30 percent of the cost of the building put aside, you probably need to show that set-aside in this year's financial plan. And if as part of that building program you intend to have 40 percent of the cost paid for by a capital fund drive starting in two years, your marketing and development staff had better be laying the groundwork for that fund drive this year. Without your strategic plan, you cannot accomplish this type of coordination.

3. Plans Allow You to Delegate More Effectively

Successful managers know how to delegate well and how to push the line staff to make as many decisions as possible. Giving up responsibility and authority is very difficult for some people, and having the framework of the strategic plan can make that action easier: The manager who is delegating has a work plan based on the strategic plan for the subordinate to work with. Also, if the subordinate was involved in the planning process, his or her understanding and ownership will be much higher and the likelihood of effective delegation will increase.

4. Plans Are Good Business—And Good Stewardship

By now you know that I consider your nonprofit a mission-oriented business. Good businesses of all types know where they are going. They know their markets and their resources, and they have a plan of how to use the second to please the first. They may differ in their products or services, and often differ in their internal philosophies, but they all have one thing in common: a strategic plan that frames the rest of their activities and provides a benchmark for evaluating their success or failure.

Planning Options

There are a variety of ways to do planning. These options include how often plans should be updated, how inclusive the planning process should be, and whether to regularly evaluate the implementation of the plan. I have summarized these choices below to point out some of the advantages and disadvantages of each. I then provide my recommendation for each area.

Frequency

While there are an infinite number of permutations of the combination of planning horizon (how long the plan is to be in effect) and planning update (how soon should the plan be redone), the following options are the most common.

- *A five-year plan updated every five years.* This is obviously the long-term view, and the advantage is that you only have to think about the plan twice each decade. The problem is that it assumes that everything will go as planned, both inside the organization and outside it, for the full five years, and that is naive, to say the least. Imagine a five-year plan written in January 1998. It could not have foreseen the 2000 crash in tech stocks, the 2000 election of George W. Bush, or the September 11, 2001, terrorist attacks.

In addition, over five years, people (on both the board and the staff) will have left, and there may be only a few of the core planning team remaining. Thus, the lessons learned and the ownership gained will be lost. In short, five years is too long.

■ *A one-year plan updated each year.* This sounds and acts an awful lot like your annual budget accompanying work plan document. It is the most capable of reacting swiftly to changing circumstances, but you lose the big picture and tend to be shaped by events rather than shaping them. We criticize the government (at all levels) for not thinking beyond the current fiscal year. Don't fall into the same trap. Strategic planning needs to be that: strategic.

■ *A five-year plan with one-year components.* This is a combination of the first two, but one that works fairly well. It allows for the long-term strategic vision to guide the flexible annual plan developed each year. The problem with this is that the overall big document is not done often enough, at least in my experience.

■ *My recommendation: A plan with a five-year horizon redone every three years.* I believe that the best way to approach the strategic planning cycle is on the basis of a five-year plan, redone completely every three years, but with annual work plans done every year. Let me explain. A five-year horizon forces the staff and board that create the goals and objectives of the plan to step back from the day-to-day concerns of the organization and do some big-picture thinking. This is essential. By reworking the full plan every three years, you accomplish three important things: You keep the planning process fresh in the organization, you can react to environmental changes, and you can have each board member take part in the creation of a strategic plan once in each of his or her three-year terms, which is the term limit that I recommend in Chapter 6. By having an annual plan of actions that support the strategic plan, you have the staff pull out the highest priority items for each year's work plan, and the board is kept apprised of the implementation status of the plan.

Process

Once you decide what planning horizon and update schedule you will use, you then need to decide what process of planning you will have. Here, you have what I think is a golden opportunity to maximize the use of the planning process itself as a tool for organizational growth, improving staff and board morale, and marketing your organization. However, your realization of that goal is dependent on the type of process you choose. Some choices are:

- *Keep it small.* The idea here is to have the fewest possible number of people involved in the planning process so that you get it done quickly. Thus, staff and board might go on a short retreat to set the goals and priorities; then the senior staff would draft the plan and bring it to the board for review and approval—short and sweet, and in the implementation stage soon. The problem with this idea is that it short-circuits one of the biggest benefits of planning: bringing more people in for their ideas and thus giving them ownership.
- *Highly inclusive.* Speaking of ideas and ownership, that is what the inclusive process is all about. Inclusion in the planning process is designed to get input from all of your staff, board, funders, community representatives, clientele (or their families or representatives), and any other group that you may need or want, such as referral sources or alumni. You do not need to put all of these people on one giant planning committee. They can be brought in three ways: having a planning committee that is more broadly representative than just board members; asking a large number of people for input through surveys and focus groups during the data-gathering phase; and encouraging a broad review and comment on the draft plan during that phase. In this way, you offer the opportunity to have input to a much larger group, they in turn now have a feeling of pride in being asked and ownership in the final product that would not have been possible in the "keep it small" philosophy. Inclusion obviously takes longer and is somewhat more expensive, but I am a strong advocate for using this method.
- *Planning committee generated.* This model has the board appoint a strong planning committee, made up of board members or board and staff combined, who generate the plan on their own and bring it to the board for review and comment. Although not exclusive of the inclusion method noted above, this type of process usually does not include a data-gathering phase that looks at more than hard data such as demographics and almost never includes outside review and comment before the board sees it. It is a variant of "keep it small," but the one that organizations with strong committee structures (which I also advocate for) tend to fall into. Again, this process is fast and controlled, but it loses the opportunity for inclusion. It also does not include the entire board in the retreat setting, which I feel is a mistake.

- *Staff generated/board reviewed.* In a strong staff model of organization, there is the tendency to allow the staff to lead the board, and this sometimes includes the development of the long-range plan. Here, a group of senior staff would develop a draft plan and have it reviewed (and usually adopted with few changes) by the board. This model leaves the board—an essential resource—out of the loop and also usually forgoes the inclusion that we have been discussing. It is fast and it is controllable, but I feel that it has more drawbacks than benefits.
- *My recommendation: Be as inclusive as possible.* My recommendation is easy to predict here: Include as many people as time and money will allow. Start with a retreat of all board and senior staff. Then give the primary responsibility for coming up with a draft plan to a planning committee made up of board, senior staff, line staff, clientele, and community members. Ask lots of people for their input. Circulate the draft plan and listen to the comments. Publish and distribute the plan widely. This method is a lot of work, but it is the best method of maximizing the value of the planning process in addition to getting the best plan.

Evaluation

Unfortunately, most people don't evaluate their plan at all, or hold off doing the evaluation until it is time to do the next plan. If you are going to use the plan as a management tool, you need to constantly be reviewing where you are in relation to where you wanted to be (your deadlines for your goals and objectives).

You need to review your progress toward your goals regularly. Otherwise, you will get to the end of the planning cycle (three to five years), look back, and discover that you have achieved only 15 percent of your goals because you got distracted.

- *My recommendation.* Use the plan as a management tool. Once a month, review it in senior staff meetings, asking the questions "Are we on schedule for this goal? If not, why not? Have conditions changed? Are the resources that we thought would be available not there?" The same holds for board meetings, but this should only be done quarterly.

Also, when the plan is complete, your planning committee needs to make written recommendations to the board about how to do the planning better the next time. These can be used by the next planning committee. If you don't write it down now, you will forget it, and the experience of this committee will not benefit the next one.

Types of Plans

There are several categories that I put plans into. I have seen literally hundreds of strategic plans, and I think that these categories are relatively fair. All of the plans that fit into these categories are intended to be strategic plans, and every one of the people who wrote them intended them to be useful and flexible. But something happened along the way, and the results are as follows.

Tomes

These are documents that rival a New York City telephone directory in size, take a professional football lineman to lift, and that nobody reads. They include everything you ever wanted to know plus a lot more, and they are too imposing and all-encompassing to be flexible and useful.

Work Plans

These are just work assignments for the staff, often put together to submit to a major government funder. They cover the "what" in minute detail, but do not relate it at all to the all-important "why" or the "how"—the mission and the strategy. They also ignore the larger issues that flow from strategies, such as which services should be provided to which constituencies.

Public Relations Documents

These documents purport to be plans but spend most of their time selling the organization. They focus on the need for the organization in the community and the wonderful things it has done in the past. This leads to a lack of objectivity and an inability to see the organization "warts and all," which is crucial to good planning. Also, a strategic plan is not an appropriate place for you to do your marketing. It is not supposed to be a sales brochure or a "feel-good" document.

History Text

These plans make up for their lack of forward thinking with a heavy emphasis on past accomplishments and how your organization was formed and grew. They are often produced by organizations that have grown rapidly and are so caught up in looking back at how far they have come that they forget to look ahead and see where they are going. This kind of plan is a great document for a student of your discipline who wants to know your history, but it usually only pays superficial attention to the changes in your community and where you want to be in five years.

Doctoral Dissertation

This is a highly technical document full of jargon and acronyms. These types of papers are written by staff people who use the technical veil to hide a lack of understanding of some of the fundamental issues, such as "What is our mission?" They cannot see the forest for the technical trees, and such a document is useless to nonprofessionals in your field, such as your board, some staff, the community, and the people you serve.

Working Document

This is a document that provides strategic vision but also practical application. It is a document that attends to the mission and a document that is written in lay language. This document is one that is true to the wants of your clientele and expresses the best of what your board and staff have to offer.

- *My recommendation.* I want you to do your best to get a working document as the product of your planning process. I'm sure you do, too, but be wary of the traps that others have fallen into and try to avoid the other types of plans listed above.

Planning Definitions

Now it is time to define what I mean in the planning process. There are lots of different definitions and ten times that many misuses of the terms listed here. But, for purposes of our discussion, here are my definitions:

- *Strategic plan.* A working document that discusses the organization's mission, the environment that it will work in over the planning period (three to five years), and the goals and objectives to realize the mission over that period. This is not a work plan, but it should be written with enough specificity that it is usable on a monthly basis by staff.
- *Goal.* A statement of desired long-term outcome. A goal may or may not be *quantified,* but it usually does have a *deadline.*
- *Objective.* A much more specific statement that supports the goal. All objectives must have a *deadline,* be *quantified,* and have an *assigned responsible agent*—that is, the person, group, or organization that is responsible for implementing the objective on time. There can be many

objectives to implement a goal. Sometimes they will be sequential, sometimes simultaneous.

- *Action statement*. The most specific item on the list, action statements support the implementation of an objective. They too need to be *quantified* and have a *deadline* and an *assignment of responsibility*. For most organizations, these statements will be included only for high-priority goals or in the one-year plan that flows out of the five-year plan.

Outcomes of Planning

What can you expect from the planning process? If you use my recommendations and renew your plan every three years, use an inclusive model, and evaluate the plan regularly, you can expect at least the following benefits.

- *Better and more effective services*. By evaluating during the plan development process what is needed and wanted and what is not; by asking people instead of assuming you know; by bringing customers, clients, patients, students, or parishioners into the planning loop, your plan will result in better and more effective services. You may find that you need to reduce or eliminate services that no longer make sense in terms of mission or in terms of markets, and you may find that services that you are sure are needed are not wanted and that certain services that you never even considered are in high demand. You will also hear a lot about current services: what works, what doesn't, small ways to make big improvements, and practical (and sometimes impractical) methods of being more effective. The planning process helps you focus your resources on what is important, and that means better and more effective services.
- *Higher ownership and morale*. If you follow the inclusive model recommended here, you will have a higher overall morale of staff, board, funders, community, and clientele. Just asking people their opinion, just including them in the loop, flatters them. If you then follow through and actually use some of their suggestions and get back to them and let them know that they were listened to, all of those who participated now have a stake in what you do and who you are. Additionally, if you are like most organizations that either (a) don't have an organizational strategic plan or (b) developed it a long time ago with only a few people, most of your staff as well as many of your board may never have been given the opportunity to see the big picture, to step back and look at the organization as a whole. Being part of an inclusive strategic planning effort allows that to happen.

- *Lower levels of conflict.* Planning and the planning process I recommend facilitate a forum for healthy debate over resources, discussions over direction, and airing disagreements over policy and the shape of the organization in the future. By providing a positive structure for healthy conflict to emerge, and for unhealthy conflict to be vented, you allow those who harbor a grudge, have not had their say in the past, have felt "muzzled," to get on their soapbox and have that say. While not a preventive for all conflict in the organization around policies and resource allocation, planning does provide the forum, and it does also let people have a clearer view, in writing, of what the organization stands for. This will confront some board, some staff, and perhaps some funders with the choice of staying or leaving, but the clarity of purpose and the focus on the future shape of the organization do make future actions more predictable, and it is often when people are surprised by actions that they are most upset. You will hear much less "nobody told me we were going to . . ." than before you developed and then published your plan, at least on major issues.

The Planning Process

Now for the planning process itself. As I said earlier, I hope that you will adopt a process that meets your own organization's needs and capabilities but still holds to this basic sequence. There is a lot of room for customization in this outline. For example, you can vary the time set aside for each activity. You may want the entire process to take three months (which is very, very fast) or allow it to take eighteen months. You may want to do focus groups only in your data-gathering phase and not to do primary research or surveys. You may decide to have the planning committee meet monthly or just three times during the process. You may decide to minimize the preparedness phase or take three months to have everyone in the organization trained in goal setting.

All of these variations are fine, as long as you don't skip any of the phases altogether. I know it is tempting to go straight to the fun part—the drafting of goals and objectives—but if you do, you miss a once in a three- to five-year opportunity for your organization. Take the time to do this right.

Preparedness

There is no point in starting this until you are ready. To get prepared, make sure that a number of things are in place. First, ensure that your senior staff and key board members agree that planning is important and that they are willing to commit the time and the money necessary to see the process through. Second, develop a planning process and get your board to agree to it. Third, using the draft planning process, develop a planning budget, both of time and cash, that will be committed to the plan. Cash costs could include a retreat facility, meals and travel, data-gathering costs such as surveys, focus groups, and possibly a consultant. I always recommend that organizations get a facilitator for their retreats, and, if this is the first time you have planned, you may also want to hire a planning consultant to help you lay out the process and advise you around the potholes. Never hire a consultant to write the plan. That is your job.

The Retreat

The best way to get started is by getting away. I strongly suggest that all board members and senior staff go away for a day to cover at least the following things: a review of your mission, an agreement on the planning process itself, a discussion of the environmental conditions under which you will be operating, the development of preliminary goals, a prioritization of those goals, and an appointment of a planning committee. Have such a retreat at the start of each revision of the plan (every three years, in my model).

 HANDS ON: Having facilitated more than sixty retreats, I strongly prefer the evening-morning model over any other. Get your group together for dinner, let them review your planning process, review the mission, and consider in what kind of world they will be operating in the evening. Then quit and socialize. In the morning, the retreat participants will return fresh and ready to set goals and put them into a priority order for you. This model produces better results because it gives people a break and also allows the staff present to socialize with the board—a key extra benefit.

At the retreat, you need to do at least the following:

- Review and agree to the planning process.
- Review and update your mission statement as necessary.
- Discuss your predictions for the world in which your plan will be implemented. What trends or activities are going to affect you and how? Walk through a SWOT analysis at this time as well (SWOT stands for strengths, weaknesses, opportunities, and threats).
- Set preliminary long-term goals.
- Discuss the goals and do an initial prioritization.

Data Gathering

Once you have the key goals, you can begin the job of data gathering. You can do this through hard data research and gathering from your internal data or at the library. Additionally, you can run focus groups and surveys of such people as staff, clientele, funders, alumni, and the like. For more information on surveys and focus groups, see the section on them in Chapter 10.

The data that you gather now will be used to help the planning committee and its subcommittees make the most knowledgeable decisions about the issues that confront you. Some data gathering will go on throughout the planning process, and you do not need to wait to begin drafting fuller goals and objectives until all the data is in.

Drafting Goals and Objectives

Now comes the fun part: the examination of the goals and the setting of objectives to support them. You can use one of two methods for this. The first is to have your planning committee do all of this work for all of the goals set at the retreat. The second, used by most of the organizations that I assist in planning, is to have specialty subcommittees that examine certain areas in depth. For example, you might have a subcommittee on Administration, one on Finance, one on Programs, one on Development, one on Marketing, and so on. The breakout of the groups will depend on your organization. A school might break the issues out by primary, middle, and secondary programs. A church might have subcommittees on Finance, Church-Based Programs, Outreach Ministries, and Buildings and Grounds.

The benefits of using the subcommittee model are that each subcommittee can go into its subject in great detail, and you can add people to the planning subcommittees who are experts in this area. More inclusion.

Whoever is setting the goals and objectives needs to look first at the goals that came out of the retreat. Can they be consolidated? Improved? Are there important issues that were overlooked in a one-day retreat? Once the goals are established, then each goal in turn should have objectives added to it. This will happen before, during, and after the data are gathered. In fact, the setting of preliminary objectives will help you identify additional data that you need to go after.

Remember that the goals are long-term statements of desired outcomes, but the objectives need to have a deadline, be quantified, and have someone or some organization responsible for their implementation.

Outside Comment

This is really the most important step for the organization as a whole. Once the goals and objectives have been fully drafted, it is time to get outside opinion. Let as many people as you have time for offer their comments. You can do this online and on paper. Post the draft plan on your Web site in .pdf form; let people know it's there by e-mail and ask for comment. In addition, distribute the plan in paper form to those who you feel will not use the online version.

I usually suggest that major funders, your banker, key referrers, community leaders, representatives of your clientele, and all of your staff get a chance to review and comment with a deadline for getting their comments to you of about two weeks. Bring all of the comments to the planning committee. Many organizations resist this step—and do so to their detriment. By asking outsiders, you get great ideas, develop relationships, and foster ownership. Don't skip this step!

Final Draft and Adoption

When the planning committee has reviewed the comments and any late-arriving data, the final draft can be written. At this time, a second prioritization should be done, and the highest priority goals should be tackled in the one-year plan for the first year of the planning cycle.

This one-year plan should be developed by staff and should include action steps to accomplish high-priority goals and objectives. The staff should run the one-year plan by the planning committee, but it really needs only a cursory review. The one-year plan is really a work plan for staff and board, and it is the plan that needs the most careful monitoring.

Once the board adopts the plan, get it printed and distribute it widely.

Implementation

As noted earlier, the plan should be a working, useful document. Its use as a tool will be discussed in a page or two, but the point of the product is to do what the plan says. You have invested a great deal of time and effort getting the plan together, and while the process has been useful, you still need to do what you've committed to. Implement!

Evaluation

I have already told you how I think you should evaluate the plan's implementation, but you also need to evaluate the planning process. Write down any things you would change or improve and file them away for the benefit of the next planning committee to benefit from.

Go to Step One and Start Over

In three years, start again. By then, you will have had three one-year plans, conditions will have changed, you will have accomplished a great deal, but probably not all of your goals, and it will be time to develop a new five-year plan.

Using the Plan as a Tool

Once you have the plan completed, printed, and distributed, you now need to use it. There are a number of uses for your plan, some of which people neglect or never even consider.

A Management Tool

It should go without saying that the plan should be written in a format that allows you to use it as a management tool. Too few organizations do, however. The plan tends to collect dust until it is time to update it, and then there is no interest in doing the update.

The progress in achieving the goals, objectives, and action statements in the *one-year plan* should be reviewed at least monthly in staff meetings, and, in some cases, every two weeks to make sure that you are still on track, that situations have not changed, or that resources have not been reduced to make it more difficult to implement the plan. The senior staff as well as the line staff need to stay on top of anticipated deadlines and work toward meeting them.

The *strategic plan* implementation should be reviewed monthly at staff meetings and quarterly at board meetings as a formal part of the session. Either staff or the planning committee can report on progress.

As new issues develop during the year, staff and board need to consider their impact on the plan. How will this affect our ability to complete the goals and objectives? If it will interfere, is this a higher priority? Which is more in line with our mission and our strategies? Use the plan as a guide, but do not be constrained by it.

A Marketing Tool

An organization that has a plan has a marketing tool. I know that I said that marketing and sales material belong in a marketing or sales piece, and that is still my position: The plan should be written as a plan, not as a sales brochure. But the very fact of your having a plan puts you ahead of many organizations, for-profit and nonprofit. It is like having a mission statement: It helps people to know who you are and where you are going. For certain people—funders, potential donors, elected officials—it lets them see who you are and where you intend to go. This is excellent marketing in and of itself.

A Policy Tool

A plan will help you do good policy because the strategies included will remind you and help new staff and board who join you to see what the belief of the organization is. For example, if you are a school for hearing-impaired children, your organization may have adopted a communications policy that calls for the use of ASL (American Sign Language—the language preferred by most deaf people as opposed to signed English) on the campus. This policy will be reflected in your goals ("Within two years the school will have 100 percent of faculty and 90 percent of nonteaching staff fluent in ASL") and objectives ("The Director of Instruction will provide four ASL courses each year for staff," "The Director of Instruction will offer three off-campus ASL courses for parents per year," "The Director of Instruction will offer ASL to the general community three times next year"). All of these push the communications policy further and actualize it with a speed that would have only happened haphazardly otherwise. If you don't agree with the policy of ASL implementation, the plan tells you right up front, and if you are an ASL advocate, you also know that the school is in agreement immediately upon reading the plan.

A Recruitment Tool

As with the use of the plan as a marketing tool, the plan becomes an excellent recruitment tool to attract the board and staff that you want. You can show people the plan, and they will know before they decide to come what kind of organization you are and where you are going. If they like what they see, they are more likely to stay. Also, the better potential candidates (both staff and board) will be impressed with the simple fact that you have a plan and are more likely to choose your organization over a competitor for their time or services.

I hope that you recognize that your plan is valuable in a number of ways beyond the process and the document. You have spent a lot of time, effort, and money to develop the plan. Now, as a good steward, it is your responsibility to use this new resource as fully as possible.

Sample Plan Formats

I have included some outlines of plans to get you started or to help you revise and update your plans if you already have them. These are templates and ideas that you can use and improve on. Do not be wedded to them if they don't work for your organization. Rather, use them as a starting point. I have included outlines only for strategic, marketing, and business plans. You'll also need a technology plan and, for many organizations, a quality assurance plan.

For each type of plan, I have included my suggestions on the purpose, horizon (how long the plan should look out), and cycle (how regularly the plan should be rewritten), as well as a definition of what the plan should support. Note that the horizon is often longer than the planning cycle. That is intentional. I want you to think long but rewrite regularly enough to keep abreast of current events.

Strategic Plan

> *Purpose.* To guide the organization as a whole toward the realization of its mission.
>
> *The plan supports.* The mission.
>
> *Planning horizon.* Five years.
>
> *Planning cycle.* Develop a strategic plan every three years, with annual components written every twelve months.

STRATEGIC PLAN OUTLINE

1. *Executive summary.* Key areas of action, priority goals.
2. *Introduction to the plan.* Why you developed the plan, how it will be used.
3. *The planning process.* Who was included, what the process itself entailed.
4. *The history of your organization.* No more than two pages on your organizational heritage.
5. *The organization today.* A three- to five-page description of your services, clientele, and funders.
6. *The world we will work in.* A listing of assumptions about the future environment and how they will affect your organization.
7. *Goals and objectives.*
8. *One-year plan.* The priority goals and their objective and action steps for the first year.
9. *Time line.* A visual representation of the goals, objectives, and action steps, usually called a Gantt or PERT chart.
10. *Evaluate and update methodology.* How and when you will evaluate progress toward implementation, and when you will revise the plan.
11. *Appendices.* Minimal supporting information for the plan.

Marketing Plan

Purpose. To guide the organization as a whole toward the realization of its mission.

The plan supports. The mission.

Planning horizon. Five years.

Planning cycle. Develop a strategic plan every three years, with annual components written every twelve months.

MARKETING PLAN OUTLINE

1. *Your mission statement.*
2. *Executive summary.* A brief summary of the marketing plan, including a list of your target markets, your core competencies, and how they match up with the wants of the markets.
3. *Introduction and purpose of the plan.* A rationale for the uses of the plan. This section can also include a brief recitation of the planning process and its level of inclusion.
4. *Description of the markets.* A full description of your major markets, their wants, their numbers, and projected growth or reduction in demand from these markets.
5. *Description of the services.* A description of each of your services, including number of people served, service area or criteria for service, and any accreditation that these services may have earned.
6. *Analysis of market wants.* A review of the surveys, interviews, or focus groups that you do to prepare the plan. The wants of the markets and how they match up to your core competencies should be included here.
7. *Target markets and rationale.* Out of all your potential markets, you will choose a few priority targets. Describe them here in more detail along with your reasoning for their prioritization.
8. *Marketing goals and objectives.* The goals, objectives, and (for annual plans) action steps that will get your marketing strategies implemented.
9. *Appendices.* Minimal supporting information for the plan.

Business Plan

Purpose. To guide the organization as a whole toward the realization of its mission.

The plan supports. The mission.

Planning horizon. Five years.

Planning cycle. Develop a strategic plan every three years, with annual components written every twelve months.

BUSINESS PLAN OUTLINE

1. *Title page identifying the business plan as the property of your organization.* This cover letter includes your name, address, and telephone number and the month and the year that the plan is written or revised. One paragraph states in simple terms who the business plan belongs to and the limitations on its distribution.
2. *Table of contents.*
3. *Summary of the plan.* A brief paragraph about your organization; a four-line description of the product or service; a four-line description of the market; a brief paragraph on production and one on distribution, if needed; and a short paragraph on the financing requirements.
4. *Description of your organization and its business with the following sub-headings:*
   - The organization
   - The product or service
   - The target consumer
   - The consumer's want for the product or service
   - The sales strategy
5. *Description of the market.* For your product or service, including information on the competition and cost price comparisons between competitors and your organization.
6. *Marketing plan that includes information on:*
   - The markets
   - Customers
   - Competitors
   - The macro-environment
   - How each of these areas affects the marketing and selling of your product or service
   - Evaluation of potential pitfalls
7. *Financial plan with sources and applications of cash and capital and:*
   - An equipment list
   - A balance sheet
   - Breakeven analysis
   - Cash flow estimates by month for the first year, by the quarter for the second and third years
   - Projected income and expenses for the first three years, and notes of explanation for each of the estimates
8. *Goals and objectives with a timeline.*
9. *Minimal appendix with:*
   - Management resumes
   - Survey or focus group data from customers
   - Other pertinent material about your organization and its work

Recap

In the first pages of this chapter, I said that without a plan, the only way you get anywhere is by accident and what you do is much too important to be accidental. Too many people depend on your organization and its services to let your management and policy setting be one long ad lib. You need to have a plan to focus you, to help you set priorities, and to guide you in the most stressful times that you will face.

In this chapter, we have covered the key parts of planning, the four reasons why it is critical, both in the process and the product, for your organization to have a consensus on where it is going. I have urged you to use an inclusive process, which will help your implementation of the plan and improve the ownership in your organization, the morale of your staff, and the positive impression of your funders. We have seen a planning process that has worked well for many of my consulting clients, and finally I have reviewed for you the outcomes and uses of planning, how to get the most out of the document that you have put so much into.

Planning is good management, and thus good mission. It is a way to get everyone involved in having your organization meet its mission commitments more efficiently and effectively. You have the time to plan. All you need to do is choose to.

Questions for Discussion

1. Are we doing all we can to focus on our future through good planning?
2. Should we consider developing (or revising) a strategic plan in the next year?
3. How can we integrate more long-range planning into our culture? Who should be involved? Should we rethink our planning process to be more inclusive?
4. What kind of plans do we need that we don't have?

CHAPTER 13

The Controls That Set You Free

Overview

All managers—for profit or nonprofit—worry. They worry about things going wrong, people messing up, accidents happening, checks not clearing, the network going down, wrong items being ordered, low-quality services being provided, donors backing out, supervisors not following disciplinary procedure, and the thousand little and big things that can occur without warning.

Over and over in my work, managers and executive directors tell me that they worry about not being on site all the time because "people won't know what to do if something goes wrong, and I'm liable if they screw up." This, of course, chains the executive director to his or her desk because it assumes that the staff people are unable to handle all but the most ordinary and routine situations.

If you agree with my suggestions and theories on delegation that were laid out in Chapter 7, you know that you cannot reach your potential as a manager nor as an organization until you delegate well, at all levels of the organization. But how can you do that and still sleep at night? You can with good controls in place, good training on how to use those controls, and accountability to make sure that those controls are used each and every time.

Let's first define controls: Controls are sets of policy and procedure that both standardize actions in your organization and clearly lay out accountability and responsibility in key areas of the organization. You want controls that protect you, while at the same time do not overly hamper your flexibility and creativity and, admittedly, that's a bit of a balancing act. Too much controlling and people have no room for personal creativity and contribution; too little control and people lose the guidance and checks and balances that come from well-written, balanced policies and procedures.

FOR EXAMPLE: When my wife and I moved to our home in Virginia in 2007, we installed an invisible fence for our then-five-year-old Brittany spaniel, Lacey. The fencing allows Lacey to roam, sniff, sit out in the sun, and enjoy being outside without either Chris or me having to watch her or keep her on a leash. A bit of training was involved on where the limits were, and Lacey tested the limits once pretty quickly, and then has respected them ever since. Both Lacey and we are happy with the results.

Obviously, you and your staff are not pets, but the concept is the same: Set a limit, allow people to roam free within those limits, and don't worry about moment-to-moment oversight. ■

This chapter will help you sleep better and leave more room for that much needed creativity time. Why? Because having good controls is the best enabler of both sleep and free brain time I know. In this chapter, I will give you my insights on how to write good, solid management control documents, ones that guide your organization, reduce risk and waste, and let you manage rather than administrate.

We'll first look at how to develop controls, and then review the following types of controls:

- Bylaws
- Conflict-of-interest policies
- Financial controls
- Personnel policies
- Media policies
- Volunteer policies
- Quality assurance policies
- Program policies
- Disaster policies

Finally, we'll examine how to train and enforce the standards and controls that you have set.

The Control Development Process

The process for control development and management is daunting if your organization has very few controls in place, or if they are out of date. However, this process can be broken down into segments and taken one step at a time. The process that is suggested below will be inclusive, bottoms-up, and as relatively painless as possible. I would suggest looking at the list of policies that you need and putting them into priority order for development.

Try to develop any policies that you need and don't currently have within the next year to six months, and get the rest updated within the next twelve. Make sure that you review the policies you have in place to assure that you consider the items that I suggest for inclusion.

- *Get examples from other organizations.* There is no point in reinventing the wheel. Ask your trade association or other nonprofits in your community for copies of their policies. Note the strengths and weaknesses but do not automatically adopt their system; it may not be the best for your organization. Look for samples online by searching for "sample nonprofit X policies." You'll be surprised how many are available to review right online and this can save you considerable time and effort.
- *Write the policy in draft.* You have to start somewhere. Write the policy in draft for your organization or have a staff person do it. Now, review the draft with a board/staff committee and, in the case of certain policies, such as financial or HR, with an expert such as your banker, certified public accountant (CPA), or local HR expert. You can make good use of a "professional volunteer" in these situations. I'll discuss that more below. Most important, make sure that you include at least one person on the committee who will *actually use the policy day to day.* For example, if it is a disciplinary policy, include a line supervisor, midmanager, and senior manager on the policy development team.
- *Float the policy for comment.* After your inner circle and experts have had a crack at the draft, let *everyone* who may have to work with the policy have a chance to comment. This means letting your funders see quality assurance policies; your entire board review conflict-of-interest and media policies; your bank, CPA, and funding auditors look at your cash controls; and your staff see discipline, reward, and compensation policies.
- *Amend and adopt the policy.* You'll remember that I've repeatedly said that boards are supposed to be all about policy. Here's a place that they get their chance. Any major policy needs to be discussed and then formally adopted by the board of directors.
- *Implement the policy.* Start by distributing the new policy and then hold orientation and training sessions for all staff and/or board who are affected by the policy to make sure that everyone understands why the policy is there, how and when it is to be used, and their responsibilities and authority under the policy. Repeat these sessions until everyone has been trained, and then repeat a refresher course, particularly for conflict of interest, interviewing, hiring, discipline, and firing at least once a year.

■ *Review and update the policy regularly.* Each policy should be formally reviewed at least every two years. Dating the copy of the policy on file will help remind you to update it.

 HANDS ON: Right on the front of each policy note two things: **the date the policy was adopted** and **the date the policy needs revision.** This front-page reminder will make it much less likely that you will forget to update and keep your policies current.   ■

 HANDS ON: In many of your policies and procedures, you will have forms: evaluation, cash receipts, travel reimbursement, time sheets, and the like. Make sure that in every case you include a sample of the form *filled in* as an example. I have yet to see a form and instructions, no matter how clearly written, that were not misinterpreted by someone. You should also have samples of all completed forms on the staff (or board) section of your Web site. Having a filled-in form as an example, in addition to blank ones for immediate use, allows the potential user to have a clear idea of how to use the form. Doing this will reduce frustration and save a great deal of time.   ■

■ *Enforce the policy.* There is no point in doing this if you are not going to enforce your expectations that people follow them. State clearly in the policies that failure to follow them will be cause for discipline for staff and for removal for board and volunteers. Put similar wording in the personnel policies and board and volunteer manuals, and make the following of policy a criterion in your evaluation process.

The development of good policies may seem to you to be tedious and bureaucratic. Is it tedious, yes; bureaucratic, no. This is good management—excellent stewardship. Why should you take the time to do control and policy development when you have so many other pressing things to do? Because having good controls will free you up to do good mission. Good controls emancipate managers from constant worry about people making avoidable mistakes; they allow you to delegate fully, and to use your time, energy, and talents on *managing* the organization rather than *administering* it. This is a crucial difference.

In *In Search of Excellence* (New York: HarperCollins Publishers, 1982), Peters and Waterman noted that those organizations that had good controls could free their managers to be the visionary leaders that were necessary to achieve and maintain excellence—the "simultaneous loose–tight" organization. Waterman later expanded on this characteristic in his book *The Renewal Factor* (New York: Bantam, 1987). Other management gurus have noted the same correlation: If you are sitting around worrying about cash controls, personnel management, or discrimination suits, you are wasting time. Those things can be (for the most part) prevented by having and enforcing good policies. Nothing is perfect, but this is a good start.

Again, this is not bureaucracy or a waste of time putting things on paper: This is good, solid management. It can turn into bureaucracy at its worst—a constricting, top-down, controlling, initiative-limiting mess—but it shouldn't. You need to work with your people to design the controls and do it with an attitude that "these will help us do our job better, will take a lot of the questions out of routine procedure, and will free us up to be creative to do more of our mission."

Types of Controls

There are numerous sets of policies and controls that you can develop. The following list is not intended to be all-inclusive, but it is extensive. It covers the types of policies I have seen organizations develop poorly, or sometimes not at all. Sometimes the latter is better than the former, because poorly written controls can be very dangerous. At the very least, you need:

- Bylaws
- Conflict-of-interest policies (usually in your bylaws)
- Financial controls
- Human relations policies
- Media policies
- Volunteer policies
- Quality assurance policies
- Program policies
- Disaster policies

Each of these areas will be discussed in some detail in the following pages. Note, however, that I am *not* contending to be an expert in each of the areas noted. Many of these controls (HR, financial, QA) are highly technical and have to do with your compliance with state and/or federal law. You will need to consult professionals in your community to ensure that you are in line with all laws as well as with your funders' regulations and your contractual obligations. What I will try to do is to point out key items that people forget to put in, and to point out places where I have observed flaws in policies at many organizations.

HANDS ON: Policy development is one of the areas where my technique of recruiting a "professional volunteer" works best. The purpose of the recruitment is to get a real expert to look at your problem—in this case, your policy—without requiring him or her to a long-term commitment as a board member. What you do, taking your personnel policies as an example, is go to the chief executive officer (CEO) of your bank or of another large company that has supported you in the past and say, "We're reviewing our personnel policies this year and wondered if you had a staff person who could provide us with his or her expertise in personnel issues for three or four two-hour meetings over the next three months?" Then the CEO gives you the name and feels like he or she has made a "donation"; the expert gives his or her time, but doesn't feel saddled with a long-term commitment; you get your expertise for free; and the expert may, in fact, become enamored of your organization and agree to help again, serve in another capacity, or donate to your organization! This technique also works for other tasks such as improving a survey, creating a logo, reviewing a media release, etc. ■

Bylaws

Bylaws are required by statute in all fifty states for a nonprofit, as well as by IRS regulations. You have them, but how recently did you and your board review them? Here are some things you should check for:

- *Mission statement.* You should review this every one or two years. You should file any substantive changes in your mission statement with the IRS and with the appropriate state official in your state (usually the Attorney General or Secretary of State). (For more on mission statements, see Chapter 4.)
- *Board selection and term.* Have the board turn over. My suggestion is that each board term be no more than three years, with two consecutive terms before a member has to go off. Perpetual boards tend to perpetuate past policy—long after it is out of date. The selection of the board can be from the membership, by the membership, or by the board itself, depending on your state and funding streams' requirements. (For more on boards, see Chapter 6.)
- *Quorum.* Don't box yourself in by saying that you need eight members for a quorum (on a fifteen-member board). What if, due to unforeseen but reasonable circumstances, four board members resign and you have no one to replace them with for six months? Suddenly you need

73 percent (eight of eleven) rather than 53 percent (eight of fifteen) to do business at a board meeting. You need to say, "A quorum of the board shall be constituted by more than 50 percent of the board members serving as of the date of the meeting."

- *Dissolution clause.* Make sure you have a clause detailing what happens in case your organization closes. You need to state that you will pay off your liabilities and that the remaining assets will then be distributed to one or more 501(c)(3) corporations. You can specify the corporation(s) if you wish.
- *Standing committees.* I urge people to name the standing committees and their responsibilities in the bylaws.
- *Intentions and restrictions.* Without being too wordy, you should state particular intentions and restrictions. If, for example, there is a second signature requirement on checks over $10,000, say it here. If, as I hope, it is the intent of the board that the committees will have a great deal of authority, say so here. If it is the intent of the board to delegate certain authority to the executive director/CEO, say so here.

Conflict-of-Interest Policies

While conflict-of-interest policies are usually included in your bylaws, they are more than important enough to discuss as a separate item. Remember in the first chapter I briefly discussed my prediction that you will operate under more and more scrutiny during the next ten years—scrutiny from the public, the press, your funders, and your donors. One of the areas where nonprofits are most vulnerable is in the writing and interpretation of their conflict-of-interest policies. Don't forget: It is not the facts that count if you wind up in the local paper or on a watchdog blog as having had board members who benefited financially from their board position; it is the *appearance of impropriety* that will sink you. You want to design your policy to prevent the appearance of impropriety, to prevent actual abuse, and to be enforceable should someone try to self-aggrandize.

There are three schools of thought on these policies, at least as far as I have observed in my consulting experience. They can be categorized as follows.

Overkill

In an effort to prevent any and all appearances of impropriety, the policy says that no board or committee member can provide any service to the organization for compensation, and if a relative of the board or committee member is under consideration for such a service contract, that person not only cannot vote on the issue but he or she has to actually leave the meeting until the discussion is concluded.

This is, frankly, a bit much. If you live in a small town like I do, there are only so many qualified people around, and automatically excluding them from providing services to you will not only prohibit you from using some valuable resources, it will also almost certainly be a disincentive to serve on the board.

Underkill

The policy says that the board shall not personally profit from its relationship to the organization, but it has no clear guidelines as to what that means, how to assess it, or how to enforce a violation. In essence, it trusts the board members to do what is right. This is living in la-la land. Board members are like all the rest of us: 98 percent honest, 2 percent not so ethical. You need to use common sense and have policies that prevent abuse, while at the same time not insulting the 98 percent of the board who are honest and upstanding.

 FOR EXAMPLE: Far too long ago, I was on the board of a social services provider and became vice chairman of the board, and thus, by default, the chairman of the finance committee. This organization was then twenty years old and had only had one executive director, who had run the organization from its infancy through the stage of having well over 100 employees. When I arrived, the board was a loose confederation of original board members, titular members (local state representatives, aldermen, etc.), and family members of persons served by the organization.

At the time I became finance committee chair, I was also the newly hired executive director of a health-planning nonprofit, and in my new job I had undertaken a complete overhaul of the financial controls, board policies, and other internal procedures. I had researched the issues thoroughly and tried to also use this fresh knowledge as part of my volunteer my board and finance committee work. Our finance committee examined the financial policies and made many changes, including requiring at least two bids on contracts more than $5,000 (a lot of money then) and reviewing insurance purchases every two years.

About two months into my term as chair, our comprehensive insurance package came up for renewal and the executive director called to tell me that I needed to sign off on the contract. I asked her if we had bid the insurance out, as called for in our newly rewritten financial policies. Her shocked reply was, "No, of course not. George (a board member for ten years—*note: ten years!*) gives us a great rate on the premiums, so we always go with him. We're *not* going to bid this." I informed her that I differed with her, and that if we were going to have policies, they needed to be followed for everyone, every time. Besides, if George were giving us such a great rate, he would certainly retain the business. The exec was very uncomfortable with this idea, noting how dedicated George had been to the organization and how his daughter was one of our first clients, and in general setting George up for immediate canonization by the Pope. So, I added, "I know you and George go back a long way, and that he has been a great help to us. Let's blame this on me, and I'll even be the one to tell George in person, okay?" "Fine," she said, still not very happy. We set the meeting with George for the next day.

George arrived at our meeting, assuming it was merely a formality and that I was there just to sign off on his contract and to pass him a check for the first month's premium. After the initial formalities, he slid the papers across the table to me, and I slid them back, saying, "George, this is *absolutely* no reflection on you, but as you know, we now have a financial policy that requires us to bid out all contracts more than $5,000. Since this premium is more than $50,000, we need to bid it out. You are very familiar with our insurance needs and may have put everything we need in the material you have today. So I can either take the papers that you have as your bid and hold them until we get two competing bids or you can rework them into a more 'bid-like' form. I have a request for proposal [RFP] here for you to look at if you would like. We have been very happy with your service and hope that you will bid for the work, but I'm sure that you understand our need to get the best price we can."

George looked at me for a moment, then smiled slightly, but didn't say a word. He simply crossed out the premium amount on the contract, *reduced it by 20 percent,* and slid it back across the table! I could hear the executive director gasp and I saw her flush red as I tried to keep from getting angry. The best response I could muster was, "Should I take that as your bid?" "Nope," he said. "I've provided good service here for ten years. I don't do bids. This is a one-time offer. Take it or leave it." "We'll take it!" said the exec. "Wrong. We'll leave it," I said. I handed George the RFP and walked out of the room. ■

What is the point? Good old George—the board member, the parent, the supporter of our organization—had been *stealing* from us for years by inflating the premium way over the market price. He got away with it because the organization had never bothered to check with the competition and he knew that. Once we had reasonable checks and balances, he was forced to play fair. Oh, and the executive director never forgave me for *embarrassing* her in front of George!

A Balanced Approach

You need to attempt to reach a balance between overkill and underkill. I suggest the following components of a conflict-of-interest policy:

- *Bid out contractual work.* Set a price threshold and get bids on purchases over that amount: contracting, equipment, supplies, food, anything. You'll need to learn how to write out your needs in an RFP, and once you learn how, and get in the habit of doing it, you will not only save money but you will avoid anyone's saying that a board member got a "no-bid" contract. Don't forget that best practice requires that you bid your audit work every three years as well.
- *If a board member bids on a contract, he or she should get it only if it is the lowest bid.* This is somewhat restrictive, but again it avoids potential bad publicity. And the board member must follow the policy to the letter. You have to play by the rules 100 percent, 100 percent of the time. The other person who loses the bid is just waiting to go to the press (or your funder) to accuse you of favoritism, or to the IRS to accuse you of "inurement of benefit," which is illegal. Play by the rules you set.
- *In discussions wherein a board member has or feels he or she may have a conflict, the board member should disclose that conflict or potential conflict immediately.* After such disclosure, the board member should be able to participate in discussion, but should recuse him- or herself from voting. The board member's participation in the discussion may bring important insights to the table and, as long as everyone is aware of the conflict, should not be inappropriate.
- *Include your staff in your conflict policies.* We always focus on board members and forget our staff. What if the husband of your vice president of finance owns a computer firm and you need computers? Can he bid for the work or not? You should specify. Can staff work on their own after hours? Can they consult with other agencies? You should spell it out.

You may need to be more stringent if you have had a bad experience with your board or if there has been a scandal at another organization in your community, but try to attain a reasonable balance. Put your policy in your bylaws and have a training session with your board and staff about what it means. Repeat that training annually.

Finally, I'm a great believer in putting your conflict-of-interest policies online as part of your transparency efforts. See Chapter 5 for more detail about this.

Financial Controls

Good financial controls can be very technical and certainly should be designed to meet your organization's unique needs. Thus, you will need to rely on your CPA and your funding source for help on these controls. I will, however, highlight the major areas that need your attention. The key to financial policies is to have good oversight in reporting, good theft prevention by reducing temptation, and good records to allow for easy auditing and analysis. It should go without saying that you need an outside audit every year, but I'll say it anyway: Get an annual audit. Think of it as more disaster insurance.

Cash Controls

You should already have cash controls in place, wherein one person logs in checks and cash, another deposits, and a third reconciles the bank statement. Even if there are only three staff, this is possible. Try to achieve it. Note: Everyone who handles any cash or checks should be bonded. It's cheap.

Receivables Controls

The person who signs for the receivables and checks them in should not be the person who writes the check to the vendor. This will help prevent collusion and overpayment.

Debt Policy

You need to spell out your policy on taking debt. Can the exec add to the line of credit without board approval? Can the executive committee approve a payroll loan without board approval? Be specific here. In Chapter 9, we discussed social entrepreneurship and why prudent debt can be a good thing and not a bad one. Whatever you decide on this issue, you want a policy and you want it to be specific.

Check Signature

Most boards let the staff write checks within the budget, but sometimes it takes two signatures above a certain threshold, such as $5,000 or $10,000. Some organizations make payroll exempt from this provision. How high or low your threshold is and how many signatures you need will in some part depend on your organization's history, the community practices on the issue, and the requirements of your funders.

 FOR EXAMPLE: Many years ago, my consulting firm received a check from a small town in Alabama for a subscription to our then-six-issues-per-year newsletter. The check was for one year's subscription—$12. It had five (that's right, *five*) signatures: the mayor, the town treasurer, the town deputy mayor, the town clerk, and the police chief. After all of us had stopped laughing, I asked our staff: "The question is, in this town, who stole how much and how recently?"

We never found out the answer to the question but the point is that you need to be reasonable. That town spent probably $50 in someone's time running that $12 check all over the courthouse getting five signatures. If you have had a bad experience with a former staff person, do take extra precautions but not absurd ones. ■

Reporting

Your policies should note who gets which reports how often. For example, your board may get quarterly financial statements but your executive committee and financial committee get monthly income and expense statements, cash flows, and an aging payables and receivables. You need to have reporting requirements and formats that meet the needs of the people reading the reports to do their jobs. That means that different groups will get different reports. How do you know what they want and need? Be a good marketer. Ask them. (For more on this, see Chapter 10 on marketing.)

Confidentiality

A lot of people forget about confidentiality, but your financials are your business. You need a statement that specifies that this information is not to be shared outside the agency except with auditors, funders, and others and only with the express written approval of the board. You don't want your numbers floating all over town.

Human Resources Policies

I know that this will seem like a cursory discussion of an all-too-important issue, but it is intentional. HR policies, and not following them, are in my view the biggest single liability you have. I describe HR policies to audiences when I speak as "Management neurosurgery: Very technical, the state-of-the-art changes all the time, and if you screw up, the consequences are dire." Why? Angry staff sue their employers more and more. We are, after all, a litigious society. We as nonprofits also do not pay our staff enough and probably never will. The one major area where angry, underpaid staff can sue us is in personnel: discriminatory hiring, sexual harassment, unjust termination, the list goes on and on. You simply *have* to have policies that meet the current law and regulation and are followed to the letter *every single time*. To get this right, you have to pay for expertise, inside the organization (if you are large enough to afford an HR specialist) or outside the organization from an HR consultant. Do NOT leave this crucial task to a board member. Get, and pay for, help.

Remember that rules and regulations in this area change regularly so keep the policies and the training for how to implement then up to date. Train your supervisory staff on your discipline process at least annually.

I intentionally did not include even a brief checklist here for fear that some reader would think that it was all-inclusive and get into trouble. Please talk to an expert.

Media Policies

The media love to sell papers, magazines, and air time—that's their business. You want to avoid being part of that sales effort by not becoming a negative story in the scandal sheets. The public's and thus the press's zest for scandal is one of the reasons that you need to develop such detailed policies in all areas of the agency: It helps avoid the things that the media love to run on the front page or the evening news—for example, BOARD MEMBERS GET SWEETHEART CONTRACT; STAFF OF AGENCY FILE DISCRIMINATION SUIT; EXECUTIVE DIRECTOR HAD VACATION ON AGENCY FUNDS. *No one* wants to wake up to see or hear those stories about the organization that he or she works for.

But what if you do? What does one do when the reporter calls for information on a story, good or bad? Your media policies should tell you. I strongly suggest that your policies include at least the following:

External Flow Control

You need to have *one* and only one person designated as the spokesperson for the agency. Usually, this will be the chief staff person but, if you are large enough, it could also be the public information officer. In some cases, your board president should be the spokesperson; in some cases, he or she should NEVER be the spokesperson. But the rule is: Limit the voices talking to the press to one voice. You want one message and one only. This rule is particularly important to impress on your board members because they can be easily contacted and are often susceptible to press badgering, as they are only volunteers and may not know the whole issue.

Internal Information Flow

Keep people informed: staff, board, the people you serve, funders, and donors. Get your side of the issue to them and quickly—before the papers hit the stands, if possible. Keep your staff fully informed of what is happening and how it will affect them and their programs. Use these opportunities to remind them *not* to talk to the press on their own.

While we are on the subject, remember these rules of dealing with the media, in good times and bad:

- *State facts only, not assumptions.* For example, if a reporter asks, "Doesn't your new program provide services in a discriminatory manner?" don't answer yes *or* no. An appropriate factual response (if true) would be, "Our board has a long-standing nondiscrimination policy in all aspects of service provision, hiring, and employment. That policy includes our new program."
- *Don't be afraid to say, "I don't know, but I'll get back to you," and then do.* It is better to check your facts and call back, but always do call back. Also, always get back to reporters by *their* deadline, even if it is inconvenient. They will run the story anyway and put their slant on it, so return their calls and try to get your two cents worth into the story.
- *State and restate your concern for the people you serve,* your prior awards and positive press, and how this issue, whatever it may be, will not affect the long-term program(s).
- *Don't try to be a "spin doctor."* Most reporters are pros and know spin when they hear it.

Volunteer Policies

Volunteer policies are being upgraded everywhere as nonprofits ramp up their volunteer management. At the very least they need to cover orientation, with an explanation of your mission and a description of all of your services; volunteer job descriptions; descriptions of expectations, responsibilities, and liability; background checks (if needed); and a list of staff positions that the volunteers relate/report to. These policies can then be distributed to staff and volunteers (online and on paper), and all can better understand the role volunteers play in your organization and how each individual participates as well. Remember what I said early on in the book: Volunteers are going to be much more important to all nonprofits over the next ten years. Get your house in order in this area.

Quality Assurance

Quality is "Job One," or so goes the classic (if ignored) Ford advertisement. However, it is true that a passion for quality is not only good mission, it is also good marketing. No matter what service you are in, you need a quality assurance (QA) program. There are many, many methods of improving quality and lots of text and online resources for you to use.

In some areas of service, there are quality boards that certify the quality of the organization. Programs like the Joint Commission on the Accreditation of Hospitals (JCAH) and the Commission on the Accreditation of Rehabilitation Facilities (CARF) are two good examples of such organizations, and there may be equivalents in your field. Additionally, you may have a trade organization that has developed standards of excellence for your field. For example, the Association of Fundraising Professionals (AFP) has standards for its members that it publishes. Your trade association may do the same.

At the very least, you want to set some standards for yourself to try to meet and exceed. These are not just goals and objectives in the planning sense, but standards of quality. For example, if you were a mental health assessment facility, you might have a standard that says that all new patients in crisis will see a counselor for initial assessment within three hours of a call 24 hours a day. If you were a church, you might have a standard that one or more of your ministerial staff will attend every church activity to facilitate counseling and fellowship. If you were a museum, you might not display any new works that have not passed a rigorous peer review of experts to ensure that the works are not forgeries.

Your goal should be to do what you do better and better. You want to earn a reputation as a quality program, and that reputation is both tough to earn and tougher to keep. Setting standards in writing will help you, your management team, and your staff and volunteers achieve those standards. My favorite book on setting standards is *Benchmarking for Nonprofits* (St. Paul, MN: Fieldstone Alliance, 2004), by Jason Saul.

Program Policies

Program policies are essential tools for you to convey your mission and your values to your staff, volunteers, funders, and service recipients. They may be short and general or long and detailed, but they should outline both the steps involved in any and all service provision and the philosophy of that provision. For example, an arts association may have a set of hands-on art exploration programs for young children. The association would need to put down its philosophy of "having children explore various creative media in a wholesome, safe environment" as well as such finite details as the need to register children, have emergency phone numbers if the children are dropped off, and perhaps (in this sad day and age of fear of child abuse) always having two adults in the room with the children. It might also put into its protocols to have the child's name added to its mailing list for future announcements of similar classes.

A second example is a health clinic, which might have very specific health care protocols for admission, screening, lab work, information gathering, insurance billing, and the like. These go a long way to ensure that staff understand each and every facet of what they need to do with each and every patient.

 HANDS ON: Don't assume that *anything* is too minute or too obvious to write down! That is why it is so critical to develop these with a group of line staff as well as with managers. I once saw a set of program policies for a health clinic that had such items as the information required on check-in, directions on how to offer coffee or tea in the waiting room in English and Spanish, what to do with blood tests, and so on, but forgot to direct the nurses to take the temperature and blood pressure of the patient! When a new nurse came on board, she was trained in the policies, and it wasn't until the patient charts were reviewed a week or two later that people noticed that these key items were not being assessed. When asked why not, she said, "You have great procedures, and I was just following them. It didn't make a whole lot of sense, but I'm new and didn't want to make trouble." I'm pretty sure that the policies in this organization were developed by management without being sent to the line nursing staff for review!

Do not fall into this trap. Include a wide review of any policy with the people who will actually use it. And let your staff know that policies are not substitutes for common sense. ■

Disaster Policies

The bumper sticker says (paraphrased) "Stuff Happens." Fires, earthquakes, tornadoes, floods, lengthy power outages, and hurricanes all do occur, and regularly. I know that you have fire evacuation procedures for all of your buildings, and I hope that you have fire drills for any residential facilities you may run. But do you have disaster procedures? Perhaps not, and you need them. Make sure that your policies have at least these parts:

- *Disaster preparedness.* What is in here will depend on where you live and work. Are you in a hurricane-prone area? An area that is regularly visited by tornadoes or earthquakes? If so, consult your local disaster preparedness agency and get up-to-date advice on being as prepared as possible. This may mean something as simple as laying in a supply of water, food, flashlights, and batteries, or as complex as reinforcing your structures.
- *Post-disaster planning.* What will you do *after* a disaster? If you lose a building to a fire or a flood, how do you get back up and running in as short a time as possible? With a good plan that has a checklist of things that need to be attended to, people to contact, and alternate sites for provision of services outlined.

 FOR EXAMPLE: During the writing of the first edition of *Mission-Based Management,* a fire at the school where my wife taught destroyed about 15 percent of the school, with extensive smoke and water damage to the rest. The fire occurred on Friday night, ending about 4 A.M. on Saturday. By Sunday evening, with a super-human effort on behalf of the administration and school district maintenance staff, the following had occurred: The entire school (a large school, with 450 students) had been cleaned and most areas repainted; all the carpeting had been removed, cleaned, and replaced; all the affected areas of the school had been rewired; transportation for 100 students and alternate sites for classes had been secured; a gym site for the entire student body had been found; medical forms had been prepared to let students and faculty know what cleaning materials had been used in case of allergic reactions; insurance had been extended to the new sites; press conferences had been held; and every student in the school had been called. By Monday evening when an open house was held at both sites, all the lost student materials had been replaced, the new classrooms (at the different site) were set up, every book in the library (which was smoke damaged) had been cleaned and reshelved, and all the computers and audiovisual equipment in the school had been cleaned and returned. Classes resumed on Tuesday, 76 hours after the fire was out. ■

There were 1,000 other things that these people did that I have not recounted, but the key for them was that they had a plan for what to do in case there was severe damage to a school. The plan was not all-inclusive, and they had to ad lib a lot, but it kept them on track and made sure that their efforts were focused and directed. You need disaster policies, and not just for fire drills.

Training and Enforcement

While policies can be a great management tool, they are a lot of work to create and to keep up to date. As I have noted repeatedly, they are also worthless without training staff and board people in their use. Again, you need to have in-services on every policy with all staff when it is first in place and then with affected staff each year. Only by repeated exposure to the policies will staff people get it right; at the same time, ways to improve the policies will be found.

Policies must also be enforced. There is no point in spending the time and money to develop these guidelines if you are not going to discipline staff and board when they don't follow the policies. Make it clear at the outset (at the training) that a wide array of staff and board were involved in development and testing of the policies and that with that involvement from all levels in development, you now expect these to be followed. Then note clearly that failure to follow the policies will lead to disciplinary action. And when someone does violate them knowingly (and someone *always* does, just to see what will happen), discipline him or her. You will be amazed at how few violations you will have in the future.

Recap

Don't miss the opportunity to have and use good controls. But remember that while controls are great, they should not discourage innovation, experimentation, and taking risks. Staff should know that policies are not excuses for total brain shutdown and that common sense is still expected.

In this chapter, we've reviewed why it is critical to your success and your ability to manage to have good, well-written, and up-to-date policies and procedures. We have reviewed the essential kinds of policies and gone over the key things that I have seen many organizations forget to include. Remember, good controls are a key to good management and mission success. Without them, you will almost surely have staff or volunteers do something, major or minor, that distracts you from your job: managing the organization. With controls, there will be less of that, although even the best controls are valueless if people ignore them. That is why we went over the issue of regular training as a key to implementation of your policies, and enforcement as a way to ensure that they are used.

Good controls set you free from administration—they allow you to be a manager. The time and money spent to develop and update them will be returned to you tenfold. Without them, your organization is a multitude of accidents waiting to happen.

Questions for Discussion

1. How are we on the list of controls? Where do we have deficits?
2. Are all of our policies available online for our staff and board to view?
3. Let's examine each of the policies and look at this issues that are identified for each of them. We can list what needs to be updated, by whom, and by when.
4. What resources can we commit to training our staff to use these policies?
5. How can we more fairly and consistently enforce our expectations of our policies?

CHAPTER 14

A National Agenda

Empowering Our Nonprofits

Overview

Up to this point, we have covered the key components of how to operationalize success at your nonprofit. You have read suggestions and applications of how to deal with your mission, your board, your staff, your markets, your money, and your long-range goals. Hopefully, by applying the ideas encompassed in the previous chapters, you can change your nonprofit for the better, become more mission oriented, more market sensitive, more transparent, and a better financial manager. But one key component remains: how your funders and the community at large view and treat your organization. These two groups can help you in your quest toward becoming and remaining a mission-based organization. Or they can impede or even negate your progress toward that goal.

This chapter will deal with those groups. It's written for you, but also for them. In the following pages, we'll address three outdated theories of how funders look at you, look at three new ways that our nation needs to view its nonprofits, and provide a specific list of action items for governments, United Ways, foundations, and corporate and individual donors to use as they consider how to assist nonprofits (or at least get out of the way) in the coming decade.

Three Outdated Theories

In Chapter 2, I recounted how nonprofits came to the state that confronts us today. I related to you the three big driving principles of most funders' views of how nonprofits really run. To recount briefly, these principles (from the funders' point of view) are:

1. *What we (the funders) say goes.* Whether it makes any sense in your community, or with your mission, since we are paying the piper, we call the tune—much more invasively and comprehensively than any for-profit customer would ever dream of doing.
2. *You can't do well doing good.* You are suspected of stealing if you are not threadbare, scrutinized well beyond the cost-benefit curve, and in general must take a vow of poverty to get our (the funders') money.
3. *What is yours is ours.* If you take our money (even if it is just a portion of your overall income), we have the right to come and strip you naked and judge you at our whim. Additionally, anything that you buy with "our" money is ours, not yours.

As I said earlier, it is my absolute belief, based on being part of and working for and around nonprofits for more than twenty years, that these policies are not only outdated but are extremely counterproductive social policy, short-sighted fiscal policy, and just plain wrong at their core. I understand how they came to pass; in small steps, each intended to improve the system, lower risk, or prevent abuse. And I know that the people who work for funders, like the people who work for nonprofits, are good people, people trying to do good, to improve society, and to spread best practices while at the same time being good stewards of *their* funds. I get all that.

But the fact remains that, in aggregate, these three operating principles do pervade and damage the sector. In sum, they presume that the funder, at the end of the day, always knows best, particularly if that funder is a government, a foundation, or a United Way; that the nonprofit is too often an inept, if not felonious, manager of public funds; and that the nonprofit should be poor to prove its honesty and dedication to its mission. They also completely ignore the fact that the relationship among government and funder and agency is really one of purchasing services. It is not parenthood. Neither is it indentured servitude.

These policies and views must change, and there are five groups of people who must change them: governments, foundations, United Ways, the public and press, and you—the staff members of the nation's nonprofits. Without fundamental change in the ways that these five groups view your nonprofit and the 1,300,000 others in the United States, there are limits to what you can achieve. For example, if your funders demand that you have no fund balance and will go to extraordinary lengths to recover funds from you, you can never be financially empowered and you can never help the community without running back to the funder for more funds, which come with all strings attached.

This concern with the way large funders contract and treat their providers of service is not, of course, unique to me. Not only have the trade associations been harping on the issue for years, our centers of academic research have been looking at the issue as well. Such notables as Brian O'Connell at the Independent Sector in a series of publications, and David Osborne, in his excellent book *Reinventing Government* (New York: Plume, 1993), have both called for a reexamination of the ways that government funds and supervises its contractual obligations. Osborne, in particular, developed a large number of examples of ways to make government more efficient and effective. Many, including the call for ending "use it or lose it" and competitive bidding, parallel the ideas that I lay out below.

But, having criticized just about everyone in the power positions, what can each group do to fix the problem? It would be unfair just to take potshots without offering solutions, so here are mine. These are not, as you will see, fine-tuning or adjustments. They are radical realignments of our national views of our private nonprofit sector. They will at some level threaten just about everyone, as they are not designed to be slow and cautious in their approach. I don't think we have the time to be slow and cautious. America's social, educational, arts, scientific, environmental, and spiritual needs are obvious to all but the most callous or out-of-touch observer. Moreover, in our current economic situation, to wait is to perhaps forgo a decade of capabilities. We cannot wait. Let's start now.

Overall Philosophy Changes That Are Necessary

In Chapter 1, I started the discussion of my three umbrella theories of nonprofits. Those three philosophies have appeared in many forms throughout the book. But how do they apply to funders? I think that they do, and as a result, they bear another examination here.

The general philosophies that follow need to be adopted and practiced at all levels. As noted previously, they require a radical rethinking of the role of nonprofits by many of us. Those nonprofit funders whose grantees and contractors are succeeding have, not coincidentally, already adopted many if not all of these tenets.

Please note that as we walk through these philosophies, I'll scold everyone, using the term "we." Why not just fuss at funders? Because we *all* have to change our viewpoint, we *all* have to compromise (or it's not a compromise), and we *all* have to move toward a more logical and more successful view of the sector if we are *all* to succeed in providing the best mission. And that's the point, isn't it? More mission, better provided, to more people. Not less cost, or more restrictions, or more reporting, but more mission.

Nonprofits Are Businesses

First and foremost, we have to stop thinking of nonprofits as *charities* and accept that they are businesses, albeit ones whose primary motivation is mission. In pursuit of that mission, a nonprofit must act as much like a business as possible without sacrificing its mission. This means adopting many of the skills taught earlier in this book: a bias for marketing, watching the bottom line, building up equity and financial flexibility, growing and retaining a strong staff, having a long-range vision, and understanding that profit is *not* a dirty word.

We also have to realize that our nonprofits contribute to our communities economically as well as in arts, human services, education, and theology. Nonprofits in the United States have—for decades—contributed over 10 percent of our gross national product, and employed over 12 percent of the workforce—that's one in every eight jobs. In many rural communities, nonprofits are major employers; in every community, they contribute to the local payroll in a significant way, in addition to the social, educational, medical, environmental, arts, and spiritual good that they do. Thus, a healthy, growing, and stable nonprofit network can stimulate job growth just as much as small businesses can, which get so much good press on the issue of economic stimulus.

I have never said, and never wish to be quoted as saying, that this business mentality should come at the expense of doing good mission. It does not mean that watching your cash flow equates with cutting all of your unprofitable programs. Doing some things that lose money is part and parcel of the service array that nonprofits should continue to provide. But, using good, sound businesslike practices at the staff and board level can make all the difference: *It means getting more mission for your money, not having more money and doing less mission.*

No One Gives a Nonprofit a Dime

Whoa, say the governments, we *give* them billions. Hold on, say the United Ways. We *give* them millions. Wait a second, say the foundations, what about our millions? And don't forget us, say the millions of Americans who dip into their wallets and purses each year to contribute to the nation's nonprofits.

To all of you who fund America's nonprofits, I say this: You're still focusing on nonprofits as *charities,* not as the mission-oriented businesses that they are. Let's look at the transactions that *really* take place when you make a donation.

FOR EXAMPLE:

- The local art museum comes to you for a $100 donation. It describes its programs, explains its funding patterns, and asks for your help in meeting its program goals. You write it a check for $100.
- The statewide drug prevention hotline calls you for a $50 monthly donation to allow it to keep taking toll-free calls from people who need drug rehabilitation services and are in crisis. You sign up for a monthly contribution.
- The county shelter for the homeless is taking contributions to pay for a holiday dinner for the residents. You chip in $20. ■

Here is the crux of the issue: In each of these cases, what did you do? Did you *give* the museum, hotline, or shelter anything? Most people would say, "Yes, I *gave* them money." No, what you did was *buy services on behalf of someone else*. For the museum, that money might go to a new display of Impressionist paintings that all can see; for the hotline, it might help pay for the toll-free 24-hour help line; for the shelter, it literally will put food in someone's mouth. Thus, you *purchased* something, perhaps not as precisely as you would purchase food from the grocery store or a repair service from your plumber, but at its core, the transaction is the same.

There is still the other side of the equation yet to be mentioned, the side that is even more important than realizing that you (and all of the other funders, the governments, foundations, and United Ways) are buying something, rather than just giving money away. It goes like this:

Nonprofits *earn* every cent that they get.

Step back and think about it. The government doesn't give money away for nothing (although I will be the first to contend that they regularly don't get their money's worth). The government wants something for its money: It *buys* services, whether they are scientific research, outreach to teenage moms, public broadcasting, or breakfasts for children from low-income families. If it buys something, then the relationship is one of purchaser (the government) and seller (the nonprofit). Thus, the nonprofit has to do something to *earn* the money, which usually means providing a service or array of services. The same is true for other funders.

The understanding that nonprofits are earning their money rather than accepting a handout is, obviously, a critical part of the philosophy change. If nonprofits are businesses and have economic worth in the society beyond their social, educational, or religious worth, then they also can and should stand up and stop being treated like a poor cousin.

There's more.

Once nonprofits earn the money, it's *theirs,* not the funder's.

None of this "use it or lose it" insanity. If the nonprofit can do the work at the level agreed to, and has funds left over, *good.* That strengthens the organization and the community. The nonprofit should not be forced to return unspent funds nor should it be punished in future funding cycles by cutting next fiscal year's grant.

Further, selling services to a government or foundation does not mean that the nonprofit should have to open all its functions for review and strip itself naked in the public square. In many cases, if a large funder purchases services and that constitutes 5 percent of a nonprofit's income, the funder demands to see all the financials, all related party transactions, and all the information about the board. I know many readers are scratching their head and saying, so? Isn't this prudent oversight? No. I'm all for good oversight, but not when it comes with the presumption of guilt.

Let's turn this around. If I as a for-profit consultant work for a government agency or a foundation (and I do), the agency or foundation doesn't ask for funds back when I'm done. They don't ask who is on my board or what other work I'm doing. No one asks me my admin percentage. I bid the work (note: I bid a *price* not a *cost*), sign a contract, do the job, send a bill, and get paid. And if I work for the agency or foundation in the future, they don't punish me for having made money on the earlier work.

As a group, are for-profit consultant and trainers like me any more trustworthy than nonprofits? Nope. And yet look at the difference in how we're treated.

The takeaway here is: If we think of nonprofits as mission-based businesses, we should treat them as such—from start to finish.

Nonprofit Does Not Equal No Profit

Here's the most important issue. Making money is good for mission. It is legal, it is ethical, and it is essential if the nonprofit is to apply best practices, innovate, and grow.

Don't believe me? Here's the truth:

Nowhere, in any state or federal law or regulation, does it say that a nonprofit must lose money or break even financially. In fact, in the IRS code, it says that "the *profits* of the corporation shall not inure to the benefit of (various people)" [emphasis added].

Thus, having profits is *fine* with the law and with IRS regulations. Still don't believe me? Look at it this way: Congress gave nonprofits a tax break. Nonprofits don't have to pay income tax on funds earned related to their mission statement. So your organization has a tax exemption from paying taxes on "income." But it is not an income tax as an individual thinks of such a tax—paying a portion of your income. No, it is a *business* income tax. Businesses pay taxes on a portion of their profits (which the IRS terms their *income*—hence the confusion). Thus, your organization really has an exemption from paying taxes on your profits. Here's the key: If you couldn't make a profit, you wouldn't need the tax exemption!

In fact, what Congress intended was for nonprofits to keep their profits and reinvest them in the community! What have we done since? In the main, acquiesced with the idea that nonprofits should be poor. Thus, it becomes okay for funders to pay costs (or most of the costs) rather than a price. If a nonprofit is "making money" (horrors!) or has a reserve or, worst of all, an endowment, that is immediately suspect and cause for a reduction in funding for the next funding cycle, a special audit, or both.

Note—we *all* have bought into this. The funders, the press, and agency staff and board. All of us. And this practice is not only absurd but incredibly damaging. And brought to you by a group of good people (all of us) believing that they are doing the best thing. The real amazement is that we've allowed this model to continue this long.

Not only is it okay for nonprofits to make money, as I said earlier, nonprofits *must* make money in most, if not every, year if they are to do their job right. Only financially stable organizations will be able to react quickly to changing needs in their communities. Only financially empowered organizations will be able to recruit and retain excellent staffs, take risks on behalf of their clientele, and do their job as it needs to be done. Finally, only financially stable nonprofits will be able to stop the cycle of dependence on government for hand-to-mouth funding. One more time: *Profit is good for mission*.

Further, profit is not a penalty on funders. Profit is accepted in every other sector of our economy, even in some sectors of the nonprofit economy (e.g., hospitals). Why, then, should profit and the stability, flexibility, and quality that it produces be such a pejorative when it is applied to nonprofits in general? And only to nonprofits?

Again, I fear misinterpretation and misquoting here. I am not contending that nonprofits should make money just to make money or just to buy nice offices or pay high salaries. The profits should be reinvested in the mission in the way that each organization's board and staff see best maximizes the use of those funds to accomplish the mission. But profits in and of themselves are not bad: They are *mission-enablers*.

Competition for Services Is a Good Thing

Here's the other side of agreeing that nonprofits are businesses. They need to compete.

Imagine that the owner of a new fast-food franchise came to a zoning hearing in your town and asked the zoning commission to rezone a parcel of land so that she could build a burger joint at the same intersection where another fast-food restaurant already operated. Now imagine the zoning commission turning the zoning request down because it "duplicates an existing service." The franchise owner would scream bloody murder and sue, and win, with a great deal of popular support in the community because we have a long and successful tradition of free enterprise and competition. Now, and this is not so hard to envision, imagine that same franchise owner sitting on a funding panel at your United Way and voting to turn *down* a funding request for a new program because it "duplicates an existing program already operating in the community."

It happens all the time. Agencies, particularly in social services, are regularly given geographic monopolies by their government, foundation, and corporate funders. This is done to "avoid duplication" and in the spirit of efficiency and economy. It is amazing to me that we let this start and let it continue when all of the evidence from every corner of the globe shows that competition (if profits are allowed and retained) will encourage better service at more economical prices than monopolies.

And, of course, while some nonprofits may think they don't compete, they already do: for the best staff, best board members, and, increasingly, for donations.

In short, competition for customers is okay and should be encouraged. I am not naive enough to say that this should be done wholesale next fiscal year. The staffs and boards of nonprofits are well trained as service monopolies and a transition time is needed and will be rocky for some. Much of the advice in this book is designed to get them ready for just such competition.

Specific Action Items

This list of action items is offered as an agenda for change for the five major groups that need to act now: the government, foundations, United Ways, the community at large, and the staffs and boards of our nonprofits. All of them are designed to mesh with the four overall philosophical changes listed in this chapter.

To be fair, I also must note here that some governments, some foundations, and some United Ways are already doing many if not all of the things I suggest here. In fact, with the exception of the idea of national management certification for nonprofits, there is little here that has not already been tested and found to work. Thus, as you read these suggestions, don't put them aside, saying, "Never happen" or "Would never work." They already are happening and already do work in other communities. What you need to do is to make them work in yours.

Government (Federal, State, County, Local)

1. *End the policy of "use it or lose it."* Let nonprofits bid on work that you want done, and then, if they do what you contracted for and have money left over afterward, let them keep it. If you bid the contract fairly, and the contractor did what you asked, why should it have to return what it didn't spend? All this encourages is waste, fraud, or both. (Note: The federal government is making major strides here, while the states in general are lagging far behind.)

2. *End monopolies.* Let the nonprofits you fund bid against each other and against for-profits. Open the markets up. To do this well, you will need to learn how to write contracts and requests for proposals in new ways, and you will have to link the end of monopolies to the end of "use it or lose it," but it will work. You will, in the end, get better services, better quality, and more productivity.

3. *Encourage productivity and quality.* Compensate contractors if they meet high-quality and productivity standards—ones that are set forth in the contract. Even small financial incentives can bring up standards rapidly. Again, this has to be linked with the end of "use it or lose it," or you will lose any beneficial effect.

4. *Pay on time and pay fair scale.* On time would be a good start for most governments, and with the improvements in technology there is really no excuse for long payment time. Paying fair will take longer, particularly in a tough economic period. But paying less than the true cost is a short-term solution that creates (and has created) a long-term problem: chronically underfunded agencies that are perpetually dependent on the government.

5. *Reduce or end the use of matching fund requirements.* The theory of the match is that it shows agency or community commitment and the likelihood of program continuity later on if funding ceases. In reality, this requirement impoverishes nonprofits and/or encourages them to

cheat by allowing "in-kind" contributions—those of time or overhead that are already paid for—often by another government agency. Can you imagine the same government asking Dell to sell a PC at 25 percent *below* cost? That is exactly what a 25 percent match does. Stop it.

6. *Develop a universal accounting and audit format.* For every type of funding, a nonprofit often has to go through a different set of bookkeeping and year-end audit and accounting forms. Sometimes this means one agency has to do ten separate types of forms. As you can imagine, this does not result in administrative efficiencies. I refuse to believe that with all the expertise in this country, governments and CPAs cannot come up with a universal set of accounting and year-end program audit protocols that would save millions of dollars in administrative oversight costs each year. If the federal government could develop this one thing and urge/encourage/require states to do it, it would be the biggest single savings (on that hated admin percentage!) available.

Foundations

1. *Require management certification for funding.* I put this on the foundation's agenda because foundations could commission such a certification effort more easily than the government. My vision here is of a management certification such as the Commission on the Accreditation of Rehabilitation Facilities (CARF) for nonprofits. All agencies that could meet the certification would be certified for three years. That would make them eligible (or more competitive) for foundation funds and could even be a prerequisite for funding continuation. Certification could also be made a competitive edge for government and/or United Way funding. I suggest that the foundations link up with any one of the many graduate programs in nonprofit management to accomplish this.

2. *Encourage and fund seed projects with business outcomes.* Program-related investments (PRIs) do this to some extent and are the most laudable development from the foundations of the past decade, in my view. However, foundations can go further to encourage financial empowerment, and seeding outside business ventures are one way to do that.

3. *Stop the practice of "use it or lose it."* See number 1 (i.e., *End the policy of "use it or lose it."*) under the earlier section "Government."

4. *Stop or reduce match requirements.* See number 5 (i.e., *Reduce or end the use of matching fund requirements)* under the earlier section "Government."

United Ways

1. *Stop funding deficits.* Many United Ways still have policies of funding only deficits, and all this does is encourage future deficits. If you accept my theory of nonprofit transactions—that donors are buying services—then United Ways should purchase the most needed services, regardless of whether the agency is making money.
2. *Require management certification.* See number 1 (i.e., *Require management certification for funding*) under the earlier section "Foundations."
3. *Encourage competition.* Do not refuse funding just because a service is duplicated: Let agencies compete to provide the best service. Demand quality, but even with higher quality, competition will ultimately lower your cost and will probably weed out the weak and inflexible agencies. This *will* be painful. People *will* scream, but the community *will* be better off for it.

The Public and the Press

1. *Stop assuming that all nonprofits are welfare recipients.* They are not. There are efficient, effective, and productive nonprofits and inefficient, underproductive ones, just like in the for-profit sector, and the ratio is probably about the same.

   Corollary assumption: All nonprofits steal. They don't. I've never seen a study done, but I wouldn't be surprised if the rate of theft and corruption in the nonprofit sector is less than the proprietary or governmental sectors. It's just that when a nonprofit staff or board member steals and it makes the headline, it is *big* news. At any rate, the public and press demands for incredibly expensive scrutiny of every dollar spent—spending millions to prevent the theft of thousands—is not only counterproductive, it is insulting to the hundreds of thousands of dedicated and honest nonprofit staffs and boards that are serving us well. Reasonable accounting and checks and balances both within and outside nonprofits are important, but we've got things way out of proportion now and our tax dollars are not well spent in this area.
2. *When you serve on a board, don't check your common sense or business expertise at the door.* I've lost count of how many times I've watched good, solid businesspeople make incredibly dumb decisions for a nonprofit "because we aren't really a business." Just because the organization is not in it for the money doesn't mean you suspend common sense in making policy decisions. You are on the board to contribute your wisdom, expertise, experience, and perspective to the discussion: Don't leave home without them.

3. *Demand productivity, flexibility, and quality from your nonprofits.* Just because it has "always been that way" is no excuse for stodgy management and outdated programming. Be as demanding of your nonprofits as you are of stores and businesses you patronize. If you donate money, you are a customer: demand quality.

Nonprofits

If the previous items are to become reality, you need to do your part. This is not a one-way street, and everyone has to help make the sector better. As a nonprofit staff or board member, there are things you need to be doing to reinforce these new ideas and make them work in your community. While everything that I have tried to convey in this book moves you and your organization toward that end, I can distill it into two short phrases:

1. *Be businesslike.* Not cold, or profit-driven, but businesslike. The more you act like a business, the more you will be treated like one. This includes dressing appropriately, using business language (markets, cash flow, quality management), and the like. Join the Chamber and get active. Nonprofit staffs regularly complain that they "don't get any respect." Part of this wound is self-inflicted. Remember, you earn your money—you are not a charity. Go out and act like it, and you will start to be treated accordingly.

2. *Be competitive—accept the marketplace and try to adapt.* This is, I know, a big change, but if the governments and foundations end "use it or lose it" and end monopolies, you'll have to get with it sooner or later. I suggest sooner. Remember, you're already competing for the best staff, for great board members, for more donations and volunteers. Take that skill and spread it to mission. Who benefits? The people you serve.

An Exhortation

These agenda items are only a start. Until all parties involved buy into the major philosophies, we won't make significant progress. Until nonprofits learn and practice the skills and policies outlined in this book, they won't become the lean, creative, and productive social entrepreneurs that would so benefit the social fabric of our society. Until the public sees our nonprofits as more than charities, they will delay realizing the full potential that this vital sector of our economy has to assist and contribute to the nation as a whole.

However, none of us has to wait for the others to get on board before starting the change. Each board member can demand better policies, a strategic plan, better financial oversight, and quality control. Each mission-based manager can value the line staff, act as if every action has an impact on the organization's marketing, and not recoil from the thought of competition. Each government agency can end the policy of "use it or lose it," even if another program does not. Each United Way can demand management training and excellence, even if there is not yet a national certification. Each citizen can trust the boards and staff to do good works and provide reasonable oversight. If each of us did, we would be well on our way. The sooner each of us starts, the better for all of us, and for the people we serve.

Recap

In this chapter, we went over the key issues that we all need to work on to fix what is broken in the nonprofit sector. First, I reiterated my beliefs regarding the fact that your organization is a mission-based business, that you earn all your income, and that it is essential for you to make money as a good steward. Then I focused in on core beliefs that need to change at the funder level and made a series of suggestions for each of the major funder groups (government, foundations, United Ways) as well as ways the public and nonprofits can move the agenda ahead. We are in this together, and need to solve the problems together. Don't delay!

Questions for Discussion

1. Which of our funders should see this chapter first? How should we approach them?
2. Should we foster a larger discussion in our community? Can we talk to a sympathetic reporter? Are our board and staff in agreement with these ideas?
3. How can we pass these ideas on to our state and national groups?

CHAPTER 15

Final Words

I hope that you feel that you are on your way to becoming an even better mission-based manager than you were at the beginning of this book. I have tried to give you the benefit of my experiences and observations about what nonprofits nationwide are doing to get more mission for their money and to be more businesslike in pursuit of their mission.

We are at an important crossroads for U.S. nonprofits, and thus for your organization as well. We can't go back to (and, frankly, wouldn't want to) the federal largesse of the 1970s. There is no money: We're more and more on our own. And we can't stay as we are—still behind in technology, assuming that the money we need will magically show up. Too many people in our communities are depending on us to provide more and better services, particularly now. We must go forward, but how? Will your organization choose the path of becoming a mission-based business? Or will you continue to think of yourself and your organization as a charity? Will you aggressively pursue the use of all of the resources available to you, including lessons from the for-profit sector? Or will you continue to do business as usual?

The answer is, of course, up to you, your staff, and your board. But if you choose the path of being a mission-based manager and want to manage a mission-based business, you have already been exposed to the keys in this book. One last time, let's review the characteristics that your organization needs to have to be successful and thrive in the coming years. In parentheses after each characteristic you will find the number of the chapter where that characteristic is discussed in detail:

1. A viable mission (Chapter 4)
2. Being ethical, accountable, and transparent (Chapter 5)
3. A businesslike board of directors (Chapter 6)
4. A strong, well-educated staff (Chapter 7)
5. Embracing technology for mission (Chapter 8)
6. Becoming social entrepreneurs (Chapter 9)
7. A bias for marketing (Chapter 10)

8. Becoming financially empowered (Chapter 11)
9. A vision for where you are going (Chapter 12)
10. A tight set of controls (Chapter 13)

You may have found that many or even all of the characteristics I tout as necessary to your vitality are already present in your organization. If so, congratulations: Your organization is well prepared to provide great services for the next decade. But wait. Is it *your* opinion only that says that you are already doing all of these things? Or did you see about the perspective of the staff and board? If it was just your opinion, remember that you do not always see things with total objectivity. Check with others, including some funders. Ask. Find out if they see your organization evidencing the same characteristics in the same way.

In Chapter 1, I suggested that you read this book as a team: Have all the senior managers read the same one or two chapters and then discuss what ideas you can or should adopt in your organization. If you didn't do that, now that you are through the entire book, try team reading. Get a group of your senior staff together and have them read a chapter or two a week, discussing them at a regular staff meeting. Going over any management text in this fashion is the best way to get the most good out of the book.

To me, the fact that you have been willing to read an entire book on managing your organization is clear evidence that you want to become a mission-based manager. But will you turn the investment of the hours you took out of your busy schedule to read this text to good use? Will you continue to put in the effort to become a mission-based manager who runs a mission-based organization? Many of the changes needed are behavioral: Developing a bottoms-up management style takes some serious change for some people, as does opening up the organization both inside and out to be more transparent. Communicating with the attitude that the key is what people hear and not what you say takes some adjusting to. Developing a culture of new ideas, in which all are encouraged, and changing methods of thinking to ask all the markets what they want instead of "knowing what they need" are disciplines that are difficult to stick to.

Psychologists who I have talked to say that a behavioral change takes two years to "take." That is, if someone adopts a lifestyle of exercise and healthy eating after years of being a couch potato full of junk food, it takes two full years before that new lifestyle becomes a habit rather than a major effort.

I suspect that it is longer for an organization. All the changes that you want to facilitate will need to be adapted to by *all* (or at least a sizable majority of) your staff and board, and that in itself will take a while. Only when they make that adaptation does the two-year clock start ticking. You need to be there leading by example, encouraging, cajoling, showing, evaluating. You are the key to the success or failure.

I sincerely hope that you succeed. Our nation and your community need every one of the nonprofits that can make the transition from charity to mission-based business. Our national needs and wants in education, the arts, social services, research, and religion are growing, not waning, and it will take a full roster of mission-based managers to bring these organizations into their fullest potential. The times demand that we respond with effective mission, and the ways of the mission-based manager *are* more effective than the old ways.

Mission-based managers are different. They see the mission first—the outcome of their organization's services—in very human terms. Outcome measures aren't just metrics; they represent people fed, children housed, a community inspired. As a mission-based manager, don't ever lose that perspective. It is what sets you apart from your for-profit peers. Yes, it makes your job that much tougher, but it makes the satisfaction of your job that much greater. It is what makes all the work worth it.

Remember that the services you provide are all provided *by* a person, and they all are provided *to* a person. In between those two people is your mission: the what and why of your organization. The mission is what brings those two people together. You are the champion of that mission both in your organization and in your community. With the skills you have learned here, you should find great success. Good luck.

Index

Accountability
  benchmarks, 67, 68, 71
  budget, 212
  characteristics of successful
    nonprofits,
    32, 289
  controls, 255
  importance of, 66
  leadership, 66, 67
  within organization, 55–58, 62
  overview, 28, 55, 70, 71
  values, 41, 58–62
Accounting and auditing standards, 284
Accounts payable, 202
Accounts receivable, 165, 166, 202, 203,
  213, 265
Action statements, 243, 247, 248, 250,
  251
Administrative (admin) costs, 204–207
Annual report, 70
Appearance of impropriety, 261. *See*
  also Conflicts of interest
Audit reports, 69, 131, 137, 138

Balance
  mission and money, 195, 205
  needs and resources, 34, 35, 37
Balance sheet, 162, 164, 203, 204, 212,
  213,
  223, 225
Bank accounts, 197, 198, 261,
  266
Banks, 224–230
Benchmarks, 67, 68, 71, 74–76, 201, 269
Berra, Yogi, 235

Blame, accepting, 102, 103
Blogs, 132, 133, 139, 261
Board manual, 90–92
Board of directors
  assessment tool, 88
  barriers to effectiveness, 77–80
  budget, drafting and adoption of, 81
  businesslike, 32, 33, 73, 285
  bylaws, review of, 81, 86
  committees. *See* Committees
  communication with, 78, 83, 86
  compliance with funding source
    regulations, 81
  compliance with state laws, 87
  composition of, 87, 88
  conflicts of interest, 86, 262–264
  directors' and officer's insurance, 87
  effectiveness, 74–76
  evaluation of executive director/CEO,
    74,
    75, 81
  evaluation of members of, 115. *See*
    also Evaluations
  expectations for members, 89
  fiduciary duties, 84–86
  financial information provided to,
    214, 218–220
  financial oversight and fiscal policies,
    81, 83, 86
  inurement of benefit, 86
  IRS forms, filing responsibilities, 86
  as key resource for organization, 73,
    84
  leadership, 79
  legal liabilities, 78, 84–87

long-range plan, 86
meaningful work, 79
Board of directors (*Continued*)
meetings, 77–79, 84, 86, 89
mentoring, 90, 91
and mission, 41, 47, 74, 77
officers, 82
orientation, 77, 84, 90, 91
overview, 73, 94–96
personnel policies, 82
policies, 81, 85, 249, 257
posting information about on Web
    site, 70, 137
public support of mission, 76, 82
quorums, 78, 260, 261
recruiting board members, 75, 82, 84,
    87, 89, 90
responsibilities, 80–82, 86, 94,
    95
risk tolerance, 145–147
role of, 74
selection of members, 260
self-dealing, 86
staff responsibilities, 77, 80, 82–84,
    95, 96
terms, 75, 260
values statement,
    developing/revising, 59, 60
volunteer work, 82, 90
Web site access, 77, 90, 137
Book clubs, 66
Borrowing. *See* Debt
Brochures, 186, 187
Budget
bottom-up budgeting, 198, 200,
    207–210
drafting and adoption of, 81
income and expense statement,
    comparing to, 203
planning, 245
posting on Web site, 131, 137
staff involvement in budgeting, 198,
    207, 212
technology, 134
Business, nonprofits as, 1–3, 289
Business financials

accounts receivable issues, 165,
    166
analysis of financial data,
    160–162
breakeven analysis, 161–163, 166
business plan, financial section of,
    162, 163
cash reserves, 166, 167
contingency funds, need for, 166, 167
costs, 167
financial condition of organization,
    162
financial projections, common
    mistakes, 163–167
and Murphy's Law, 166, 167
operating expenses, 160
pricing information, 159, 167
pro forma statements, 161–166
reviewing, 163, 164
sales targets, 158, 159
start-up costs, 159–161
working capital, 160, 161
Business plan, 148–154, 162, 163, 167,
    168,
    251, 252. *See also* Business
    financials
Business ventures, 147, 148
Businesslike nonprofits, 286
Bylaws, 81, 86, 260, 261

Career opportunities, 130
Cash
controls, 265
future cash and capital needs,
    planning for, 220–222
reserves, 166, 167, 197–199
Cash flow
analysis, 161–166
projections, 200–202, 211, 213–215,
    217–219, 225
Census trap, 176, 187
Certifications, 269, 283–285, 287
Chambers, John, 168, 198
Change, 286, 287, 290, 291
Characteristics of financially
    empowered nonprofits, 196–200

Characteristics of successful nonprofits, 9, 31–34, 36, 289, 290
Charity versus mission-based business, 2, 3, 291
Checks, signature requirements, 261, 266
Chief executive officer (CEO), 74, 75, 81, 99, 100. *See also* Management
Chief information officer (CIO), 127, 140
Coach/conductor style of management, 107, 122
Collins, Jim, 27
Commission on the Accreditation of Rehabilitation Facilities (CARF), 284
Committees
  assignment to, 93
  board manual, listing in, 91
  board member service on, 89
  board of directors, role of, 75, 76
  chair, appointment of, 75
  effectiveness, 93, 94
  finance committee, 218
  leadership, 75, 76, 94
  meetings, 84
  orientation, 90
  overview, 92
  planning committee, 239, 240, 244–248
  role of, 92
  staff, role of, 84
  standing committees, 261
  structure, 79–80
  technology, 131
  Web site, information posted to, 93
Communication, 35, 36, 78, 83, 86, 108–112, 115, 122
Compensation, 117–119, 122
Competition, 26–28, 175, 185, 186, 282, 284–287
Compliance with laws and regulations, 81, 87
Computers. *See* Software; Technology; Web sites
Confidentiality, 266

Conflicts of interest, 86, 138, 257, 261–265
Consultants/facilitators, use of, 245
Contingency funds, 166, 167
Contracts
  bids, 262–264
  versus grants, 222
Controls
  benefits of, 258
  board responsibilities, 85, 86
  bylaws, 260, 261
  characteristics of successful nonprofits, 34, 290
  conflict of interest policies, 257, 261–265
  defined, 255
  developing, 256–259
  disaster policies, 270–272
  discussion questions, 273
  enforcement, 258, 272, 273
  experts, use of in drafting and reviewing policies, 257, 259, 260, 265
  financial, 265, 266
  human resources policies, 267
  media policies, 267, 268
  overview, 255, 256, 272, 273
  program policies, 269, 270
  quality assurance, 269
  training, 257, 272, 273
  types of, 256, 259, 260
  volunteer policies, 268, 269
Core philosophies, 1–7, 197, 277–280
Cost of capital, 214
Cost shifting, 205, 206
Costs, 159–161, 167, 185, 186, 204–207
Crandall, Robert, 200, 201
Credit cards, use of for online donations, 131
Current ratio, 204

Debt, 199, 224–230, 265
Debt-to-fund balance, 204
Decision processes, 61, 74
Delegation, 112–115, 122, 237, 255

Demand for services, future trends, 25, 26
Development. *See* Fundraising
Directors' and officer's insurance, 87
Disaster policies, 270–272
Dissolution of nonprofit, 261
Donors, 3, 4, 125, 131, 137

Economy, impact of, 7, 8
Educational function of Web site, 130, 137
E-mail, 127, 128, 130, 134, 135, 139
Employees. *See* Staff
Empowering nonprofits
    action items for, 282–286
    and change, 286, 287
    competition, 282
    discussion questions, 287
    and outdated theories, 275–277
    overview, 275, 287
    philosophy changes, 277–280
    profit, need for, 280–282. *See also* Profit
Endowments, 198, 204, 223, 230, 231
Ethics, 32, 55–66, 70, 101, 289
Evaluations
    of marketing efforts, 189
    staff, board members, and volunteers, 115–119, 122
    of strategic plan and planning process, 240, 247
Executive director. *See* Chief executive officer (CEO)
Expectation of outcome, 3, 4
Expectation of service, 4
Experts, use of, 245, 257, 259, 260, 265

Feasibility study, 150, 151
Feedback, 139, 168, 209
Fiduciary duties, 84–86
Finance committee, 218
Financial controls, 265, 266
Financial empowerment
    accounts payable, 202
    accounts receivable, 202, 203, 213
    administrative costs, 204, 205

balance sheet, 203, 204, 212, 213, 223, 225
banks, selecting, 228–230
benefits of, 231
bottom-up budgeting, 198, 200, 207–210
cash flow and cash flow projections, 200–202, 211, 213–215, 217–219, 225
characteristics of financially empowered nonprofits, 196–200
characteristics of successful nonprofits, 33, 34, 290
debt, use of, 199, 224
discussion questions, 232
endowments, 198, 204, 223, 230, 231
expenses, 203
financial flexibility, 199, 211
financial ratios, 204
financial reports, use of internally. *See* Internal financial reporting
and foundations, 202, 204, 212, 222, 223, 225, 230, 231
income, tracking, 202
income and expense statement, 203, 209, 213, 214, 216, 218
lenders, working with, 224–227
leveraging, 199
management principles, 198, 199
measurable outcomes, 197, 198
mission focus, 199
nonfinancial indicators, 205
numbers viewed in context, 200, 201
and outdated perspectives, 275–277
overview, 195, 196, 232
planning for future cash and capital needs, 220–222
and pricing, 184. *See also* Pricing
process, timeframe for, 196, 200
and profit, 185
profit and loss, 205–207
restricted funds, 198, 213, 223, 231

retaining funds, 222–224
subsidiary corporations, 198, 223
working capital, 195, 197, 213, 214,
    218, 220–223
Financial oversight and fiscal policies,
    81, 83, 86
Financial ratios, 203–204
Financial reports, use of internally. *See*
    Internal financial reporting
Financial statements. *See* Business
    financials
501(c)(3) organizations
    and board responsibilities, 81
    dissolution, 261
    endowments, 230
    foundation corporations, 223, 230.
        See also Foundations
    and history of nonprofits, 14
    and profit, 4, 147, 197. *See also* Profit
    and restricted accounts, 198
    subsidiary corporations, 198, 223
    tax-exempt status, 4, 5, 39
Five-year plan, 237, 238, 240, 242–244,
    248
Focus groups, 180–182, 239,
    244–246
Forms
    IRS forms. *See* Internal Revenue
        Service (IRS)
    sample forms as part of policies and
        procedures, 258
Foundations, 202, 204, 212, 222, 223,
    225, 230, 231, 278–280, 282–287
Friedman, Thomas L., 124
Funders, outdated perspectives of,
    275–277
Fundraising, 6, 7, 48, 82, 131

Generation change, 24, 25
Goals
    management and staff, 116
    strategic planning, 239, 242, 245,
        246
Google, 59, 60
Government funding, 14–21
    action steps for change, 283, 284

capitation funding, 176
and financial empowerment, 196
funders as customers, 189–192
future trends, 22–24
and methods of retaining funds, 222,
    223
outdated perspectives, 275–277
use it or lose it funding, 15, 16, 277,
    280, 283, 284, 286, 287
Grants, 14, 222

Health system agencies, 20, 21
Human resources (HR) policies, 82, 267

Income, earned, 3, 4
Income, tracking, 202
Income and expense statement, 203,
    209, 213, 214, 216, 218
Innovation, 35, 37, 57, 58, 195
Insurance, officer's and director's,
    87
Internal financial reporting
    board of directors, 214, 218, 219
    cash flow projection, 217
    CEO, 213–215
    income and expenses, statement of,
        216
    off limits information, 211
    overview, 210–213, 219, 220
    policies, 266
    senior management, 214
    service staff, 214
Internal Revenue Service (IRS)
    501(c)(3) organizations. *See* 501(c)(3)
        organizations
    Form 900T, 81
    Form 990, 69, 81, 86, 137, 138, 204,
        205
    Form 990N, 69, 86
    Form 990T, 69, 86
    forms, filing responsibilities, 81,
        86
    foundations, 223, 230. *See also*
        Foundations
    mission statement, filing with, 41
Inurement of benefit, 86, 264

Inverted management pyramid, 99–106,
    112, 119, 121, 168
Jordan, Michael, 52

Leadership, 51, 61, 64–67, 75, 76, 79,
    97, 98, 101. *See also* Management
Leases, 223
Legal liabilities, board of directors, 78,
    84–87
Lencioni, Pat, 51, 61, 101, 118
Leveraging, 199. *See also* Debt
Listening, 138, 139, 180–184

Management
    certification, 284
    coach/conductor style of, 107, 122
    communication, 108–112, 122
    delegation, 112–115, 122, 237, 255
    enablers versus restrictors, 100
    ethics credos, 62–64, 70
    evaluation, 115–119, 122
    financial empowerment principles,
        198, 199
    financial information needed by, 214
    inverted management pyramid,
        99–106, 112, 119, 121, 168
    leadership and willingness to follow,
        101
    "management by wandering around,"
        101, 113
    mission-based managers, 34–37, 291
    posting information about on Web
        site, 70, 137
    risk tolerance, 145–147
    staff recognition, 119–122
    strategic plan as management tool,
        240, 248
    styles, 106–108, 122
    traditional management pyramid, 98,
        99, 259
    "treat others the way you want to be
        treated," 101
    trust, 108–110
    two-way relationship with staff, 100,
        101
Marketing

asking customers what they want,
    177–182, 184, 189–192
assistance with, 179, 180
brochures, 186, 187
census trap, 176, 187
characteristics of successful
    nonprofits, 33, 289
discussion questions, 193
evaluation of, 189
flowchart, 173, 174
focus groups, 180–182
fundamentals of, 173–189
funders as customers, 189–192
identifying target markets, 174–176,
    187, 188
importance of, 172, 173, 192
internal markets, 175
listening, importance of, 180–184
market segmentation, 176
market wants, assessment of, 176–182
overview, 171, 172, 192, 193
payer markets, 174, 175, 186
plan, template for, 251
pricing, 184–186
product or service, development and
    redevelopment of, 182–184
product-driven, 173
promotion, 186–188
providing the service, 188, 189
referral markets, 186
service markets, 175, 186
steps of marketing process, 171
strategic plan as marketing tool, 248,
    249
surveys, 178–181
Marriott, J. Willard, 122
Marriott Hotels, 99, 105, 106
Matching funds, 283, 284
Maxwell, John, 64, 101, 102
Media, 267, 268, 275–277, 285, 286
Meetings
    agendas, 79
    attendance, 78, 79, 86, 89
    board of directors, 77–79, 84, 86, 89
    communication, 112
    effectiveness, 79, 80

minutes, 86, 137
orientation, 77
quorums, 78, 260, 261
staff attendance at board meetings, 84
staff support for board meetings, 77
Mentoring, 90, 91
Metrics
accountability, 67, 68
measurable outcomes, 197, 198
Mission
board awareness of, 77
and board of directors, 74
characteristics of successful
nonprofits, 32, 289, 290
as criteria for staff evaluations, 117
and differences in perspective, 43–47,
77
discussion questions, 37
importance of, 39, 55, 195, 291
investment in, 144. *See also* Social
entrepreneurs
mission statement. *See* Mission
statement
money as enabler of mission, 195. *See
also* Profit
public support of by board members,
76, 82
as reason for staff, 99, 100
technology as accelerator of, 27, 33,
124, 129
Mission reserve, 199
Mission statement
and business plan, 148
and differences in perspective on
mission, 43–47
filing copies of with state and IRS, 41
formal adoption of, 41
as frequent reminder of mission, 41,
42
as fundraiser, 47, 48
leadership action, 51
legal implications of, 39, 40
as a management tool, 47
as motivator, 47, 48
and need for leadership, time, and
training, 49–52

overview, 39, 52
posting on Web site, 135, 136
reviewing, 40, 41, 260
rewriting, 41
and tax-exempt status, 39, 40
visibility of, 42, 48, 49
as volunteer recruiter, 47, 48
Mission-based business versus charity,
2, 3,
291
Mission-based managers, 34–37, 291.
See also Management
Moore's Law, 126, 127
Motivation, 35, 47, 48
Murphy's Law, 166, 167

Nonprofit Technology Network
(nten.org), 133

Objectives, 242, 243, 246
O'Connell, Brian, 277
Operating expenses, 160, 206, 207
Operating income, sources of, 198
Organization of book, 10–12
Orientation, 77, 84, 90, 91
Osborne, David, 183, 277
Overhead costs, 206, 207

Payer markets, 174, 175, 186
PayPal, 125, 131
Payroll, 203
Perot, Ross, 50
Peters, Tom, 101, 113, 258
Planning
action statements, 243, 247, 248, 250,
251
benefits of, 243, 244
budget, 245
categories of strategic plans, 241,
242
comments on draft of strategic plan,
246, 247
committee, 239, 240, 244–248
consultants/facilitators, use of, 245
data gathering, 246
definitions, 242, 243

discussion questions, 253
evaluation of plan, 240
Planning (*Continued*)
    evaluation of plan and planning
        process, 247
    five-year plan, 237, 238, 240,
        242–244, 248
    focus groups, 239, 244–246
    frequency of, 237, 238, 248
    for future cash and capital needs,
        220–222
    goals, 239, 242, 245, 246
    inclusiveness, 239, 240, 243
    long-range plan, 86
    objectives, 242, 243, 246
    one-year plan, 238, 243, 247, 248
    overview, 233, 253
    phases of, 234
    preparation, 244, 245
    process, 238–240, 244–248
    reasons for, 234–237
    retreats, 234, 239, 240, 245,
        246
    strategic plan, posting on Web site,
        131, 137, 247
    strategic plan as working document,
        242, 247
    subcommittees, 246
    surveys, 239, 244–246
    SWOT analysis, 245
    templates, 249–252
    uses of strategic plan, 240, 242,
        248–249
Podcasts, 132, 138
Policies and procedures. *See* Controls
Policy setting, 81, 85. *See also* Controls
Poverty chic, 16, 17
Pricing, 159, 167, 184–186
Profit. *See also* Social entrepreneurs
    and business ventures, 147, 148
    ethical perspective on, 5, 6
    and financial empowerment,
        185
    legality of, 4, 5, 147, 185, 197, 205,
        280, 281
    need for, 5, 197, 280–282

and risk tolerance. *See* Risk
Profit and loss, 161, 162, 164, 205–207
Profit margin, 204
Program policies, 269, 270
Program-related investments (PRIs),
    284
Property, leasing from subsidiary
    corporation, 223
Public perceptions, 285, 286

Quality assurance policies, 269
Quorums, 78, 260, 261

Recognition
    and idea generation, 168
    praise, 102
    staff recognition programs, 102,
        119–121
Recruitment
    board members, 75, 82, 84, 87, 89,
        90
    mission statement as volunteer
        recruiter, 47, 48
    strategic plan as recruitment tool,
        249
    through Web site, 138
    volunteers, 47, 48, 61
Related-party transactions, 223
Restricted funds, 198, 213, 223, 231
Retreats, 234, 239, 240, 245, 246
Return on investment (ROI), 6,
    154–157
Revenue, 197, 198. *See also* Profit
"Right thing to do is the smart thing to
    do, and vice versa," 62–64, 70
Risk
    assessment tool, 146–148
    and bottom-up budgeting, 208, 209
    and debt, 224
    reasonable (prudent) risk, 143, 144,
        147, 151, 153
    and social entrepreneurship, 143,
        144, 152–154, 157, 163, 169
    tolerance, 145–147

Ryan, George, 66

Sales targets, 158, 159
Self-dealing, 86
Signature requirements, 261, 266
Smith, Roger, 50
Social entrepreneurs
 business plans, 147–154
 and business ventures, 147, 148
 characteristics of, 144, 145
 characteristics of successful nonprofits, 33, 289
 definitions of, 143
 financial information, preparing, 158–163
 financial projections, common mistakes in, 163–167
 flexibility, 196
 innovation and creativity, encouraging, 167, 168
 internal risk assessment tool, 146, 147
 mission-based managers as, 35
 overview, 143, 144, 169
 return on investment, 154–157
 and risk, 143–148, 151–154, 157, 163, 169
 stewardship, 144
Software
 antivirus and antimalware, 135
 open source, 133–135
 types of, 127, 129, 131
 updating, 140
SourceForge.net, 134
Spreadsheets, 201, 211
Spybot-Search and Destroy, 135
Staff
 board meetings, attendance at, 84
 characteristics of successful nonprofits, 33, 289
 communication and interaction with, 101, 102
 compensation, 117–119, 122

 delegating authority to. *See* Delegation
 evaluation of, 115–118
 financial information needed by, 213, 214
 full-time equivalent (FTE), units of service provided by, 205
 as internal market, 175
 mission statement, review of, 41
 orientation, 61
 personnel policies, 82, 267
 recognition programs, 102, 119–122
 relationship to CEO, 74
 responsibilities to board, 77, 80, 82–84, 95, 96
 time sheets, 206, 207
 values statement, developing/revising, 59, 60
 Web site access, 130, 131, 137
Standards, 269
State law, compliance with, 87
Stewardship, 144, 237
Strategic plan. *See also* Planning
 categories of, 241, 242
 defined, 242
 final draft and adoption of, 247
 outside review of, 246, 247
 posting on Web site, 131, 137, 247
 templates, 249–252
 uses of, 240, 242, 248–249
 as working document, 242
Subsidiary corporations, 198, 223
Surveys, 178–181, 239, 244–246
SWOT (strengths, weaknesses, opportunities, and threats) analysis, 245

Tax-exempt status, 39, 40
Team approach to use of book, 9, 10, 290
Technology. *See also* Web sites
 as accelerator of mission, 27, 33, 124, 129
 backups, 135

blogs, 132, 133, 139
budget, 134
characteristics of successful
    nonprofits, 33, 289
checklist, 131–135, 141
Technology (*Continued*)
chief information officer (CIO), 127,
    140
cost-benefit ratio, 127, 128, 134
e-mail, 127, 128, 130, 134, 135, 139
future trends, 27, 28
"geek quotient," 127, 140, 141
and generational differences, 124,
    126
impact of, 8, 22, 124
Moore's Law, 126, 127
Nonprofit Technology Network
    (nten.org), 133
operating systems, 133
overview, 123, 124, 141
periodicals, reviewing, 140
plan, 130, 132, 134, 135, 139, 140
podcasts, 132, 138
price checks, 140
resources, 133, 134, 140
security, 135
SourceForge.net, 134
team, 131, 139–141
TechSoup.org, 133, 135, 140
as tool, 128, 129
and transparency, 55. *See also*
    Transparency
ubiquitous nature of, 123–125, 127
updating, 139, 140
voice mail systems, 128, 129
younger staff and board members,
    need for, 126, 132, 133
TechSoup.org, 133, 135, 140
Testimonials, 135, 136
Traditional (top-down) management
    pyramid, 98, 99, 259
Training, 51, 52, 257, 265, 267, 272, 273
Transparency
benefits of, 69
characteristics of successful
    nonprofits, 32, 289

and ethics, 61, 62
within organization, 55–57, 62
overview, 28, 55, 69, 71
as part of core values, 41
values, 41, 61, 62, 70
values statement, 58–60
Web site, documents posted on, 61,
    69, 70, 131, 135–138, 247, 265
"Treat others the way you want to be
    treated," 62, 63, 70, 101
Trend analysis, 179, 200
Trends affecting nonprofits, 22–29
Trust, 108–110

United Ways, 275, 276, 278, 279,
    282–285, 287
Unrelated business income, 40, 41, 81
Use it or lose it funding, 15, 16, 277,
    280, 283, 284, 286, 287

Values, 41, 61, 117
Values statement, 58–60, 70
Video, use of on Web site, 130, 132,
    136, 138
Vision, 34, 290. *See also* Planning
Voice mail, 127, 129
Volunteers
board members, 82, 90
evaluation of, 115. *See also*
    Evaluations
future trends, 24
as internal market, 175
policies, 268, 269
"professional" volunteers, 24, 260
recruiting, 47, 48, 61
satisfaction survey, 179
tradition of in U.S., 13, 14
Web site information, 130, 136–138

Waterman, Robert, 258, 259
Web sites. *See also* Technology
accessibility and ease of use, 136
board members, access to
    information, 77, 90, 137
budget, posting, 131, 137
careers page, 130, 136

comments section, 139
committee information postings, 93
design, 135
documents posted on, 61, 69, 70, 131, 135–138, 247, 265
donations through, 125, 131
donor information, 137
educational function of, 130, 137
feedback, 139
framework for, 135–139
as main source of information, 125, 126, 137, 138
mission statement, 135, 136
mission statement, posting on, 135, 136
Nonprofit Technology Network (nten.org), 133
promotion of services, 186, 187
recruiting through, 138
SourceForge.net, 134

staff-only section, 130, 137
SurveyMonkey.com, 179
TechSoup.org, 133, 135, 140
testimonials, 135, 136
testing, 136
video, use of, 130, 132, 136, 138
volunteer information, 130, 136–138
"What is yours is ours" philosophy, 17, 21, 276
"What we (the funders) say goes" philosophy, 15, 20, 276
Working capital, 160, 161, 195, 197, 213, 214, 218, 220–223

"You can't do well doing good" philosophy, 15, 21, 276

Zero-tolerance culture, 64, 65